Black Music in Britain

Popular Music in Britain

Black Music in Britain

Essays on the Afro-Asian Contribution to Popular Music

Edited by Paul Oliver

Open University Press
Milton Keynes · Philadelphia

Open University Press
Celtic Court
22 Ballmoor
Buckingham MK18 1XW

and

1900 Frost Road, Suite 101
Bristol, PA 19007, USA

First Published 1990

British Library Cataloguing in Publication Data

Black music in Britain : essays on the Afro – Asian
   contribution to popular music. – (Popular music in
   Britain)
   1. Black pop music
   I. Oliver, Paul, 1927–
   780'.42

   ISBN 0-335-15298-8
   ISBN 0-335-15297-X (pbk.)

Library of Congress Cataloging-in-Publication Data

Black music in Britain : essays on the Afro-Asian contribution to popular music / edited
   by Paul Oliver.
      p.   cm. – (Popular music in Britain)
   Includes bibliographical references (p.
   ISBN 0-335-15298-8:   ISBN 0-335-15297-X (pbk.) :
      1. Popular music–Great Britain–African influences. 2. Popular music–Great
   Britain–Asian   influences.   3. Blacks–Great   Britain–Music.   I. Oliver,   Paul,
   1927–   . II. Series.
   ML3492.B58 1990
   781.64'0941–dc20
                                                                    90-6720   CIP   MN

Typeset by Best-set Typesetter Ltd., Hong Kong.
Printed in Great Britain by St Edmundsbury Press,
Burn St Edmunds, Suffolk

Contents

List of Illustrations

Editorial Preface

What *is* British popular music? Does such a thing exist? What makes certain music and songs popular? And who made the musical cultures of these islands? What did Scots, Welsh, Irish and North American people have to do with the process? What part did people in the English regions play – the Geordies, Cockneys, Midlanders and all the rest? Where did the Empire fit in? How did European 'high' culture affect what most people played and sang? And how did all these factors vary in significance over time? In the end, just how much do we know about the history of musical culture on these tiny patches of land? The truth is that we know very little, and this realization led to this series.

The history of British people and culture has been dominated by capitalism for centuries; and capitalism helped to polarize people into classes not only economically, but culturally too. Music was never *simply* music: songs were never *simply* songs. Both were produced and used by particular people in particular historical periods for particular reasons, and we have recognized this in the way in which we have put this series together.

Every book in this series aims to exemplify and to foster inter-disciplinary research. Each volume studies not only 'texts' and performances, but institutions and technology as well, and the culture practices and sets of social relationships through which music and songs were produced, disseminated and consumed. Ideas, values, attitudes and what is generally referred to as ideology are taken into account, as are factors such as gender, age, geography and traditions. Nor is our series above the struggle. We do not pretend to have helped produce an objective record. We are, unrepentantly, on the side of the majority, and our main perspective is from 'below', even though the whole musical field needs to be in view. We hope that by clarifying the history of popular musical culture we can help clear the ground for a genuinely democratic musical culture of the future.

Dave Harker and Richard Middleton

Notes on Contributors

John Baily is a former research fellow in Social Anthropology at Queen's University Belfast; he now teaches ethnomusicology at Columbia University, New York. He is the author of *Music of Afghanistan* and has published extensively on musical cognition and ethnographic film making.

Sabita Banerji was born in Kerala, South India. A graduate from Bristol University, she has worked with the Commonwealth Institute in London, has published in British and Indian periodicals, and is now a freelance writer, music critic and arts administrator.

Gerd Baumann studied ethnomusicology and social anthropology at Belfast and Oxford Universities and conducted field research in Sudan. He teaches anthropology at Brunel University and since 1986 he has been engaged in resident research with the Asian community in Southall, Middlesex.

Thomas Chatburn is a conductor, composer and lecturer. He studied at the University of Wales and Princeton University, USA, and is currently Principal Lecturer in Music at Oxford Polytechnic. His interests include jazz, Indian music, steelband, and ethnic music in the UK.

John Cowley has published many articles on blues and black music. He produced the Flyright-Matchbox Library of Congress series of LPs and is a contributor to the *Blackwell Guide to Blues Records*. His doctorate thesis at the University of Warwick is on calypso and Caribbean music.

Jeffrey Green worked in Uganda 1968–70 and has travelled widely in the USA. He is the biographer of *Edmund Thornton Jenkins* and he has written for *Black Perspective in Music, Journal of Caribbean History, Immigrants and Minorities* and the *New Grove Dictionary of Jazz*.

Anthony Marks studied musical composition and has worked extensively as a writer, editor and music critic. He contributed articles about pop and soul to the *New Grove Dictionary of American Music* and has played various instruments in pop, soul and jazz groups.

Paul Oliver writes on Afro-American music and his books include *Blues Fell This Morning, Conversation with the Blues, Savannah Syncopators, The Story of the Blues* and *Songsters and Saints*. He co-edited with John Baily 'South-Asia and the West', a special issue (7/2) of *Popular Music*.

Michael Pickering is Senior Lecturer in Mass Communications and Popular Culture at Sunderland Polytechnic. He is the author of *Village Song and Culture* and, with Tony Green, of *Everyday Culture: Popular Song and the Vernacular Milieu*, and has published articles on nineteenth-century music.

Howard Rye took his BA at St Edmund Hall, Oxford University. He edits the discographical magazine *Collectors Items*, writes many articles on discography, and his continuing research on Afro-American music appears in *Storyville*. He contributed to *Under the Imperior Carpet*.

Chris Stapleton has written on African pop music since 1982 when he took on the 'Afro-Beat' column for *Black Music*. He has written for *Blues and Soul* and was co-author with Chris May of *African All-Stars*. He taught in Sierra Leone in the 1970s, and is now a sub-editor on a daily newspaper.

PART ONE

The Background of
Black Music 1800–1950

Conflicting and ambivalent attitudes to black music heard by white audiences in Britain are evident in this advertisement for the appearance of the Southern Syncopated Orchestra in Nottingham, in April 1920. *Courtesy of Nottinghamshire County Library Service*

Introduction

PAUL OLIVER

These have been notable years for black* music in Britain. For instance: in the wake of the nation-wide success of the Bhundu Boys from Zimbabwe the previous year, many African bands and solo musicians were to be heard in clubs, concerts and festivals throughout the British Isles within a single year. Amayenge came from Zambia. Combining the *kalindula* of their country with the *rhuma* rhythms of Zaire, their lead singer Kris Chali was backed by guitars, keyboards and talking drums. Shalawambe was another Zambian band, with Dolenzy Kabwe taking the vocals. The high audibility of the Zambians was challenged by the *soukous* rhythms of the bands from Zaire, like Sam Mangwana's or Taxi Pata Pata, with its heady mix of *soukous*, jazz and high-life.

Some of the African bands combined the traditional, contemporary or high-life dance rhythms of the drummers, with the saxes, trumpets, keyboards, electric guitars and bass of western jazz and rock. But it's hard to generalize on size or style; groups ranged in scale from the Four Brothers of Zimbabwe, to Remme Ongala's Orchestra Super Matimila from Tanzania, or the twenty-eight musicians of Adzido and the Pan-African Dance Ensemble. The ensemble was 'pan-African' in a musical rather than a political sense, drawing upon the diversity of forms that continues to spring from the continent. But a feature of some of the African bands and soloists heard in Britain was its syncretic character, deliberately bringing together elements that were 'pan-Atlantic'. Julian Bahula's Jazz Africa, the Afro-Funk-Jazz of Dudu Pukwana's Zila, or the African reggae of Harare Dread and Dande Lenol, underlined this cultural hybridization.

If jazz and reggae were prominent, there were also strong parallels with the blues, evident in the playing and singing of Youssour N'Dour or Baba Maal from Senegal, S.E. Rogie's 'Palm Wine Music' from Sierra Leone, or the playing of Ali Farka Toure from Mali. It is problematic whether this blues-

---

* Throughout this book the words 'Black' and 'White' have capital initial letters where they are used as nouns, and lower case where they are used as adjectives.

related music is evidence of the Savanna traditions and their link through slavery with the development of blues, or the reabsorption of Afro-American elements within the idioms of Islamic West Africa. Some of the Africans maintain that they are perpetuating their traditional musics on *kora* or *khalam*, but the use of western guitars argues a more complex cross-fertilization. Nevertheless, the talents of Salif Keita from Mali, or of the *oud*-player from Sudan, Abdel Gadir Salim, emphasize the accomplishment and artistry of many contemporary African musicians from this region.

Visiting black jazz musicians from the USA during the same period included the hard bop saxophonist Sonny Rollins, veteran bebop trumpeter Dizzy Gillespie, Don Cherry, improviser on the pocket cornet, the pianist Cecil Taylor, the virtuoso trumpet player Wynton Marsalis and even Ornette Coleman playing with the Philharmonic Orchestra at the Royal Festival Hall. The Harlem Blues and Jazz Band with Al Casey and George Kelly played the Brecon Jazz Festival, as did blues singer Louisiana Red. Many other blues singers visited Britain, including the influential Oklahoma guitarist, Lowell Fulson, Chicago guitar players Luther Allison and Joe Louis Walker, and the boogie-woogie pianist Big Joe Duskin from Cleveland, Ohio. There were fewer black jazz musicians from Britain, but the Jazz Warriors, a nineteen-piece big band led by the youthful sax player Courtney Pine successfully toured with a 'homage' to the role model black jazz saxophonist, the late Joe Harriott.

Such a summary can be no more than a catalogue of names of bands and musicians and their countries of origin: similarly diverse if unreadable lists could be drawn up for many other genres, whose ancestry may be much shorter but whose black credentials are no less valid, though they stem from the city ghettos. Rap and hip-hop received an aggressive shot in the arm from the visits of Run DMC, Derek B and Public Enemy, but home-grown rap flourished too, with the rapid-fire wit of Overlord Six, Gold Top and the London Rhyme Syndicate. The male dominance of this idiom was challenged in 1988 by a number of 'She-Rappers', including the Wee Papa Girl Rappers – the witty sisters Total S and TY Tim (who reluctantly admit to their given names of Sandra and Timmy Lawrence).

Reggae bands, soul singers and steel pan orchestras flourished during the same year, 1988, with the West Indian and American-derived sounds wholly integrated in British black culture. But the many forms of music to be heard from the Indian subcontinent were as varied, if less clamorously attracting popular attention, included the *qawwāli* of Nusrat Fateh Ali Khan's singers, the *sitar* of Ravi Shankar, or Ghasi Ram Nirmal playing the *jal tarang*, or tuned bowls of water. More than 150 performers appeared at the Asian Music Festival at Crawley, Sussex, in the summer.

This list of black musicians who performed in Britain in 1988 is in no way exhaustive; it's not even representative, especially of the many forms of pop music which are addressed to large, unspecified audiences. Popular American artists like Tracy Chapman and Gail Ann Dorsey (American, but resident in Britain), and soul singers like Freddy Jackson and Womack and Womack, appeared in concerts. Nina Simone at the Royal Festival Hall and the sensational Michael Jackson at Wembley underscore the crowd-pulling power of star performers. A nimble-footed and well-heeled enthusiast eager to hear a variety of black performers could have attended the Warwick Folk Festival and the Norwich Jazz Festival, sat in on the World of Music, Arts and Dance (WOMAD) festivals in Cornwall and Bracknell, taken seats at the St David's Hall, Cardiff, and the Philharmonic Hall, Liverpool, queued for the Crucible Theatre in Sheffield and the Mayflower Theatre Southampton, packed in at Dingwall's or the 100 Club – or shared in the (free) spectacle and music over the two days of the Notting Hill Carnival.

Few who listened to these artists, whether groups or soloists, would question whether they were 'black', or that what they were playing and singing was 'black music'. It would be convenient, and certainly more comfortable, to leave the matter there. But this is a book that is intended to be on 'black music in Britain' and the question as to what *is* 'black music' and by whom it is played cannot be avoided. The problems that arise from the simple assumption that music performed by black musicians is 'black music' are many, and by no means are they easily resolved. For instance, among other black artists performing in Britain during the year were such varied performers as Miriam Makeba, Joan Armatrading and Jessye Norman. If Miriam Makeba's staged performances of traditional Xhosa songs may qualify them as 'black music' for some, if not for all of her audience, are Jessye Norman's interpretations of songs from Schumann's Op 39 'Liederkreis' 'black' by any definition apart from her colour?

Black people, black culture

The problem of black music is that it cannot be defined by any wholly unassailable criteria. On the one hand it cannot be assumed that all that black singers or musicians perform is black music, simply because of their ethnic origins, while on the other it may not be defensible to argue that black music can be performed only by black artists. Though many would prefer to think such is the case, and would have good evidence in terms of examples of white bands and singers who have been less than successful in performing black music, the argument gets close to an inverted or over-compensatory racism.[1]

There's a glib answer to this, and it has been used to explain away or sometimes to discredit black concert artists, or even some jazz musicians and popular music entertainers whose work has gained them large audiences: Blacks alone play black music, but *some* Blacks have compromised themselves and their musical inheritance to perform the music of Whites, or to play for Whites. This is not a particularly edifying argument, and it is one that accepts unquestioningly, that Blacks inherently play black music.

Inevitably this line of reasoning leads to the 'all Blacks have rhythm' stereotype, which in the past has justified the imposition of inferior status on the grounds that the skills and qualities that they may have are based on 'primitive' intuitions, rather than on intellect or sensibility. Concepts of innate abilities among members of a particular race or ethnically identifiable group are based on the belief that the same genetic differentiation that accounts for say, skin pigmentation, physical build, hair section or other racial markers, also accounts for the presence of specific abilities, such as an aptitude for the use of colour, or the playing of percussive instruments. Such an argument has also been used to justify a belief, by those who consider themselves to be racially superior, in heightened sexuality or a predilection for violent behaviour among Blacks.

To follow the argument through one has to confront the problem of genetic admixture through intermarriage and cross-fertility between races. The outcome of miscegenation between people of different racial stocks over generations, inevitably leads to the diminution of some genetic traits and the dominance of others. They're expressed most visibly and physically in, for instance lightening of skin hue, or differences in hair section and hence, changes in hair growth. If abilities *are* genetically related, the diminution or dominance of some would also seem to be the inevitable result of such racial cross-breeding, but the vast literature on race does not bear this out. Nor does common experience: in the jazz field, for instance, dark-skinned Louis Armstrong, Bessie Smith or Charlie Parker are not rated as being the musical superiors (or inferiors, for that matter) of light-hued Jelly-Roll Morton, Billie Holiday or Lester Young; at least, not on account of the presumed 'blackness' of their genes.

Associations of the distinctions of colour with distinctions of culture have been consistently made, first perhaps by Whites in defence of slavery, and later by Blacks in the crusade for liberty. Whether they arose as expressions of white discrimination rooted in the myth of racial superiority, as demands for equality of rights and opportunity of 'race leaders' such as W.E. Du Bois, as protestations of white purity of the Ku Klux Klan, or as the declarations of James Brown and his followers of being 'black and proud', the motivations for such distinctions have been consistently ideological and political. Nevertheless, if it is accepted that the creativity of jazz musicians cannot be related directly to the measure of blackness in their skin pigmentation the corollary has to be acknowledged also: aptitude for music, or for any other aesthetic expression, is not racially predestined. When taken to its conclusion, an argument for innate abilities becomes not racial, but racist.[2]

Yet the phenomonen of 'black music' is profoundly evident to all who are interested and involved in popular music from any point of view, whether as participants or listeners, dancers or teachers. In many different genres of folk and popular (or folk *into* popular) music, Blacks have been the innovators, the inspiration, sometimes the sole exponents and performers. Mississippi blues, Kansas City jazz, Jamaican calypso, Ghanaian high-life, South African township *kwela*, Trinidadian steelband, Cuban *guaguanco*, Gujarat *ghazals*, Nigerian *juju*, Punjabi Bhangra are literally but a few forms that have flourished on four continents in this century. Superficially it might be argued that 'rhythm' is common to all of them, but a unifying theory that embraced the enormous diversity of rhythm patterns that these and other black-initiated genres represent would be immensely difficult to construct.

The extension of conventional instrumental techniques and the invention of new ones, the wit and often poetic expression of many lyrics and the improvised topicality of others might be identified as elements common to many, if not all of these genres. A number it seems, share what some ethnomusicologists, such as Richard A. Waterman and Bruno Nettl, have identified as 'African features that were carried into the New World': adding the 'metronome sense' of adherence to metre and tempo, the use of syncopation, the employment of call-and-response patterns, the love of instrumental music, the interest in improvisation, the variety of tone colours in vocal technique, and the employment at times, of polyphonic singing. As I have myself argued at length, there are many retentions of musical and vocal practice from the West African savanna regions traceable in the blues.[3] But again, many of these musical forms are as notable for their diversity as for their similarities. Some cross-influences can certainly be traced: jazz and calypso on forms of high-life, for instance. And there are musical lineages: ska into blue-beat into rock-steady into reggae. All the same, it is the special nature of each popular music that justifies its being identified by name and which make its distinctive characteristics at least as, if not more important than, those that it has in common with others.

Of course, it may well be argued that Gujarat ghazals and Punjabi Bhangra have no place in such a list; that as musics of Asian origin, or rather more specifically, as musical forms of peoples from the Indian subcontinent, they have no place in the company of genres of African, Afro-Caribbean or Afro-American origin. Apart from any musical differentiation, the argument might run, the makers of these musical types are not 'black'. Identification of groups according to their colour has a long history which is bewilderingly imprecise, as Jack D. Forbes has shown: 'By the sixteenth century the English and Scots were referring to the people of Africa as Moors, and then later as Blackamoors, Ethiopians and negroes'.[4] Whereas in 1619 twenty 'Negroes' were brought to Virginia, by 1670 there were some 2,000 'black slaves' in the colony, evidence of the early use of 'Negro' and 'black' which would be reliable were it not for the fact that native Americans ('Indians' as they were to be designated in the eighteenth century) were included in the terms.

Faced with the fact of people of mixed racial ancestry the British tended to adopt the Portuguese 'mulatto', but the term implied interracial unions between native Americans and Africans and not necessarily between Africans and Europeans. These were designations that were intended to be descriptive and did not necessarily imply anything derogatory. But there were, and are, numerous insulting terms, some of them employed innocently, even with a certain patronizing affection. While 'darky' and 'coon' were often used with offensive intent, this was by no means always the case; indeed, some black bands and vocalists used them of themselves earlier in the present century. Later, 'coloured' was used to describe persons of brownish hue, and eventually was extended to all dark-complexioned people. In some circles 'colo(u)red' was an acceptable designation (e.g. the National Association for the Advancement of Colored People) but by mid-century and until the 1970s, 'Negro' was the preferred term, until the polarizing 'Black' began to replace it once more.

Even in the early 1980s some writers were still referring to 'Black and Asian', making a loose distinction (which, however, would have had to include people from Turkey to China to be in any way accurate) between two uncertainly defined groups. It was an alternative to the equally flawed 'Afro-Asian' (which implies an interracial link), or the 'coloured minorities' of some other commentators, sociologists and authors. Today, for expediency and often for reasons of solidarity, the elastic term 'black', even if it isn't wholly accepted, has been stretched to include residents in Britain of Afro-Caribbean, African, Indian and Pakistani origin or ancestry. With some misgivings we have used both 'black' and 'Afro-Asian' here, though where the historical context, a reference or a quotation makes it anachronistic, we have retained other terms.

A UNESCO report on *The Race Concept* concluded that 'genetic differences are of little significance in determining the social and cultural differences between different groups'.[5] As anyone in the street or dance-hall can confirm, 'black' as a description is no more than a term of convenience which defines with accuracy neither racial group, nor ethnic identity, nor even skin hue. Furthermore, it is by no means an accurate way of bringing together a diverse range of musical forms, except that it serves to identify musics which have as their origin or as their exponents, people who have been designated, or who designate themselves, as 'black'.

The terminology of race generally fails to provide acceptable terms to describe people who acknowledge some origins in Africa, the Americas or South Asia, but who have settled in a western country, have taken its citizenship, or have a right to it by birth through the inter-marriage of their parents. Faced with this terminological dilemma some anthropologists have accepted 'ethnic' as a working term, not as a biological definition from outside the society but as an identity from within it. In other words, those that believe themselves to be 'African', whatever the genetic evidence, are understood to *be* African. On this basis, those who consider themselves to be 'black' are indeed black. And by extension, 'black music' is that which is recognized and accepted as such by its creators, performers and hearers.

It is discussed in this sense in this book, encompassing the music of those who see themselves as black, and whose musics have unifying characteristics which justify their recognition as specific genres: peculiar patterns of 'sonic order' in John Blacking's phrase. Blacking observed that 'Music can express social attitudes and processes', and reflected, 'could "soul" music affect Black Americans if its forms were not associated with a whole set of extramusical experiences which Black Americans share?'[6] What these extramusical experiences in different black (I shall use the term without further comment from here on) cultures may be and which may be common to a number, or all of them is a complex issue.

Over fifty years ago the distinguished anthropologist Melville J. Herskovits applied some concepts of psychoanalysis to 'Negro cultural behavior', in particular those of repression and compensation. In a number of African and New World black cultures he argued that 'there exists both a recognition of the neuroses as induced by repression, and of the therapeutic value of bringing a repressed thought into the open' through song.[7] While this is far from being the only function of black music it is convincingly an important one.

Within specific musical cultures, many of the functions summarized by ethnomusicologist Alan P. Merriam undoubtedly apply: for the confirming of social norms and the validation of social institutions, for instance. Merriam argued that music functions by contributing to the continuity and stability of the social structure and to the integration of the society, as well as by providing entertainment, aesthetic enjoyment and channels of communication.[8] In the context of, say, reggae and Rastafarianism, these functions seem evident. Black music may be both therapeutic and socially reinforcing. But, as Blacking noted, 'it is useful and effective only when it is heard by the prepared and receptive ears of people who have shared, or can share in some way, the cultural and individual experiences of its creators'.[9] His observation has considerable bearing on the audiences for black music in the early years.

Black performers, white audiences

While their first appearance in Britain may not be known, black musicians played at Court from the first decade of the sixteenth century. In his comprehensive history of Blacks in Britain, Paul Fryer notes many who played, sometimes in groups, sometimes singly, in the seventeenth and eighteenth centuries. A number were probably native Americans – the term 'Tawny' was used to distinguish them from 'Moors', and was later applied to Asians – but Queen Elizabeth I had ten black musicians and dancers at her Court, and later black military bandsmen were employed in many regiments in the eighteenth century. To maintain their favoured occupations it seems certain that the black trumpeters and drummers among the militiamen would have meticulously played the military musical repertoires of their day. There is some evidence that occasionally, African 'drolls' performed curious music on kitchen utensils, but there is no indication that they won any converts.[10] If Britain heard the music of ex-slaves it is unlikely to have been much before the nineteenth century.

While Blacks did bring their music to Britain it is an open question as to how much influence their music exerted. They made an important contribution to the shanties of seamen working under sail following the re-establishment of the British Merchant Service in 1815. Slaves from the American South and ex-slaves from the British West Indies worked at capstans and halyards to the chanting of their songs and often to the playing of a fiddler. Black fiddlers played between decks too, and West Indian sailors brought their songs to the ports of Liverpool, Bristol and London. Theirs was a 'folk' music, that is, one functioning within their defined world, with an 'audience' of fellow seamen who shared their culture.[11] But some shantymen's songs reached a larger audience, for a number were printed in the pocket-sized 'Ethiopian Songsters' which were published in large quantities in the nineteenth century.

'Folk music', like 'popular music', with which this book is primarily concerned, requires some explanation. Precise definition of these much used and abused terms has eluded many writers but for our purposes 'folk' music idioms are understood to arise from, and be largely expressive of, the values of discrete societies. Their exponents may be illiterate, and such literacy as obtains may have no bearing on a music whose vocals are orally transmitted and whose instrumental techniques are passed on by copying or demonstration. Performance skills, expression and creativity exist within prescribed limits in folk societies, where adherence to tradition is usually marked.

'Popular music', on the other hand, reaches its audiences beyond the limits of a local community by transmission through mediating means. These can include published song-sheets and music, radio programmes and phonograph records, concert performances and tours, video and television appearances – indeed, all disseminating media. In the process, popular musics and their exponents may be subjected to commercial pressures to adapt for unseen audiences, and may be further subject to change through the constraints or extensions of media technology. Literacy may not be a necessary component of popular music, but it is required of the media middle-men, if not of the performers.

While some popular music idioms may be products of a sophisticated milieu it is noticeable that a great many, even most of those that are black music, have their origins in folk music. A popular music may well develop from a folk idiom as it gains a wider audience through personal contact, transmission by travel or by the media. It is widely believed that while a popular genre has a massive following it should retain its contact with its folk roots. These origins, real or presumed, represent the 'authentic' in a popular music, recognised by the audiences in the vocal timbre or playing techniques of performers, or in the content and form of the songs. In these terms black shanties were a folk music.

In the second half of the nineteenth century the black population grew in the East End of London. Accounts of the music heard there lie buried in obscure memoirs, for example, of missionary workers like Joseph Salter, who spent over forty years there with London's Africans and Asiatics. He described an occasion when some fifty Africans on the dockside formed a circle round two musicians. One had:

> a guitar of homely manufacture, with three strings and the hard shell of the fruit called the Zeezee. The instrument of the other was extemporised, being made by thrusting a stout bamboo through a disused *bouilli boeuf* tin, on the side of which the dark musicians kept beating with a marrow bone. To this music the Africans joined chorus and sprang about.

Indian musicians were to be heard behind the Royal Sovereign, a decrepit pub in High Street, Shadwell, where 'thirty noisy Mahommedans' listened to sitar and tambour players. In the 'Black Hole', Whitechapel, lived a group of Hindu mendicants.

> A well-known character was a professional player on the native tum-tum . . . in native garb with his noisy instrument suspended from his neck . . . his bony fingers would wriggle over the parchment of his drum, he would shout his song with

vigour, and his skinny legs, spinning round and round would perform all the antics which only Asiatic exhileration can produce.

In 1872 the first of the 'Foreigner's Fetes' was held at Streatham. Sponsored by the London City Mission these events continued well into the 1880s, and included 'Asiatics (representing most of the nations of the East), and many of the tribes from Central Africa . . . Turks, Arabs, Gujeratis, Bengalese, and a few from unusual localities'. Londoners had opportunities to hear Indian and African musicians at the international exhibitions of the 1870s and 1880s and 'Zulus, Maoris, Japs, Chinese, even American Indians and Dahomian Amazons, have appeared among us and have been amply applauded and rewarded by the public'.[12] Salter's accounts make it clear that they played the authentic folk musics of their countries.

The transition from minority applause for folk music to wide acclaim for popular music was made with the arrival of the American Minstrel shows. Minstrelsy was far from being a matter of black-face parody alone; though black folkways and speech were mimicked and were a source of low comedy, much of the dancing was based on black 'capers' and many a 'Genuine Negro Jig' (so captioned) was featured. Banjoes and fiddles, tambourines and bones were played by 'Ethiopians' with a spirit which may (or may not) have caught the spontaneity and freedom of the original, but which undoubtedly created an audience for uninhibited music-making. Nevertheless, when minstrel companies toured Britain in the 1880s with black rather than white performers, they soon accorded with the conventions of the Minstrel genre. Black or white, most shows were played in black-face.[13]

No company was more popular in Britain than the Moore and Burgess Minstrels, who played for over thirty-five years at St James's Hall, Piccadilly. Like many companies they included operettas, and in the 1890s presented 'Musical and Vocal Tableaux Vivants' which enacted Harriet Beecher Stowe's highly influential *Uncle Tom's Cabin*. The combination of minstrel show and 'Uncle Tom' encapsulates the effects of the minstrel era on the reception and expectations of white audiences for black music in the nineteenth century. Not all the laughter was condescending, and not all the tears shed over Topsy were false. But parody on the one hand and sentimentality on the other dominated the presentation of popular black music and song – most frequently through the smoked glass of white interpretation.[14]

Receptive ears were also open to black religious music, but the problem of sharing the cultural experiences of their creators existed here too. Slave songs and spirituals performed by the Fisk Jubilee Singers moved the hearts of tens of thousands of their hearers, inspiring many other companies. Williams' Colored Singers, 'the World's Greatest Harmonizing Octette' formed in 1904, were extremely popular, giving 130 performances in an 18-week run at the London Coliseum. The slave songs and spirituals that the Jubilee companies performed were not sung as they had been on *ante-bellum* plantations or as they were sung in camp meetings. Most of the Williams' Octette were trained singers, who brought dignity and professionalism to their work; with a more legitimate approach they sought to counter the impact of the minstrel shows and bridged the cultural gap with their audiences.[15] Black-face minstrel troupes and Jubilee Singers alike published their songs enabling their hearers to try to play the new melodies and master the unfamiliar rhythms. Sheet music of 'Spirituals', 'Parlour Songs', 'Heart Songs' and 'Familiar Plantation Ditties' were sold in single copies and in folios for musical evenings, Glee Clubs and provincial amateur minstrel shows. Banjo pieces, jigs, cakewalks and coon songs arranged for piano were selling in millions by the 1890s, with many companies having offices in London and New York.

Many of the songs were intended to be comic: black artists Bert Williams and George Walker brought their comedy musical show *In Dahomey* with a cast of fifty to the Shaftesbury Theatre in April 1903. A performance at Buckingham Palace before King Edward VII provided the accolade that ensured the success of the national tour that followed.[16] It was a trail-blazer for many all-black shows, including Will Garland's *A Trip to Coontown*, which played three venues in London in 1906 before going on tour, and the first of several under his direction, including *Coloured Society* in 1917 and *Coloured Lights* a decade later. Their titles confirmed that he had devised a formula which readily appealed to British theatre-goers.[17]

For a black, or even a black-faced, entertainer there were clear advantages in conforming to the expectations of white society, while being sufficiently skilled or innovative for colour to be a sign of quality. A number of burnt-cork performers took the steps from minstrel show to concert stage by way of the music halls, like Eugene Stratton or the 'Chocolate Coloured Coon', G.H. Elliott, who affected a genteel manner in his act. The respectability which they gained was an inducement to black artists who followed suit, such as the team of Haston, Mills and Tuck, 'The Versatile Three', whose white-tie versions of plantation songs were coupled with parlour airs. In the performances of Layton and Johnston, their black contemporaries in the 1920s who played the Café de Paris in London and won the approval of the Prince of Wales, all links with black styles had been discarded in favour of the cultural mores of their bourgeois audiences.

By this time much had happened in the dissemination of popular music. Piano rolls, cylinder recordings and, in the years preceding the First World War, gramophone records made cakewalks and ragtime banjo pieces widely available. The Turkey Trot, Bunny Hug, Grizzly Bear and Boston dances brought sensuous pleasure to thousands of young people – and outraged their parents. Following the success of Ethel Levey and the all-white *Hallo, Ragtime!* show at the London Hippodrome in 1912, which 400,000 people paid to see, ragtime – or what passed for it – captivated the nation, and prepared the way for the Original Dixieland Jazz Band's uproarious tenure at the Hammersmith Palais de Danse when the war was over. It was a white band, but those who complained of its 'jungle rhythms' sensed the black elements, however caricatured, that underlay its raucous improvisations.

Will Marion Cook's Southern Syncopated Orchestra, Jim Reese Europe's Society Orchestra, Bennie Peyton's Jazz Kings and the other visiting black bands from the USA between 1910 and 1930 played music with elements of cakewalks, ragtime, military music and jazz. The 1920s was the period of clubs, cabarets and all-night dance halls: Rector's, Ciro's and Murray's gave employment to black bands who played for enthusiastic dancers, though their audiences were necessarily limited. A greater impact was made by *Dover Street to Dixie*, 1923, *Blackbirds of 1926* and *1928*, and many other scintillating shows, which brought such artists as the singers Florence Mills, Adelaide Hall, Mae Barnes and Edith Wilson to the London stage, to be followed by Buck and Bubbles and Bill Robinson. In the orchestras a roster of jazz stars included Johnny Dunn, Garvin Bushell, Tommy Ladnier, and eventually, fronting his own orchestra in 1932, Louis Armstrong at the London Palladium. Black music may not have 'arrived', and even Armstrong did not play to full houses, but there was nevertheless a large and appreciative audience for it, which no longer needed the mediation of white musicians to make it palatable.[18] When the Hampton Singers, a company of over fifty men and women, toured Britain in 1930, the reporter for the Johannesburg (South Africa) *Sunday Times* wrote of the 'band of blacks at Westminster Abbey', in words revealing of attitudes both in Britain and in the colony: 'one gets rather nauseated with the manner in which London loses its heart to anything black'.[19]

Black music and Empire

Even this rather breathless summary serves to emphasize that many factors affected the slow recognition of black music in Britain since the early nineteenth century. Over a span of more than a century it is probable that only the shanties were directly influenced by Blacks from the British colonies, and even in this instance Afro-American shantymen played an important part in the process. By far the majority of black artists who performed on the public stage in Britain were from the USA; West Indians and Africans were relatively few in number, though as the 1930s advanced their contribution became more significant. This curious situation reflects the small number of Blacks living in Britain in the period up to the First World War.

Estimates of the black population at the beginning of the nineteenth century seldom exceed 15,000. More remarkable is the fact that the number may not have been much higher at the end of the century: 'the majority of them seem to have been absorbed in the population', concluded Field and Haikin somewhat enigmatically.[20] A modest phase of settlement in docks areas occurred in the 1900s but no conspicuous growth in numbers occurred until the First World War. Disbandment of the black crews of requisitioned ships, direct recruitment into munitions factories and post-war demobilization contributed to the increase, though the numbers were still measured in hundreds. They were large enough to lead to race riots in 1919: in Cardiff, for example, where the number of Blacks, mainly unemployed, had quadrupled and stablized at 3,000 in the war years.

While the resident black population was probably too small to make significant inroads into popular culture, the attitudes and values of imperial Britain would not have promoted them. In the late 1870s the exploration of Africa stimulated the interest of the European powers in the potential of the continent. The ensuing 'scramble' with the arbitrary partition which took place between 1884 and 1890 led to the squalid 'wars' – or massacres – which resulted in colonization, and dominance over some 40 million Africans. British glorification of conquest in the name of Queen, Country and Christianity promoted patriotism and xenophobia. Tommy Atkins was glorified in song in the aftermath of the Matabele war of 1893: 'to keep our flag a-flying, he's a doing and a-dying, evr'y inch of him a soldier and a man'. Six years later 200 Matabeles, Hottentots and Swazis among others were displayed in their kraals and re-enacted the war in Frank Fillis's extravaganza, 'Savage South Africa', at Earl's Court.[21]

Africans were being Christianized and 'civilized' by the British, which included introducing them to the exploitation of their lands, their labour and their minerals. Slavery had been finally made illegal in the Empire in 1833, but the 'friend and brother' was still subject to virulent abuse from many racists in power or with access to the press. Conversely however, members of the Abolitionist movement and their successors rejoiced in the Emancipation following the war between the states, and applauded the black visitors who brought their slave songs to Britain. Watching the shows, concerts and other entertainments which featured black artists or their burnt-cork parodists, audiences of either conviction could find support for their beliefs and attitudes. In the opening chapter of this book Michael Pickering considers the nature of Victorian black entertainment and the complex responses of its audiences to the 'jet ornament in society'.

As we have seen, some musicians were determined to detach themselves from the stereotypes of black performance. Seeking equality and comparability in their chosen fields they played on the concert stage. They did not represent a single musical approach; some were players of popular music, others of popular classics; some were composers. But, as Jeffrey Green shows in Chapter 2 on popular concert hall performers from the start of the twentieth century to the Second World War, the expectations of the audiences were also influenced by their own stereotypical concepts of what the black artist should perform.

This period was also the time when Britain first encountered black jazz; not jazz of the brash and often grotesque kind purveyed by the Original Dixieland Jazz Band, but with a light swing and, in Sidney Bechet, musical improvisation of genius. But, as Howard Rye recounts, in Chapter 3, in the mid-1930s a Musicians Union ban, endorsed by the Ministry of Labour, severed the artery of black American music. Versatile West Indian musicians resident in Britain fed new blood into jazz, tempered by their Caribbean inheritance. In the war years West Indians came in considerable numbers – 7,000 served in the RAF alone – and the legacy of calypso recordings made post-war is documented by John Cowley. His Chapter 4 brings us to the years of a greatly expanding immigrant community, and a new era of black popular music.

Those whose ears are 'prepared and receptive' to black music are by no means only black. As the initial chapters repeatedly confirm, the audiences for black music in Britain were mixed, by far the majority being white, and of different age groups. These audiences were neither consistent in size and composition, nor were they uniformly appreciative or for that matter, hostile. It is easy to assume a certain homogeneity of both music and audiences which the all-embracing 'black music' might appear to imply. In fact, the musical forms which Britain encountered over the space of a few decades were diverse and most of them were new. Research is only now being conducted on a number of genres, and on the artists who visited these shores. Painstaking combing of old newspapers, music magazines, concert programmes and other ephemera, the examination of ships' registers and passport applications, the piecing together of data on recordings and interviews with surviving performers are together slowly revealing a clearer, if complex picture.

Black Music in Britain lays a groundwork which brings together for the first time much of the fruits of this research. Part One examines aspects of the British experience of black music up to the end of the First World War, relating the visits of touring groups and soloists, and the musicians of the small black community prior to the Second World War, to the milieux of theatres, concerts, club engagements and recording sessions in which they appeared. All the writers in Part One have been engaged in original research in the uncovering of this neglected aspect of the social history of popular music. Together, their studies of the diverse forms of popular music to which audiences in Britain were introduced indicate the measures of popular success and critical response with which they were met, and provide a foundation for an examination of the musical forms which proliferated in Britain with the expansion of the black population in the post-war years.

LORD   KITCHENER

recording   exclusively   for ...

MELODISC

Latest records :   **THE GREATEST CALYPSO LABEL in the WORLD**

MARJORIE'S   FLIRTATION
MY   WIFE   WENT   AWAY
WITH A YANKEE   1300   Listen to the latest recordings of the following Calypso
A MAN IN THE WARDROBE   Singers
V10   **LORD BEGINNER   ·   THE MIGHTY TERROR**
CONSTABLE JOE   1318   **THE LION · KING TIMOTH · TONY JOHNSON**

Advertisement for Calypso recordings on 78rpm records, issued in London by Melodisc, 1950s. *Collection: Paul Oliver*

1 'A Jet Ornament to Society': Black Music in Nineteenth-Century Britain

MICHAEL PICKERING

Introduction

There were black musicians in Britain in every decade of the nineteenth century, and they performed for every class of people. The material they sang and played was extremely various, ranging from 'classical' music to popular songs and ballads. Yet their public performances always occurred within the context of the white host culture, and that context exerted a considerable shaping pressure, in a variety of ways, on their repertory and style of presentation. Any discussion of black musicians and their performances in Britain is, therefore, inextricably bound up with white aesthetic tastes and conventions, and with the determinant factors generating and perpetuating those tastes and conventions across what was always a highly stratified cultural terrain. It is for this reason that it is impossible to talk of 'genuine' black music or culture in Britain during this period, even though white people at the time considered, at different points, that they had encountered the 'real thing'. Indeed, belief that this was so was a considerable source of appeal and pleasure.

The situation was rather one of mutual cultural interchange. This process involved Blacks on the one hand borrowing, imitating, adapting and accommodating themselves to white musical genres and modes of performance at the same time as, in certain cases, whether as a result of access or appropriate form, blending these with the performative material and practices of vernacular Afro-American culture. On the other hand it involved Whites in their own use of elements of black culture, or what purported to be elements of that culture, often mediated by other Whites who were only ostensibly representing black vernacular music and black styles of performance. In this unequal two-way exchange, the transatlantic phenemenon of 'nigger' minstrelsy acted in many cases as a filtering mechanism of immense significance, both for the audiences in Britain of white 'Negro delineators' and performers of, say, plantation or 'coon' songs, and for black popular entertainers who had to work within the black-face mode.[1] We have therefore to talk of a series of cultural translations on both sides where Whites always had the uppermost hand because of assuming, and holding, a position of racial and social superiority. How black performers signified for white British audiences was inevitably mediated by a whole host of assumptions and expectations of the Black, and many of these were constructed in reverse perspective to that of white people's self-image. The Black thus provided in many instances a convenient, exteriorized composite made up of aspects of 'self' denied, inhibited or repressed in the social and cultural order of the time. The fear of Blacks as well as the fascination with which they were met has inevitably to be seen in this regard.

It is important not to subsume white response to black musicians in nineteenth-century Britain entirely within this interpretative framework. Through the connection of much Afro-American music with slavery – from minstrelsy's slavery songs and plantation ballads to the jubilee singers' whitened versions of their own black spirituals – the black singer and musician was regarded as an object of pity and pathos. This way of seeing the Black, following from the abolition of slavery in British colonial territories, was a significant determinant of white response, but it would be too easy to assert that the feelings of sorrow and sympathy evoked by black music's slavery associations were merely self-serving: symbolic collateral for British civilizational advance. It is true that in the years up to the American Civil War, John Bull prided himself on having liberated the Negro from the chains of slavery ahead of Cousin Jonathan. In contrast to the plantation autocracy of the Deep South, Britain was self-styled as 'the land of the free'. The image operated throughout those years in different ways, being a spur to well-intentioned humanitarian reform as well as a fillip to self-righteous and complacent patriotism. Yet sympathy for, even indignation incurred by the plight of the black American slave, cannot be explained wholly in terms of national chauvinism, or a guilt-ridden bourgeois sentimentalism. Of course, feelings of sympathy and identification co-existed with racialist attitudes and values, among all social classes, but what must be recognized is that every manifestation of white response – even where it involved imaginative leaps or incited flights of fantasy – was necessarily rooted in the socially and culturally specific circumstances in which the response occurred. The sympathy of a collier for black suffering cannot be seen as synonymous with the way heart-strings were plucked by parlour renderings of plantation ballads.

One must emphasize, as well, the sheer excellence of some of the singing and music performed by Blacks in nineteenth-century Britain. When this was accomplished within 'classical' modes, the measure of assessment was set by pre-existing aesthetic standards operative within that realm of musical production. But white people in Britain also thrilled to previously unencountered styles and idioms of performance, and as for instance in the case of black spirituals, to song material that was relatively new. Whether as side-show exhibits or musical prodigies in the tradition of institutionally accredited music, the novelty value of black performers was considerable. At the same time any undue strangeness of content and form was usually diluted in order to conform with white aesthetic criteria. The appeal of black musicians on grounds of racial or cultural 'difference' always existed in tension with a counter-pattern of implicit or explicit requirements to conform to *a priori* standards or entrenched expectations, and much of the response of their white audiences is likely to have resonated within this to-and-fro movement between delight in what was strange, and satisfaction with what was culturally recognizable and familiar.

There were cases of black musicians who became relatively integrated into local communities, such as Jospeh Emidee or Tom Rutling, to take examples from either end of the period covered here, but to a great extent black musicians had the status of social 'outsiders', often caught in the double-bind of not being accepted fully on their own terms, and rarely being accepted without equivocation or qualification on the terms of the host culture. Their cultural status was largely confined to what an *Athenaeum* reviewer of John Brigg's *The History of Jim Crow* called in 1840 'a jet ornament to society'.[2] This status was manifest in variable ways across a range of personae and roles, yet all of them were deeply infiltrated by the contradictory racial stereotypes of the Black that were operative in British cultural life, up and down the social scale.

It was through the perceptual grid of those stereotypical views that the two thematic sources of white response to Afro-American and African musics were established: primitivism and affectivity. These ascribed psychological and cultural qualities spoke more of the groups responding than of those represented, in that they constituted either reversals or extensions of white conceptions of national character and culture. We have lived in the long shadow of these stock ideas ever since. There have been on the one hand conceptions of an earthy barbaric or semi-civilized fervour, of a raw and reinvigorating directness, of a libidinous excitement and a passionate involvement, that have tended to be morally excluded and repressed in the name of civility, respectability and suburban restraint. On the other hand there has been an emphasis (not wholly one-sidedly) on sentimentality and nostalgia, spirituality and moral uplift. Carnal exuberance and soulful effusion have constituted the central modalities of black music in white British perception and expectation, structuring appeal and pleasure in ways from which Whites are only now beginning to extricate themselves.

Buskers, bandsmen and concert virtuosos

Prior to the nineteenth century, black musicians had managed to find various niches for themselves amidst the host culture, as for instance in pageants and military bands; in the late eighteenth century London's black community organized what were known as Black Balls, where Blacks of both genders 'supped, drank, and entertained themselves with dancing and music, consisting', according to one report, 'of violins, French horns, and other instruments' played by an all-black band. A few of these 'black hops' were exclusively for Blacks, but at others in the last two decades of the eighteenth century, 'white Londoners as well as black were dancing to black dance music'. The opportunity to do this on any concerted scale would not present itself again to white people in Britain until the early twentieth century, after the advent of what John Buchan described as 'that hideous ragtime'. Britain had by then become a much more avowedly racist society.[3]

The fairly sizeable black community in Britain in the second half of the eighteenth century continued to exist into the early nineteenth century, particularly in London, where it was 'vibrant and organic, even if depressed'. But a gradual process of decline began from around the 1800s, primarily as a result of poverty, disease and maltreatment, a significant diminution in the flow of immigrants, and intermarriage with white people (particularly by black men, who greatly outnumbered black women in Britain at this time). By the time 'nigger' minstrelsy began to develop in Britain in any significant way, on stage and in street culture, Blacks had become a much less common sight, and this undoubtedly added to the novelty attraction of black-face musical entertainments. By the mid-century a steep decline in the black population was confirmed, but in the decades preceding the advent of the Jim Crow craze, there was none the less a fair number of Blacks in London, where minstrelsy first developed, and in pockets in the larger maritime cities as well.

Most Blacks in those decades were among the very poor, and many of them joined the swelling ranks of beggars that were a regular sight in the street-life of the time, especially in the years after Waterloo. The Society for the Suppression of Mendicity dealt with around 400 black beggars in the first half of the 1820s, a ratio of one in every forty beggars, though these figures relate only to those who fell into their clutches.[4] Among those who used some form of musical entertainment as a way of eliciting coins from passers-by, two Blacks in particular achieved notoriety.

Joseph Johnson had been forced to leave the Merchant Navy – without pension or compensation – after being seriously wounded; as he could not claim parish relief, he began to earn his living as a street-singer. Gradually becoming a 'regular chaunter', he gained renown particularly for his eccentric headgear: having built a model of the ship *Nelson*, he attached this to his cap, to which 'by a bow of thanks, or a supplicating inclination to a drawing-room window', he was able to 'give the appearance of sea-motion'. 'Black Joe' frequently travelled around the south east, hitching lifts on farm waggons and singing in market towns and villages as well as in the metropolis. It is clear from the songs mentioned as in his repertory – George Alexander Stevens's 'Storm', 'The British Seaman's Praise', and H. Green's 'The Wooden Walls of Old England' – that he chose material in close response to the tastes and sentiments of his majority audience, rather than for any expressive quality in relation to his own immediate experience or feelings. Though that is a common enough compromise among all street entertainers, it was, in varying degrees, to remain the case for all black musicians who came to public attention in nineteenth-century Britain. Contemporary writers commented on how much better 'many of these ebony personages' fared as beggars and buskers by comparison with Whites. Johnson, it was said, never failed to gain the farmer's penny on his rural rides, and many believed that some black mendicants had amassed small fortunes. The possession of black skin was to some extent an advantage in that it could draw on the anti-slavery public sentiment of the time. It was primarily because of this that many Blacks were said to 'possess lucrative stands', and to be well patronized as serenaders. Their success is indicated as well by the opportunistic 'lamp-blacks', white men who blacked up and 'stood pad' as real Africans.[5]

The other of the two most celebrated black street entertainers of this period certainly had a lucrative stand. Billy Waters, one of the St Giles 'black birds' and dubbed 'King of the Beggars' in London, regularly busked outside the Adelphi Theatre in the Strand, trying as he put it to obtain an 'honest living by scraping de cat-gut!' He wore a ribbon-decked cocked hat and feathers, and as he sawed away on the fiddle, would engage in various 'peculiar antics', grinning madly and suddenly turning and kicking out his wooden leg. This he had gained while serving in the British navy, having lost his own after falling from the top-sail yard to the quarter deck on the *Ganymede* sloop of war. He received only 'a trifling pension' after he left the navy and, like Johnson, turned street-singer in the effort to earn his daily bread. For a while at least, he did well. The burden of his well-known ditty

> Kitty will you marry me,
> Kitty will you cry –
> Kitty will you marry me,
> Kitty will you cry! cry-cry!

was probably as much echoed in the London streets at that time as Rice's 'Jump Jim Crow' chorus was to be some twenty years later.

Waters was exceptional not only because of his comparative success as a street-singer, but also for a short time as a result of his performances within the Adelphi Theatre itself, where he played himself in the stage version of Pierce Egan's widely read *Life in London*. He and his companion African Sal were among the favourite characters in Moncrieff's highly successful production there. The Adelphi was also one of the two London venues where T. 'Daddy' Rice first made such a spectacular splash with his grotesque song and dance act in 1838. In many ways, as a musician and dancer, Waters prefigured Rice's black-face act, though without of course the aid of burnt cork. On his death-bed in St Giles workhouse in 1823, Waters cursed 'dam Tommy Jerry', attributing his appearance alongside the stage versions of those two notorious Regency bucks as the reason why the 'fickle British public refused to be as liberal as they had been'. He was forced to pawn 'his old friend, the fiddle' for a meagre sum prior to entering the workhouse, and he died an indigent pauper. His renown as an eccentric popular figure outlasted him, however: Catnach cashed in on it by publishing a mock Last Will, and he and African Sal were featured later in a Staffordshire pottery series of 'English Characters'.[6]

Blacks undoubtedly continued to provide musical entertainment for both 'respectable' and 'vulgar' classes, in London and perhaps also in the old slave ports, though with what frequency this was true of specifically poor, working-class groups one cannot say. Pierce Egan noted in 1821 that at a party in the East End, 'Lascars, blacks, jack tars, coal heavers, dustmen, women of colour,

old and young, and a sprinkling of once fine girls . . . were all jigging together'.
By that time Black Balls were a thing of the past, for the black community
lacked the cohesion to mount them.[7]

Blacks like Waters and Johnson not only exploited the role of victim but also,
equally self-consciously, slotted into the commonly held white assumption that
racially they were possessed of an innate musicality, an exuberant sense of
rhythm and musical expressiveness that were peculiar to their African origins.
The view of socio-cultural characteristics as manifestations of deep-seated,
ethnic traits continued to serve throughout the century, in some ways with
increasing rigidity, as the major template by which black people were understood. Black musicality, seen as quintessentially a 'spontaneous and emotional
creation, an uninhibited, dynamic expression of vitality', was a central element
in this understanding, and one which antithetically confirmed the ascendant
bourgeois self-image and culture.[8] In contrast to a self-ascribed bourgeois
musicality that was spiritual and elevated, a physically uninhibited and emotionally impulsive musicality was integral to black cultural stereotypicality.
Nevertheless, a distinctively black subcultural musical identity is likely to have
existed only embryonically in Britain at this time. Although an occasional 'wild'
vocalization would have been in line with the exploitation of black performers
of notions of an innate primitive musicality, it was perhaps only in the second
half of the eighteenth century, at black hops, that shades or inflexions of
African idiomatic expression might have been introduced into black musical
performance.

The same point holds for black military musicians. Blacks had been employed as regimental bandsmen from the seventeenth century, but the tradition
was extended and expanded by the vogue for 'Janissary' music. This Turkish
band music became fashionable in western Europe from the mid-eighteenth
century and lasted well into the nineteenth century. Blacks were prominent as
members of British army bands, and the Turkish music was performed by them
from the outset, 'undoubtedly because their dark skins added the necessary
touch of glamour and their skill in playing percussions made them indispensable'. The Janissary movement, and Blacks along with it, then spread into
secular popular music.

Henry George Farmer has written extensively and appreciatively of black
army bandsmen, and set their achievements in proper perspective, while
Wright and Fryer have more recently provided useful summaries of their
history.[9] In his account, Fryer claims that black army musicians constituted 'a
privileged sub-culture of an alien society'. The presence of a distinctive identity
and orientation is a defining feature of subcultural groups. For black musicians
in His Majesty's Service, this must to some extent have been built up through
pride in their gorgeous and outlandish dress, with its oriental accoutrements,
through their enthusiasm, swagger and skill in movement, in timing, in
acrobatic movements and virtuosity, and through the admiration of their
comrades and of the crowds who thronged to see and hear them. Yet the extent
to which their group identity, and their orientation to the wider social and

imperial order in which they existed, was distinctive in a specifically subcultural sense, remains debatable, particularly in view of the strict army discipline of the time.

Besides bandsmen, the only other exception to the struggle for survival which most black musicians faced in Britain was the handful of gifted individuals upon whom was conferred the even greater privilege of aristocratic or royal patronage. By the second quarter of the nineteenth century, this had largely been withdrawn, and was then only extended to visiting black performers like Elizabeth Taylor Greenfield or the Fisk Jubilee Singers. One reason for this patronage at the turn of the century was that the image of the Black had not yet rigidly hardened into the antithesis of the English gentleman. Blacks who could evince a bearing of refinement, cultivation and good manners – Afro-American abolitionists or African students for example – were hospitably received by the gentry and nobility and judged more on the basis of their social accomplishments than their ethnic identity. In the second half of the century, and particularly from the 1860s, the 'gentleman of colour' became seen as a contradiction in terms, since by then only white skin could ensure the true presence and mark of a gentleman.[10]

This shift in attitude was part of the wider rigidification of racial values, the growth of a specifically racist ideology in Victorian Britain out of a matrix of ethnocentric assumptions and perceptions. Such ethnocentrism may have allowed a greater expression of tolerance, but Blacks were nevertheless utilized, in the early nineteenth century, as 'a jet ornament to society'. The convention of black servants grew up in the eighteenth century when, in a variety of offices, Blacks were a common appurtenance of fine living, dressed in court livery and indulged in as household pets and symbols of prestige. The patronage which some of them enjoyed extended to musical tutelage. Their appeal to the English aristocracy and gentry was inseparable from their ethnicity. Black Pompeys and Darling Blacks were taken up, encouraged and hailed to a great extent as a result of their intense curiosity value. The demonstration of their talents in music and the other arts as equal to those of well-educated white people created among their audiences and patrons a sense of amazement and awe, the *frisson* of an extreme unlikelihood disproved. To Bridgetower's immaculate skill as a violinist was added his status as a black child prodigy. When he played at concerts in the fashionable spa of Bath, he drew record-breaking audiences who 'were gratified by such skill on the violin [which] created general astonishment, as well as pleasure'.[11]

It would be ungracious to focus the accomplishments of Blacks like Soubise, Bridgetower, St Georges and Sancho, and the response with which they were met, entirely around the alternating play of positive and negative feelings associated with their blackness. The West African Sancho, for instance, was a widely read individual of considerable self-generated achievement in various realms, of which musical composition and performance was only one. Audiences as well no doubt felt as profound a delight in accomplished black musicianship as they did in white. Yet despite Sancho's English cultural models, his 'broad talents, white friends … endless patience and good humour', he was always to remain the black 'outsider', never 'truly at home in England', as he himself, without bitterness, was acutely aware. Blacks 'to the English', he wrote, 'from Othello to Sancho the big . . . are either foolish – or mulish – all – all without a single exception'. Whether performing at the top or bottom end of the polarized musical world, Blacks were never fully assimilated into white society (miscegenation being the only exclusion to the rule). English race-thinking at the time was certainly tempered by the humanitarian philanthropy of the opponents of slavery, and some white people seem to have disengaged themselves from – or to have freed themselves in large measure from – hostile prejudicial assumptions in evaluating black talents. Parke, for instance, in speaking of one black man's musical ability on the oboe, felt that this proved 'that an African with a cultivated mind differs from an European in nothing but his colour, which is not the effect of *sin*, but *sun*'. Yet colour was always a possible barrier in social life, as the experience of Joseph Emidee attested. His performances on the violin were evidently greatly admired at parties and concerts in Cornwall, where he lived after being impressed for seven years as ship musician on board Sir Edward Pellew's the *Indefatigible*, playing hornpipes, jigs and reels for the crew's evening dancing and revels. But the proposal that he should give a public performance in London in the late 1800s was opposed (despite the success of musicians like Bridgetower) on the grounds that 'his colour would be so much against him, that there would be a great risk of failure'.[12]

Song and dance men

The cultural frames in which black performers operated in Britain remained, throughout the nineteenth century, predominantly either those associated with the status arts of the structurally powerful, or those of the travestied and blanchified version of Afro-American culture that was represented by the 'nigger' minstrel phenomenon. Certain Blacks continued to 'play de skientific' like 'massa Pagganninny', and did so within the appropriate ritualized contexts of polite musical performance, while others worked within the popular vein of entertainment. This distinction, however, is rather too neat. There is considerable evidence of bi-musical competence and cross-over between the opposed worlds of musical communication. This stylistic mix in repertory continued into the twentieth century, as for instance in the concert performances of Paul Robeson.

Minstrel acts and shows on the professional stage were performed almost exclusively by white men in burnt cork or 'nigger' black make-up, with occasional appearances by white female performers, up to the 1870s, when Blacks themselves began to appear more regularly as stage entertainers, both within the minstrel form and in jubilee choirs. This was true also of alfresco and street minstrelsy in Britain. The busker practice represented by the likes of Waters and Johnson had radically diminished by the mid-century. Only one genuine 'Negro' figured in Mayhew's estimate of the fifty black-face buskers working the streets of London in the early 1850s, though he encountered a number of black beggars. There were some significant exceptions to this pattern between 1840 and 1870, at least on the professional stage. To date, the relatively greater degree of attention paid to British minstrelsy within the serious historical study of popular entertainment has tended to obscure the music of Blacks themselves, particularly outside the minstrel context. 'Daddy' Rice's black-face success in England from 1838 is thus much more commonly referred to than the acclaimed visit the previous year by Frank Johnson, and yet Johnson was a far more accomplished artist than the opportunistic Rice. Although there was strong rivalry from other Blacks within his home town, Johnson was regarded as Philadelphia's leading bandmaster, and the small group of his musicians which he took across the Atlantic was the first American band to give concerts in Britain.[13]

As well as being a celebrated violinist and bugle player, Johnson (1792–1844) was a prolific composer. 'His output included cotillions, quadrilles, marches, and other dances, sentimental ballads, patriotic songs, operatic arrangements, and even minstrel songs.' Added to this was the even greater versatility in the various musical styles offered by his bands and orchestras, moving between the provision of music for aristocratic balls and parties, military parades, sacred-music concerts, Black Balls and funerals, and the 'promenade concert' – an institution which Johnson first established in the USA after his return from Europe. His repertory in England, where he gave concerts in all the principal cities, included operatic arias, comic songs, instrumental numbers and arrangements of English and American patriotic pieces, a mixture of material that evidently went down well in London: his band's 'scientific' performances of music culminated in a command performance for Queen Victoria, who presented him with a silver bugle. It was said that Johnson had 'a remarkable taste for distorting a sentimental, simple and beautiful song into a reel, jig, or country-dance'. In the kind of confrontation between black and white values which this playful, subversive approach represented were the cultural seeds of later stylistic distillations, such as ragtime and jazz.[14]

Following Johnson, another black musician made a significant visit to Britain in 1843, the same year as the white minstrel Dan Emmett. Joe Sweeney was a singer and banjo player who rejected the Jim Crow-type plantation costume and attempted to improve the image of the Black, but he is noted more for the fact that he introduced the modern form of the banjo to Britain. Even before Johnson's tour, England had been toured in the 1820s by two black entertainers from New York. James Hewlett (d. 1840s), the principal actor of the African Grove, worked in London and the provinces as a singer and mimic, and was followed by the black tragedian, Ira Aldridge (1807–67), who 'shipped for Old England' in *c*.1824. In view of the racist press campaign against him by the pro-slavery forces in London in the early 1830s, it is perhaps adding insult to injury to lump Aldridge with the minstrel song and dance men who subsequently appeared in Britain, but along with his brilliance as a 'serious' actor, Aldridge excelled in performing the popular song material he commonly sang on stage to his own guitar accompaniment. His repertory included ballads, comic songs and proto-minstrel pieces. Of the latter, 'Opossum up a Gum Tree' was just as much associated with him as with Charles Matthews. 'Let Me, When My Heart is Sinking' and 'The Negro's Lament', for which Aldridge was also renowned, both came from Bickerstaffe's *The Padlock*, a musical enterainment of the time in which Aldridge played the part of Mungo, who, though a slave, was 'not the usual abject, servile creation of the nineteenth century melodramas' but 'a man of spirit, protesting against his ill-treatment, and daring to voice his protests even to his master'. The light-hearted song 'Let Me, When My Heart is Sinking' ends with an appropriate sting in its tail:

> We dance and we sing
> Till we make the house ring,
> And, tyed in his garters,
> Old Massa may swing.[15]

The most significant exception to the dominance of the white black-face performer in the 1840–70 period was the celebrated William Henry Lane (*c*.1825–52), popularly known by his sobriquet of Master Juba. At the height of his fame in the 1840s, Lane was commonly acclaimed as the most outstanding contemporary exponent of popular dance. One of the earliest historians of minstrelsy, Edward Le Roy Rice, claimed that the 'world never saw his equal'. Yet today, despite the enormous influence he exerted on the art of solo dance forms, he is relatively unknown, although one writer in particular, Marian Hannah Winter, did produce a well-rounded appraisal of his achievement over forty years ago. As she wrote then: 'Almost legendary among his contemporary colleagues, the Juba epic dwindled into oblivion'; even black historians, 'intent on apotheosizing Ira Aldridge, the African Roscius, ignored him'. The 'Greatest Dancer in the World', as the handbills called him, 'did not excel at an art which had prestige'.

In Lane's dancing the Irish jig was assimilated into Afro-American vernacular and not only considerably embellished, but also forged into a new form that had a profound impact on the developing minstrel tradition. While his achievement must be set within the rich matrix of vernacular dance steps, capers, theatrical gestures and acrobatics from which his art emerged, credit for his excellence and his many innovations must also be fully paid. As Winter put it in 1947: 'The repertoire of any current tap-dancer contains elements which were established theatrically by him'. His exceptional qualities as a dancer were acknowledged shortly before he came to London, when he achieved the unprecedented distinction of receiving top billing with four white minstrels. Juba was also 'a first-rate singer and tambourine virtuoso', but it was his dancing which was exceptional, equivalent in effect to a musical instrument. He arrived in London in the summer of 1848 with Pell's Ethiopian Serenaders.

Juba stole the show when Pell's troupe appeared at a crowded Vauxhall Gardens. The *Illustrated London News* (5 August 1848: p. 77) considered his versions of the 'Virginny Breakdown', the 'Tennessee Double-shuffle', the 'Louisiana Toe-and-Heel' and the rest as authentic 'nigger' dances, and stood in awe of the way he 'could tie his legs into such knots, and fling them about so recklessly, or make his feet twinkle, until you lose sight of them altogether in his energy'. The review praised Lane as well for his 'intricate management' of the tambourine, from which he produced 'marvellous harmonies': 'We almost question whether, upon a great emergency, he could not play a fugue upon it'. Also noted for its singularity was 'the rapidity with which he sings one of his favourite songs'. Dicken's widely quoted description of Juba's dancing in New York is closely matched in enthusiasm by the London reviews. The general consensus was that in style and execution Juba's dancing was 'unlike anything ever seen in this country'. Lane appeared before the Queen at Buckingham Palace, and went with Pell's troupe to Liverpool, where one witness spoke of him dancing 'demisemi, semi, and quavers, as well as the slower steps'. He stayed on in England, but died three years later, in London, in miserable circumstances. He was still only in his late twenties, and had quite literally danced himself to death. Years of poor diet and irregular sleep only exacerbated his physical breakdown.[16]

The critic for the *Theatrical Times*, in August 1848, considered Juba's performances as 'far above' those of 'the mountebanks who give imitations of American and Negro character'. An interest in the 'genuine article' remained – fuelled by the small size of the black population at home – and black talent undoubtedly served to revive minstrelsy and raise audience levels at various times, though particulary after the Civil War. Success was by no means guaranteed, however, simply by the inclusion of black performers, as one of the first people to bring a real black minstrel troupe to England in the *post-bellum* period discovered to his cost.

Sam Hague (1828–1901) was an English clog dancer who had worked in the USA and become a minstrel business manager. His twenty-six man ex-slave troupe had been freed from plantation existence only a few months before their first performance in England, at the Theatre Royal in Liverpool on 9 July 1866. This explains why Hague's Georgia Minstrels were lacking in professionalism, with little if any prior experience of the popular stage. They were mainly required to offer a portrait of life on the old plantation, and their only stage costume consisted of garments identical to those worn in their slavery days. Small wonder that the public, as Reynolds puts it, found 'this crude representation of real negro life' poor in entertainment value by contrast with 'the educated, refined minstrel companies that were then so popular in England'.[17] Their inability to read, write 'or tell a note of music from a horseshoe', since they 'all played and sang by ear', obviously precluded any short-term shift to a repertory more in line with contemporary English taste. Hague was forced to compromise, shipping back at his own expense those who wanted to return home, and engaging a number of white professionals to work with the black performers who remained.

Reynolds disapprovingly notes that those remaining lived a 'fast and dissipated life' that soon led to the grave, the only one remaining alive suffering a paralytic stroke rendering him unable to work, but his account of Hague's subsequent minstrel successes mentions four accomplished black entertainers who worked under him, so it is clear that Hague was willing to continue drawing on black talent of various kinds. The dwarf 'Japanese Tommy' (Thomas Dilward) worked as a fiddler, singer and dancer. Neil Solomon and Abe Cox were comics; Cox's *pièce de résistance* was a 'Hen Convention' song, with vocal farmyard imitations. Aaron Banks was 'tall, good looking' and 'with a very pleasing voice'. His most renowned song was 'Emancipation Day', which usually met with a double encore when he sang it. 'No white man could have put the same amount of enthusiasm and realism into this song of jubilation as did Aaron Banks, the freed slave.' Banks continued to work with Hague at least into the late 1870s, operating as a corner man with his touring troupe (one troupe remained resident in Liverpool) 'at all the principal towns in Great Britain'.[18]

George Hicks (*c.*1840s–1902), one of the earliest of the black minstrel managers, toured Europe with a few of his minstrels in 1870, and then also joined Hague's Slave Troupe with his black colleagues in the summer of that year, playing throughout England and Ireland during the course of the following twelve months. Hague's success in England, after the initial hiccup, was significant, according to Toll, in helping black minstrels establish themselves as entertainers in the USA. Hague and Hicks had a violent disagreement, and in the early 1870s Hicks drew Dilward, Banks and Cox across to the USA, although not permanently in Banks' case. The comedian Bob Height, later compared to Bert Williams, was another Black to work with Hague in England after emigrating in the early 1870s in disgust with Charles Callender's economic exploitation of black performers.

Hague's minstrels subsequently toured the USA in the early 1880s and were extremely successful, particularly because of the fine quality of their music. But where British minstrelsy was offering novel features in the USA, so American minstrelsy trail-blazed a bumper version of the minstrel show on a scale not seen before in the British Isles. The minstrel show format by this time provided a loose but dynamic framework within which all sorts of popular entertainments could be presented and developed. This prototypical variety show framework undoubtedly contributed to the continuing success of minstrelsy during the later nineteenth century. Haverly's visiting troupes worked this *melange* at an exciting high speed, and added to it grand scale, superb talent, and all sorts of spectacular effects, preceded by lavish advertising campaigns up and down the country. His initial success in Britain encouraged him to bring over an all-black troupe in 1881, consisting of sixty-five 'real negroes', both male and female and of all ages, from 'the ancient Uncle Toms and Aunt Cloes, smart young coons and wenches, down to the little Piccanniny'. Along with plantation ballads, concerted numbers and 'comic nigger ditties and witticisms', the programme at Her Majesty's Theatre included spirituals, first introduced to the English, Scots and Welsh eight years previously by the Fisk Jubilee Singers, who were in turn burlesqued in the show. There were various individuals of particular merit in Haverly's Coloured Minstrels, such as Tom McIntosh, Wallace King and Richard Little. But perhaps of greatest significance were the principal comedian, Billy Kersands; James Bland, one of the most notable black songwriters of his day; Horace Weston, a musician, dancer and actor who had toured Britain several times before his visit with Haverly, as for instance with Jarrett and Palmer's Uncle Tom company in 1878, when he 'scored an enormous hit' as the 'Black Bonanza' with his virtuoso banjo playing; and the Bohee Brothers, also banjo players of outstanding distinction, and tutors on that instrument to the Prince of Wales.

Haverly's success with black performers in Britain – the show toured the provinces over 1881–2 – was followed up by similar enterprises, such as Callender's All-Coloured Minstrels. James Bland and the Bohee Brothers were among about half a dozen Blacks who stayed on in Britain after Haverly's return. Bland (1854–1911) was a black troubadour, credited with having written over 600 songs, although his 'Carry Me Back to Old Virginny', 'Oh, Dem Golden Slippers' and 'Hand Me Down My Walking Cane' are among the handful best remembered. Bland wrote mainly within the vein of the old-time 'darky' plantation melody so notably developed by Stephen Foster, but he was for obvious reasons more directly influenced by black vernacular, ex-slave song, in the post-Civil-War period in which his talents prospered. Though he had to struggle initially to gain recognition, Bland was a tremendous success in Britain, achieving for himself the sobriquet 'Idol of the Halls', and although he wore black-face when appearing in minstrel shows, he managed to discard the use of 'nigger' make-up for his solo performances with the banjo in the concert halls, clubs and restaurants of the metropolis. Some of his most famous songs were launched in London and, according to his semi-fictionalized biography, he was a success with critics and people alike.

James and George Bohee were noted for their soft-shoe dances as well as their prodigious banjo-playing skills. They ran a banjo studio in London, and regularly toured the provinces for six-month spells, always preceding their shows with street parades, as did various other troupes. According to *The Era*, the Bohees' 'novel business' had many imitators, and every 'barrel-organ played their favourite banjo song and dance' 'I'll Meet Her When the Sun Goes Down'. James Bohee, who died in Ebbw Vale while on tour in 1897, was, according to W. MacQueen Pope, 'about the finest banjoist the world ever saw, or listened to'. George, with his fine tenor, did the singing in their act. Along with Bland and others, the Bohees gave command performances, and were popular at society functions and private entertainments as well as in the halls, both on their own and with their troupe, who at one time included the Black Swan Trio (which featured the black female singer, Carlene Cushman).

Toll describes Kersands as the most famous, and highest paid, black minstrel star. He 'acted out the caricatured role of the ignorant, slow-witted black man', and was renowned for the 'comic contortions of his gigantic mouth'. This included feats of dancing with a cup and saucer inside his mouth, or giving a monologue with several billiard balls in his cheeks. It would be too easy to see this kind of grotesque humour as simply rubber-stamping the demeaning character of black stereotypicality as portrayed by Whites. To some extent the injury was exacerbated, but in other ways Kersands – along with other black performers – indirectly or covertly offered a black subtext, and utilized Afro-American vernacular culture much more than any white minstrel ever did. This was more obviously the case with his songs, like the celebrated *Old Aunt Jemima*, and with his buck-and-wing and Essence of Old Virginia dances. Undoubtedly acting Sambo on stage for the sake of professional success was deeply humiliating, but artists like Kersands in certain ways transcended the barbed-wire circle of racist response through the sheer brilliance of their skills, and through carrying a stereotypical feature to the point of utter absurdity, thereby cathartically draining off some of its venom. 'Son, if they hate me', he once said without a smile, 'I'm still whipping them, because I'm making them laugh'.[19]

The luxury of an entirely new sensation

The command performance became a common occurrence for outstanding black artists visiting Britain. Elizabeth Taylor Greenfield (*c*.1824–76) was born a slave in Natchez, Mississippi, but manumitted when her mistress joined the Society of Friends. Given encouragement when she taught herself to play guitar, she showed considerable musical talent, to the degree that, after she began singing publicly, she became dubbed the Black Swan and the African Nightingale (after Jenny Lind). She arrived in Britain at Liverpool Docks in April 1853. The person with whom she had drawn up a contract for her tour 'was unfaithful to his promises', and left her destitute, but she found ready patronage from Lord Shaftesbury, and from the Stowe-Sutherland circle that had gathered around the ideological focus of Stowe's *Uncle Tom's Cabin*.

At her Stafford House concert the Black Swan sang to the 'choicest' of London's elite, including foreign ambassadors and 'ladies in demi-toilet and bonneted'. The highlight of her performance appears to have been a rendition of Foster's 'Old Folks at Home', giving one verse in the soprano, another in the tenor voice. Harriet Beecher Stowe wrote: 'Her voice, with its keen searching fire, its penetrating vibrant quality, its timbre . . . cut its way like a Damascus blade to the heart'. Greenfield's first public concert was at the Queen's Concert Rooms in Hanover Square. The London papers all commended her singing; *The London Advertiser* found her voice 'peculiarly effective in ballad-songs of the pathetic cast', such as 'The Cradle Song' and 'Home Sweet Home'. She then went on to appear in Brighton, Dublin and Lincoln, among other places, culminating in her performance before the Queen. She returned to the USA in the summer of 1854, having established herself as the most notable black concert artist of her day.[20]

'Blind Tom' Bethune (1849–1908) followed Greenfield in 1866 as the next major black sensation on the British concert music scene. Whereas Greenfield's accomplishments were explained in terms of the romantic ideology of genius, Blind Tom was classed as an 'idiot savant'. He was financially exploited by his master, both before and after the Civil War,[21] and exhibited initially as a blind Negro Boy Wonder, and later as a vaudeville attraction, but he also gave many 'serious' concert performances in the USA and Europe. Although Tom could undoubtedly pick up by ear and with great facility extremely complex piano compositions, the considerable evidence of his rigid practice schedule severely undermines the idea that he was simply a 'natural', untaught prodigy. And, while he attracted an unfortunate amount of attention as a 'musical curiosity' whose feats had to be rigorously tested, his reputation was not merely based on his 'scientific' exhibit value. He was also seriously regarded as a musician and composer of considerable merit.[22]

Yet what characterizes many of the reviews of his British performances is the way recognition of his talent, intelligence and sensitivity is controverted by the label of 'imbecile'. This was undoubtedly fostered by his promoters who understood the economic value of staging an unusual spectacle, even before 'a decidedly "genteel" and select assembly'. But the contradictory ideas built up around Tom also fitted the racial stereotype of the 'Negro' as exhibiting a 'natural' musicality and the sub-rational features of primitivism and affectivity accompanying that 'instinct'. Allied with this were the physical ape/artistic angel antinomy that could give such a delicious thrill to the educated White, and the notion that blindness leads to an uncommonly advanced development of other faculties, such as the memory. Certainly Blind Tom seems to have possessed a powerful memory, but his classification as 'idiot savant' has hardly any more historical credibility than a Barnumesque puff. As James M. Trotter wrote: 'Who ever heard of an idiot possessing such power of memory, such fineness of musical sensibility, such order, such method as he displays?'[23]

Perhaps the biggest black music sensation of the Victorian period was the troupe of singers from Fisk University, Nashville, Tennessee. The story of the Fisk Jubilee Singers was among the best-known in the annals of black musicians in Britain. The intention to raise money for the Negro Fisk University by touring the Northern States and Britain with a choir performing black spirituals, was brilliantly realized. They made two major tours of Britain, from April 1873 to May 1874, and from May 1875 to October 1877 (with an intervening two-month visit to Holland). One of the original members of the troupe, Frederick J. Loudin, returned in 1884 and 1887 with another choral group, and later settled in Britain. After the first tour, two of the singers stayed behind, one of them to study music, while a third, Tom Rutling, after seven and a half years with the Jubilee Singers, settled in Harrogate to teach singing, perform popular concerts and give lectures on slave life in the *ante-bellum* South 'with its tragedy, pathos and humour . . . illustrated by its quaint music'.[24]

Although the category of verisimilitude was fraught with problems of appropriate evaluative yardsticks and criteria of assessment, minstrelsy's realist credentials had always vied with its other sources of attraction and appeal. This delight in what was perceived as 'authenticity' was true also of the reception of the Jubilee Singers, who were contrasted with their black-face counterfeits just as performers like Juba had been before them.[25] Yet the origins of black spirituals or 'anthems' are obscure; 'the ways in which they were first sung are probably unknown'; and there is uncertainty about the extent to which spirituals were an original black genre.[26] What is certain is that the refinement of their material and the diminution of black performance features underpinned the tremendous success of the Fisk Singers in the Old World, as did the inclusion in their repertory of other non-spiritual religious material, sentimental songs and, as a set-piece yet again, 'Old Folks at Home'.

The generally highly favourable reception which the British gave to the Fisk Jubilee Singers ranged from the hauteur of Queen Victoria's 'Tell them we are delighted with their songs' to the unaffected joy of the 'simple' Highland girl who exclaimed, 'It filled my whole heart!'. The gatherings at which they performed were invariably under the patronage of the aristocracy, gentry, local dignatories and clergy, including those of Nonconformist denominations, and their packed audiences were generally 'highly respectable' and/or 'highly fashionable': in Hawick, for instance, 'most of the elite of the town and neighbourhood [were] present'. The sentimentalist philanthropic interest of the aristocracy and gentry in the anti-slavery cause in the third quarter of the nineteenth century has been well chronicled, and this clearly accounts for one line of attraction to the Fisk Singers. But *Uncle Tom's Cabin* was among the most widely read books of the Victorian period, and its broad popularity (regardless of its ideological misrepresentations) attests to the depth of anti-slavery feeling among all sectors of the population. Sympathy for the black experience of slavery in the USA undoubtedly impelled many to attend the performances of the Fisk troupe's 'sorrow songs', and when the troupe evinced themselves as noble, dignified, devout 'pilgrims' with 'quiet and unassuming manners', the strength of their appeal 'to the sensibilities of the religious and philanthropic public' was singularly reinforced.[27]

All of the newspaper reviews which I have so far located expressed considerable enthusiasm for what was heard. The *Standard* valued it as 'the best entertainment of its kind that has ever been brought out in London'. The *Hull News* called their performance 'one of the richest treats which has ever been provided in this town'. In Sheffield their 'beautiful voices' were felt to 'manifest the perfection of vocal euphony', while in Leicester the programme, 'at once varied and attractive', was considered to have been 'rendered throughout in a manner which, for taste and skill, could hardly be surpassed even by vocalists of greater pretensions'. These reports echoed the general response of the singers' audiences. In Derby, for instance, the 'audience listened with rapt attention, and applauded with boundless enthusiasm, and *encored* the singers most unmercifully', while the solos of Minnie Tate and Maggie Porter received 'great applause' in Hawick and were 'loudly encored' in Derby. The *Birmingham Morning News* summed up the situation in speaking of the unmistakeable evidence that 'the immense audiences which gathered to hear were gratified with the exhibitions'.[28]

Yet there are clear signs in the reviews of uncertainty as to how to respond to the Jubilee Singers' 'plaintive wild plantation hymns and melodies' with 'their pathetic heart stirring strains'. This is at least partly explained by the struggle to put into words the beauty of the harmonies, the thrill of the glides, inflections and tonal extensions, the sense of what a *Daily Telegraph* reporter called 'the luxury of an entirely new sensation'. As another London review attempted it: 'There is something inexpressibly touching in their wonderful, sweet, round bell, voices, in the way in which they sing, so artless in its art, yet so consummate in its expression, and in the mingling of the pathetic with the unconscious comic in the rude hymns, shot here and there with a genuine golden thread of poetry'. The *Hull News* spoke of their 'quaint compositions, which called forth alike smiles and tears', while a Sheffield reporter wrote that their songs were 'so full of pathos, and withal so grotesque and comic that you unconsciously rejoice with them in their happiness, and grieve with them in their misery ... [they] sing as if they have been taught by nature'. What this West Yorkshire reviewer was striving to express was the sense of 'something altogether novel in their songs', in their time and pronunciation as well as their content, along with the wondrous quality of the vocal performance: 'Steal Away to Jesus' floated 'along the hall with softest cadence as though angels sang', while the chanting in unison of the Lord's Prayer touched 'the deepest recesses of the heart'. The music was 'unique – almost rude to a refined taste, but yet it is singularly sweet and genuine; and although it is possible that educated musicians might pooh-pooh it, still it has a chaste novelty'.[29]

Educated musicians and writers were equally if not more confused in their reaction to the Fisk Singers. *The Orchestra* described their music as an odd mixture of German part-song, Scottish national airs and Dutch traits! But the most common confusion in characterizing their performances was in identifying them with 'the merry "nigger" refrains of ordinary Christy minstrels'. Even though sharp distinctions were usually drawn between spiritual singers and the 'coon' minstrel, some shreds of association unavoidably lingered, particularly in view of the idea of the spiritual as plantation song, itself a mainstay of the minstrel tradition. Hence the references to comic and grotesque features, to a curious 'compound of the touching and the ridiculous'. Racial arrogance also surfaced. The *Birmingham Morning News* not only referred to 'exhibitions' (evoking images of circus savages) but also described the Fisk songs as 'specimens of a kind of art developed amongst a people of a semi-barbaric race brought into contact with the more cultivated'.[30]

Any notable innovation and success in popular entertainment engenders its genuine successors and its fake imitators working a racket. Loudin's re-formed Fisk troupe and Orpheus McAdoo's Virginia Jubilee Singers nobly followed the original Fisk troupe on the British tour circuit. The Canadian Jubilee Singers toured Britain in the 1880s with the purpose of raising money for a black theological seminary in Ontario. A 'native' South African choir, derived from seven distinct tribes, sucessfully toured Britain in 1892 in order to raise money for the establishment of black technical schools in the colony. Their 'worthy cause' attracted many public figures, and in what was now long-established practice, they sang before the Queen. They were said to have 'excited a new interest in our dusky fellow-subjects at the Cape'.[31] But as with the early-nineteenth-century lamp-blacks, other troupes appear to have existed only to milk human sympathy for the benefit of their own pockets – the Wilmington Jubilee Singers (taken over by Hague) and Sherwood's Missionary Band, who toured Britain in 1876–7 and 1894, are cases in point. Minstrelsy shows also cashed in on the huge public interest in 'sperichuls', both by satirizing them and by absorbing them into the gallimaufry of their repertory.

More importantly, black religious music has continued 'to furnish a reservoir of inspiration to the entire jazz tradition', and that tradition has spawned or catalysed a wide range of highly significant developments in popular music as a whole.[32] The basis for such cross-fertilization was laid in the nineteenth century. Indeed, the process of assimilation, adaptation, collision, synthesis and reassimilation has operated continuously across the boundaries between black and white musical traditions and genres since the start of the period covered here, and yet historical research on its dynamics within the British context has only barely begun. I have attempted here only to clear the ground for that work and to gain some sense, however inchoate, of the contemporary experience and evaluation of black musicians in nineteenth-century Britain. How we 'hear' their voices now is a further problem, encircled with thorny historiographical briars and hidden analytical snares, yet it is one which must become central to the task of historical music scholarship.

Veteran members of the Fisk Jubilee Singers on their way to perform before the Royal Family at Windsor Castle, 1925. *Collection: Paul Oliver*

2 Afro-American Symphony: Popular Black Concert Hall Performers 1900–40

JEFFREY GREEN

At the beginning of the twentieth century the most popular composer living in Britain was a black man named Samuel Coleridge-Taylor. His music was performed in concert halls across the land, by choirs and instrumentalists, amateur and professional. Errand boys whistled fragments in the streets; piano rolls were manufactured; sheet music was sold in the thousands; on parlour pianos up and down the land beginners stumbled over 'Demande et Response' from his choral suite *Hiawatha*. Arthur Sullivan and Edward Elgar praised him; Americans, black and white, welcomed him to their shores three times; festivals requested his presence to conduct or judge; he was invited to Germany, and a German reputation and experience were seen as the hallmark of European music for German instrumentalists were famed and its present and past composers dominated the concert hall programme. His sudden death from pneumonia in September 1912 was reported in the world's newspapers and his funeral in Croydon, where he had lived almost all of his thirty-seven years, saw crowds lining the route from the church to the cemetery. His obituary in *The Times* expressed the widespread belief that he would have produced more and enduring works had he lived into maturity. Coleridge-Taylor's ambitions and achievements inspired black people in Africa, in the Caribbean, in the USA and in Britain.

Daniel Taylor from Sierra Leone was educated in Somerset before studying medicine in London; his liaison with Alice Hare Martin led to their son's birth in London in August 1875. Called Coleridge by his mother, he showed his African descent in colour, features and hair. His mother, now married to George Evans, encouraged his violin lessons with local teacher Joseph Beckwith. Funded by a silk merchant named Herbert Walters, the promising musician went to the Royal College of Music in London and there in 1893 he was awarded a scholarship which enabled him to study composition with Charles Stanford. Stanford conducted his Symphony in A minor in 1896 and took his Clarinet Quintet to Berlin, where it was performed by the violinist Joachim in 1897. Queen Victoria's private orchestra played one of his waltzes;

in 1898 his operetta *Dream Lovers* was performed. Associations with the Afro-American dialect poet Paul Dunbar led to *African Romances*; he composed for the Gloucester festival and was written about at length in the prestigious *Musical Times*. He overcame family objections and married Jessie Walmisley, a college colleague, in 1899. His *Hiawatha* works met with immediate and sustained success, and he was invited to the USA by black Americans. This led to anxiety, as his wife wrote in June 1903:

> Take care of him and try and spare him the racial prejudice which I know is so bitter in the South. Some, if not all, our colored friends here wish to prevent him from taking the proposed visit.

Coleridge-Taylor had artistic success but little financial reward from *Hiawatha*, and his professional activities included writing for the theatre, notably for Beerbohm Tree at His Majesty's Theatre in London. The brilliance of *Hiawatha* was never repeated but it remained in performance into the 1950s, and his instrumental pieces are today found in light-classical renditions, but not alongside the 'masters' (for other compositions, see Chapter 5). Contemporaries rated his music higher than that of Elgar; but attitudes have changed. Today it is difficult to find much of his music on disc.[1]

Coleridge-Taylor's black friends included those working for greater influences in the affairs of the world of Africa and African peoples, among them barrister Henry Sylvester Williams from Trinidad, medical practitioner Dr John Alcindor (a Trinidadian graduate of Edinburgh University, who worked in London from 1899 to his death in 1924) and photographer John Richard Archer, of Barbados-Irish parents born in Liverpool, active in politics in south London's Battersea (he was mayor of that borough in 1914). These four men had participated in the Pan-African Conference of July 1900. Williams died in Trinidad in 1911 but Archer and Alcindor attended the composer's funeral.[2]

Another black man who had achieved fame in the performing arts in Britain, albeit in mid-century, was the New-York-born actor Ira Aldridge, whose two daughters by his Swedish wife were very positive about their identity as Blacks. Luranah (born 1860) and Amanda (born 1866) had a musical education: Luranah Aldridge impressed Charles Gounod and her friendships included the Wagners; her sister was a foundation scholar at the Royal College of Music in 1883 where she studied under Jenny Lind, Frederick Bridge and George Henschel. All three had high reputations which survive today in an age when musical achievements are so often measured by the sales statistics of discs. Luranah's career as a singer ended when she was crippled by rheumatism. She and her pianist sister had performed together; Amanda then turned to composition under the name Montague Ring and taught singing. The sisters were part of London's black community, well known to Dr Alcindor for example, and associated with visiting Americans including the singers Roland Hayes and Paul Robeson.

The Times reported Amanda Ira Aldridge's concert at the Steinway Hall on 5 June 1905, which included items by Dvořák, noting 'the subtle quality which enables Miss Aldridge to place herself on good terms with an audience'. This was not a minstrel show or a grotesque and demeaning show, but a performance solidly within concert hall traditions. When back in June 1898 she had performed Coleridge-Taylor's 'A Coon Song' it was not in the sense of that word in the decades-old traditions of music hall and minstrel shows. Luranah sang to her sister's piano at the Queen's Small Hall in central London on 16 December 1905, and the pair were working in Bath in April 1908. Included in Luranah's programme were 'Big Lady Moon' and 'Sweet Baby Butterfly' by Coleridge-Taylor with the words by the Sierra Leonean student Kathleen Easmon.

The sisters appeared at the prestigious Queen's Small Hall in June 1912 and June 1913, and Amanda Aldridge's compositions (as Montague Ring) in the latter recital included 'Where the Paw-Paw Grows (African Serenade)', which had words by Henry Downing, an Afro-American resident of London and long-time friend of the Coleridge-Taylors. Downing had worked in Angola, which seems to rule out his influence in the West African origins of the Fante and 'Togo' themes to Montague Ring's 'Luleta's Dance', performed at the Queen's Small Hall in May 1914.

The children of London's professional or middle-class black community went to Amanda Aldridge's Kensington home for music lessons in the 1920s, and into the 1940s she remained in correspondence with Blacks in Africa and the USA. She influenced Edward Scobie, whose *Black Britannia* of 1972 was a pioneering study of black people in Britain. She died in 1956, knowing that her father's career would be published in Marshall and Stock's biography, which duly appeared in 1958.[3]

Cosmopolitan influences can be seen in the music of Kaikhosru Sorabji, born in Essex in 1892, son of a Parsi engineer from India and an opera singer of Spanish and Sicilian descent. His works are eccentric, for inherited wealth meant that he required no income from performances, some of which require a soloist to play for over two hours. Indeed, one work takes nearly four hours. He retired in 1982 and died in 1988; his writings include two books and hundreds of articles. Sorabji's compositions are well regarded by instrumentalists although opportunities for public performance have been severely restricted.[4]

One composer who was seen by contemporaries as stepping into Coleridge-Taylor's shoes was Edmund Thornton Jenkins from South Carolina. Jenkins arrived in London in 1914 aged twenty after training with Kemper Harreld (also the tutor of the American band-leader, Fletcher Henderson), in the bustling colleges of Atlanta, Georgia. He had first been exposed to formal music at the orphanage his father ran in Charleston, South Carolina, as had another clarinettist. Emerson Harper was also in the orphanage band that played at the Anglo-American Exhibition in London in the summer of 1914, but he returned to the USA, where in the 1930s he pioneered black instrumental contributions on New York radio and began a friendship with poet Langston Hughes, who voiced the ambitions of black America of the 1920s in the so-called Harlem Renaissance. That Edmund Jenkins had to return to Europe in 1924 because there was no substance behind talk of 'black uplift' suggests that opportunities for skilled black musicians could be found in Europe.

Jenkins studied at the Royal Academy of Music for seven years, eventually teaching the clarinet there. Prize-winner and holder of scholarships and medals, Jenkins had considerable instrumental skills, notably the piano, the organ, the violin and the clarinet. His tutor in composition was Frederick Corder, who had been influenced by Wagner and other German composers. Jenkins attempted to merge the folk songs of his native black America into the orchestral traditions of Europe, and sought to keep their emotional and stylistic qualities. He had a broad experience of Afro-American music, having travelled widely in the USA with his father's orphanage band. With the assistance of largely Caribbean student friends he staged and conducted a concert of Coleridge-Taylor's works in London's Wigmore Hall in December 1919 before an audience that included the composer's widow and his teacher Stanford. One piece from Jenkins's pen, a South Carolina fisherman's song, later became his *Charlestonia* theme which was premiered in Belgium. It is to be regretted that he died in Paris in 1926, aged thirty-two.[5]

It is tempting to regard his death as enabling George Gershwin's opera *Porgy and Bess* (first performed in 1935) to be classed as the first American classical style work, combining black themes in a performance that can only be American. It is also arguable that Jenkins's death permitted the Arkansas and Ohio-trained William Grant Still's *Afro-American Symphony* performed in 1931 to be regarded as a breakthrough by black American musicians. Both Jenkins and Still had worked in dance music around 1921, for instrumentalists at academies often worked in theatre and music hall bands. Jenkins's Academy colleague, later the famed conductor Sir John Barbirolli, worked in theatrical pit bands (as had Jenkins) and this, as with dance music, afforded valuable experience of what the public wanted from music, and formed part of the apprenticeship of music students that can be easily overlooked. One of Jenkins's colleagues in the dance band he led with great success at the Queen's Small Hall in 1921–2 was pianist Jack Hylton, who became a very popular and successful promoter in the 1930s. Jenkins had the technical and artistic skill and training to create what Coleridge-Taylor had inspired. The barriers preventing Blacks from performing outside certain areas of popular music reduced the opportunities for Jenkins in America, from which he fled to Paris where he established a music publishing business and wrote an operetta on South Carolina themes.

Those composers of British birth but non-European descent such as Sorabji and Coleridge-Taylor did not have an education that exposed them to the wealth of themes and musics that existed in Africa, Afro-America and the Caribbean. After his contacts with Paul Dunbar and choirmaster Frederick Loudin from Ohio, Coleridge-Taylor did bring in African and West Indian themes into his compositions and he arranged *24 Negro Melodies for the Piano* (1905) before he made his first visit to the USA. Composers from the tropical empire had to overcome the restrictions of colonial life, although music-making in genteel surroundings was not absent from the urban centres. Thus Nicholas

Ballanta-Taylor from Sierra Leone spent many months in the USA around 1920 (where he met Kathleen Easmon) including a spell visiting isolated black communities in Georgia, and training in New York. He traced African themes in Afro-American music, briefly visited Britain, and spent decades teaching in Sierra Leone but without the finances to exploit his ideas of an African piano and compositions in European notation but with African musical styles and harmonies.[6]

When the Georgia-born and Tennessee-raised singer Roland Hayes arrived in Britain in 1920 he was assisted by members of London's black community including Amanda Aldridge. He took lessons from George Henschel, met the Nigerian nationalist and engineer Herbert Macaulay (whose daughter he introduced to Miss Aldridge, for singing lessons), travelled to France and met with general acclaim. His concert hall recitals included Negro spirituals. Here we could see that white audiences expected a black American to sing black church music – but we could also see that Hayes placed those songs in his programme to show a black element in concert music, taking its rightful place alongside songs by Handel, Beethoven, Debussy – and Coleridge-Taylor and Montague Ring.

Hayes's recitals were reported in the press, the *Daily Telegraph* of 23 April 1921 heading its account 'A Negro's Recital' and detailing a Yoruba song Hayes had presented at the Wigmore Hall. 'The versatility of Mr. Hayes is remarkable', the *Telegraph* noted. The report in *The Times* was headed 'A Fine Singer', stating that he was 'a first-class musician' and 'there was everything to praise in his conception of a song as music'. Hayes included songs in Swahili, performed in aid of the African Progress Union which was led by Dr Alcindor, met other African nationalists with Macaulay and the radical John Archer, and also sang for King George V at Buckingham Palace and at a promenade concert at the Queen's Hall. During these years 1920–3 Hayes was accompanied by pianists Lawrence Brown or William Lawrence, who were both active in arranging Negro spirituals. These musicians had fine qualities and were able to perform black music to packed audiences in the concert hall without a suggestion of novelty. Brown, during his early years in London, arranged spirituals for the piano. Of course Coleridge-Taylor had done that, but it had been the success of Harry Burleigh – yet another American singer who had visited Britain (in 1908 and 1909) and whose arrangement of 'Deep River' had taken sacred themes into the secular concert hall performance style – which had broadened the market for this music. The music did not pass through the degradation of minstrelsy, burnt cork and plantation theme shows. Brown and Robeson toured Britain in the late 1940s; Hayes returned to wartime Britain to sing for the blitzed citizens of London.[7]

Another singer active in the 1920s was the Jamaican soprano Marie Lawrence (Mrs Pearson), who first moved to Britain in 1906 with the so-called Native Choir of Jamaica. That choir of a dozen men and women presented American and Jamaican secular and sacred music. In pianist Henry Nation it had a classically trained performer whose career seems to have been ignored, as it is difficult to grasp the concept of a concert hall instrumentalist of African descent. Marie Lawrence knew another member of the Native Choir, Louis George Drysdale, who had settled in London by 1918 and taught many singers there in the 1920s. Drysdale supported himself by tailoring but his list of pupils, like that of Amanda Aldridge, is a veritable who's who of Afro-American singers. Most of them worked in the stage shows that had brought black performers before white audiences since *Shuffle Along* played to packed houses in New York in 1921. Those shows were in the plantation-minstrel traditions but gave steady employment to black singers and instrumentalists including pianist James P. Johnson, who was in London in 1923. Johnson also turned his hand to compositions in the concert hall traditions, joining black themes to European concepts, but without much success. It remains conjecture that he was inspired by his contacts with Jenkins in London. He was able to broaden his horizons for he played for the South African nationalist and ANC official Sol Plaatje (see Chapter 5); and so did Marie Lawrence who sang at the farewell concert for Plaatje at the Mortimer Hall in October 1923. She also sang in respectable London restaurants in the 1920s, and worked in films in the 1930s.[8]

One of the films, *Sanders of the River* (1935), featured Paul Robeson, a lawyer who turned to singing and became politically involved in the advancement of his people. Robeson made his home in London in the 1930s, and his powerful bass voice can be heard on records and in several films. It is easy to be scornful of those films but it was by contacts with African actors that Robeson was stimulated to explore his roots and from that take a political stance. He travelled to the Soviet Union and in Britain was taken up by liberals and left-wing Negrophiles, as well as by well-heeled socialites, which led to a public scandal around Lady Edwina Mountbatten. The most effective establishment figure in such circles was Nancy Cunard, whose massive *Negro* anthology has merit. Her friendships with Blacks left deep wounds and her pianist lover Henry Crowder's autobiography *As Wonderful As All That?* (1987) should be read as widely as Anne Chisholm's *Nancy Cunard* (1981).[9]

There are arguments that would place Robeson in the category of black musician and sex symbol, which cannot be applied to John Payne in the same way. Payne, from Alabama, first arrived in Britain in 1919 and soon had many musical connections, aided by the charity of Lady Mary Cook. Contralto Marian Anderson was one of the guests at Payne's London home in the 1920s. She returned to the USA to become highly praised – and persecuted by racists – for her concert hall performances and recordings of Christmas songs. Payne's pupils also included Don Johnson (born in Cardiff of Welsh-Barbuda parents) who worked in the swing band music style of the late 1930s. The pieces by pianist and composer Reginald Foresythe, a British-born Black, whose music was played by American and British dance bands, are as distinctive as their titles, which are whispy and hint at an unearthly delicacy; they show a merging of orchestral and dance band styles.

Conditions for Blacks were better than in the USA, where reports of institutional prejudice included the Scottsboro incident (when black youths were arrested for alleged rape) and lynchings, but there was severe prejudice at all levels in Britain. Efforts to reduce this led Dr Harold Moody, a Jamaica-born doctor who qualified and settled in London in the 1910s, to establish the League of Coloured Peoples in 1931, a grouping that was largely middle-class professionals in which concert music and other skills such as tennis were recognized.[10] Chicago newspaper magnate Robert Abbott was refused accommodation in twenty hotels in London in 1929; Louis Armstrong's orchestra was rejected by hotels in the 1930s. Details of such events were sent to Afro-American newspapers by Rudolph Dunbar, a skilled clarinettist from Guyana who had been trained in New York and Paris before settling in London around 1930, aged thirty-two. Dunbar wrote a well-respected clarinet tutor book that went into several editions, but his ambitions to conduct were generally thwarted. He died in London in June 1988; his obituary appeared in the *Daily Telegraph* and in the *Independent*.[11]

One of Rudolph Dunbar's musical associates in London in the 1930s was Ufela Sowande from Nigeria, who studied music at Trinity College from 1935. Sowande supported himself by playing in a jazz style in nightclubs, which assisted his contacts with American jazzmen and entertainers. He made radio broadcasts and worked with Dunbar and other Caribbeans in London. One veteran recalled that they performed one of his serious compositions over the radio around 1938. Certainly his *Africana* was broadcast by the BBC in 1944. He moved to the USA and is regarded as the first African to combine African elements with European concert traditions and styles.[12] His contacts with other black people in London in the 1930s, like those of Coleridge-Taylor, the Aldridge sisters, Hayes, Robeson, Drysdale, Jenkins and Ballanta-Taylor, show how cosmopolitan black elements were available in Britain.

One of the musicians active in London in the 1930s was Leslie Thompson from Jamaica, who had studied music in the West India Regiment and had been a medal winner at the British school of military music at Kneller Hall in 1920. He settled in London in 1929 and worked in show orchestras for Charles B. Cochran. By this time the American recordings of Louis Armstrong and the enthusiasm for jazz or swing led many dance band musicians in Britain to believe that such musical skills were the product of a racial element, and so the schooled musician Leslie Thompson was welcomed into dance bands because of his colour.

By 1935 it was financially sensible to establish an 'all-coloured' orchestra, but Thompson's Emperors of Jazz had no Americans. The instrumentalists were of African descent but born in Jamaica, England, Trinidad, Wales and, in the case of Bruce Vanderpoyce who played the bass, South Africa. Thompson had worked with Constant Lambert and others of the concert hall avant-garde in Britain, who had shown different degrees of interest in jazz, including Spike Hughes, William Walton and Noel Coward. He moved into Latin American music and after the Second World War took formal tuition at London's Guildhall School of Music. Thompson's autobiography was published in 1985; he died at the age of eighty-six in December 1987 and at his London funeral had the music of his favourite composer, Mozart.[13]

Black American musicians visited Britain despite the restrictions placed on foreign performers by the British Musicians Union. Recordings of folk music were issued (the earliest commercial recording of African music was in 1905; the next was in 1922) including calypso. The social disadvantages experienced by Blacks in the USA, and under colonialism in Africa and the Caribbean, led to some Whites' expressing sympathy with Blacks, and they sought out black people both as cultural curiosities and as victims of white prejudice. Membership of Dr Moody's league was mainly white although it had wide links into the world of Africa and Africans. Financial pressures led African students such as future president of Kenya Jomo Kenyatta to take demeaning roles in films and plays, in which grass skirts and bwana-knows-best dialogue largely featured.[14] The sounds of ethnic America, and of the Caribbean to a smaller extent, were available on disc, and to many Britons interested in black music there ceased to be any concert hall element.

Aspiring black artists such as Guyana's Alyce Fraser, who gave a concert at New York's town hall in 1927 and was in London in 1929, worked in plantation roles in the minstrel traditions which had been revived due to black writers and showmen from the *Shuffle Along* success. *Plantation Days* and the *Blackbirds* shows indicate their contents in their names. Cardiff-born Lilian Jemmott, who had passed the piano examinations set by the Royal College of Music, seems to have abandoned music to marry a Nigerian medical practitioner. Ida Shepley from Trinidad (of West African and Canadian descent) arrived in Britain in the 1920s when she was three, and was having lessons from Amanda Aldridge by 1944 when she sang on the radio.

Amy Barbour-James, of pure African descent born in London in 1906 of Guyanese parents, knew both Marie Lawrence and Basil Rodgers of the 1906 Jamaican choir, and like them sang spirituals in London in the 1930s. Her father, John Alexander Barbour-James (1867–1954), had been involved in gatherings of Blacks in London since 1918 when he retired from the colonial service in Ghana; in the African Progress Union, the Islanders Club, and then the League of Coloured Peoples, which he helped to establish, he had included concert music presentations. He was vice president of the League in 1937, the year before he left for the Caribbean. His daughter Amy died in May 1988, her Harrow home full of the published music of black composers. Her piano had once belonged to Dorothy Callender, the London-educated daughter of Guyanese lawyer W.E.S. Callender. She had been a prize winner at Trinity College of Music. Her brother was a radio announcer for the BBC in the 1930s before establishing a law practice in the Bahamas. Such middle-class people were unlikely to have mixed with Blacks who had been raised within folk music traditions. Indeed, Amy Barbour-James recalled that some of the bit-part actors in *Sanders of the River* were roughs from the dockland slums of London. Her brother John Victor, who had trained as an engineer, also appeared in that Robeson film, and became a British version of Robeson until an accident at a film studio ended his short life in 1938.[15]

The Second World War and the realities of post-war Britain made the British more aware of Blacks. The anti-colonial struggles, the work of agitators such as George Padmore, the obvious inequalities of Robeson's USA when his passport was withdrawn, a government action which was later reversed but which prevented his travelling in the 1950s, and the exposure of many Britons to the 130,000 black American servicemen in wartime, all enlarged British white knowledge of Blacks. And then there were the thousands of Caribbean migrants from the 1950s.

The black musicians named in this chapter largely drew their repertoire from all over the world of Africans as well as from the Europeans. They presented a global music, and in so doing their attempts showed that Blacks were capable of taking a mature place in the world. Their background was slavery, oppression, lynching, segregation, colonialism and racism, and in presenting the music of their kin they were making a racial statement that, at the same time, presented those musics as equal to the European school. Those presentations also were of black men and women as individuals of achievement and distinction, not as unsophisticated peasants or semi-minstrels apparently ready to strum a banjo and dance an exotic step or two.

Once the numbers of black people in Britain reached levels, from the 1950s, where African descent was no longer a novelty, the white audiences for concert presentations seem to have disappeared. Promoters and the audiences wanted Blacks performing black music. And so it was that the schooled pianist from Trinidad, Winifred Atwell, earned a living in Britain from the early 1950s by playing a pastiche of ragtime, selling thousands of discs of a superficial version of a music of black America of the 1890s. There was no room in Britain for a black concert hall performer by the 1950s.

It has taken a generation for black instrumentalists and composers to overcome some of the prejudices of Britain and the effects of stereotypes in entertainment. Now, as the children of the 1950s and 1960s migrants enter adulthood, we can see composers such as Shirley Thompson (London-born of Jamaican migrant parents and a graduate of Liverpool University) working within the international once-European concert hall tradition.[16] The Guyana-born organist and teacher Ian Hall graduated from Keble College, Oxford, in 1962, played regularly in churches, chaired the UK committee of the Second World Black and African Festival of Art and Culture of Nigeria, worked in Ghana, and has conducted his music at Westminster Abbey. His early inspiration was Bach's Fugues. Exposure to other musics in Britain, and then to drums in Ghana, changed his musical direction.[17] Some years ago an especially crass interviewer asked an opera singer of Afro-American origin why she did not sing spirituals; the extremely polite response was that such music was not part of her personal cultural experience.

Exactly how much pressure is from within Britain's black community to press its musicians to play in more popular music styles is a question that needs a great deal of investigation, but a black style is expected from black musicians. As recordings of and books about ethnic musics such as blues, jazz, high life and reggae show the strengths of some black musics, there seems to be no understanding that Britain has a history of black musicians which is largely distinct from ethnic or traditional musics.

Trained instrumentalists and singers who could fill halls with ticket-purchasing audiences who would hear music by black and white composers did exist in Britain but their time has gone. Some, perhaps with tongue in cheek, participated in recordings and concerts by calypsonians and jazz musicians in the 1950s, for a black skin did not and does not mean an untrained or untutored instrumental or vocal skill.

White composers, exposed to jazz in the 1920s, adapted their music to the more superficial aspects of jazz such as the plunking banjo and the unlyrical saxophone, but not to the essence of the new black music. The instrumentalists produced by British academies and colleges were deliberately not taught jazz or the techniques developed in its playing.[18] This myopic stance combined with the misunderstanding of the white composers may well have been the major motivation in the move by concert hall audiences, who voted with their feet when a living composer's music was on the programme. Concert hall perform-ances were distanced from the music of the majority, and so-called classical music became out of reach for many. Perhaps black composers in the concert hall traditions, merging the sounds of black musics into the orchestral performance styles, will discover the way that was lost by European musical chauvinists.

Perhaps when black people are allowed positions of authority, respect and prestige outside the fields of popular entertainment and sport, will the white British treat black musicians as individuals rather than as stereotypes. If the effect of Blacks in the British concert hall is a fraction of the impact of Blacks in more popular music since the 1930s, it will be both profound and irreversible. If, like Coleridge-Taylor and other black musicians in the concert halls of Britain 1900–40, such composers and instrumentalists of African descent widen the base of concert hall music, then, as at the beginning of this century, there may be a composer of African descent like Samuel Coleridge-Taylor who is known and respected for music and not for colour.

Many people in Britain who profess an interest in black music have scant knowledge of the musicians named in this chapter, and those who have a knowledge of concert hall performers in the early years of the twentieth century often have not noticed that some were black artists and performers. Still ignored and overlooked, today's black concert hall performers may well be part of a process that will lead to fame for musical qualities and not for so-called racial ones. The success of black singers in opera suggests that the process may well be underway.

Acknowledgements

The recollections of veterans who told me of their experiences and of their relatives and friends were invaluable, and my thanks go to Frank and Evelyn Alcindor, the late Amy Barbour-James, Leslie Brown, Joe Deniz, the late Rudolph Dunbar, Marjorie Evans, the late Ronald Green, Don Johnson, Josephine Harreld Love and the late Leslie Thomp-son. I have also benefited from the comments, assistance and archival material obtained from Esme Bahn and colleagues at the Moorland-Spingarn Research Center of Howard University, Washington DC; Christopher Fyfe; Len Garrison; Richard Hadlock; Ian Hall; Diana Lachatanere and colleagues at the Schomburg Collection of the New York Public Library; Bernth Lindfors who told me where the Amanda Aldridge papers were stored; Rainer Lotz; Paul McGilchrist; Ian Pegg; Paul Richards; the librarian and colleagues at the Royal Commonwealth Society; Howard Rye; Eileen Southern; Shirley Thompson; Brian Willan, and the staff at the Colindale newspaper library of the British Library. Ron Gould's comments on the first draft of this paper were wise and encouraging.

Samuel Coleridge-Taylor (1875–1912) circa 1904. *Courtesy Jeffrey Green*

3 Fearsome Means of Discord: Early Encounters with Black Jazz

HOWARD RYE

There is no clear dividing line, either in fact or in public consciousness, between the minstrelsy of the nineteenth century and those forms of Afro-American music which have been known since 1920 as jazz and blues. In Britain, visiting entertainers were presenting music with distinctive Afro-American content from the middle of the nineteenth century and by 1900, as Michael Pickering has shown (Chapter 1), black artists were commonplace on the music-hall circuits, where they were evidently widely appreciated and perceived to offer a characteristic type of performance. In the absence of sound documents, either of the music played in Britain or of its American prototypes, it is only possible to speculate how far these presentations were adapted to British taste as discerned by the artistes or their backers.

Queen Victoria still reigned when an Afro-American musician first recorded in Britain. Seth S. Weeks, a mandolinist born in the 1860s, recorded 'The Chariaton March' (*sic*) (Berliner 7353) in London in December 1900. He recorded at least two dozen more numbers, though not all are likely to be performed in distinctively Afro-American styles. Whatever hopes may be entertained of 'Georgia Camp Meeting' (Edison Bell 442), such titles as 'Laburnam Gavotte' (Pioneer 131) are likely to be conventional instrumental showpieces, a guess supported by contemporary accounts of Weeks's concert appearances. Weeks did later work in jazz groups and in 1920 was leading his own Le Weeks Jazz Band at the Paris Apollo.

The Edwardian era brought further visits to Britain by Americans active in the emerging syncopated styles of dance music. In 1905 Joe Jordan brought to Britain a band described by James Weldon Johnson as 'the first modern jazz band ever heard on a New York stage'. A British reviewer of the day heard their performance as 'plantation songs and negro dances',[1] and thought that the act's appeal would be improved if the singers and dancers were accompanied by the Palace Theatre's pit band rather than by the Afro-American band.

Repeated claims have been made of visits to Britain in this period by such lions of the new musics as ragtime-pioneer Scott Joplin, New Orleans trumpeter

Bunk Johnson, and the New Orleanian pianist and pioneer jazz composer Jelly Roll Morton. Recent research suggests that the two last named were too young to have visited Britain at this time.

Such evidence as is available suggests that Afro-American music was seen by Edwardian observers essentially as one novelty turn amongst many, albeit sometimes imbued with a bitter-sweet nostalgia for 'slavery days' and the *ante-bellum* South. In the period 1910–20 visiting black performers began to exert a direct influence on popular music and to be perceived to be making an artistic contribution. This change was probably associated with a growing vogue for Afro-American sounds in high-class dance clubs. The Versatile Four were embarked on a long-term residency at Murray's Club in Beak Street as early as 1913. Their numerous recordings (1916–20) reveal extreme versatility, with a repertoire ranging from sentimental pap, played straight, to lively ragtime performances.

A turning-point was the arrival in 1915 of Dan Kildare's Clef Club Orchestra. The Clef Club had been formed in New York in 1910 to act as a centre and promotional organization for black musicians in Greater New York, its aspirations rather uneasily spanning symphonic music and an emerging awareness of distinctive Afro-American styles. Kildare was initially vice president and from February 1914 was president of the Clef Club. The band came to open the London Ciro's Club in a converted swimming baths in Orange Street behind the National Gallery. The management already owned high-class restaurants in Paris, Deauville and Monte Carlo, and the new venture successfully appealed to those with the highest social status. This did not prevent the club's being closed for the duration in 1917, but apart from wartime vicissitudes it remained in existence until March 1954. In its earlier years especially, it frequently played host to both visiting and resident Afro-American performers, and was extensively patronized by younger members of the royal family. At the inaugural dinner on 18 April 1915, the band's selections 'were greatly enjoyed'.[2] Its seven members included two seminal figures in the establishment of Afro-American jazz on the London scene.

Pianist Dan Kildare was born in Kingston, Jamaica, on 13 January 1879. He continued to lead the band at Ciro's at least until late 1916 and thereafter teamed up with drummer Harvey White as a music-hall duo. They also contributed to the Palace Theatre show *Hullo America* (1918), and co-led Dan and Harvey's Jazz Band on record. Ciro's reopened in mid-October 1919 and Kildare began a new engagement there in January 1920. By this time he was quarrelling with his English wife, the landlady of The Bell public house in Little Titchfield Street. On 21 June 1920 he became the first jazz musician to achieve notoriety in Britain, by murdering his wife and her sister, and then killing himself. He immediately became the stuff of legend and it is clear that already the serious jazz musician was regarded with a mixture of awe and incomprehension as a wayward untutored genius. As the *News of the World* related:

> Kildare's genius was killed by drink. His compositions numbered many hundreds, but they were never published, because he forgot all about them a few hours after they were composed. Night after night, when he arrived to take charge of his jazz

band, he would sit at the piano, compose a melody, decide it was good, and give his musicians their instructions; they would promptly swing into it and make a hit.[3]

It is a story which has become familiar to students of the romantic view of jazz and its practitioners. How far it is true in this case we can only speculate.

Drummer Louis Mitchell was to make a more durable mark on the course of Afro-American music in Europe. Born in New York City on 17 December 1885, he had visited Britain in the summer of 1914 to accompany a dance act at the Prince's Restaurant. In later years, he claimed, not entirely incredibly, to have been the first man to bring jazz to Britain. He left the band at Ciro's in July 1915 to embark on a career as a music-hall artist, which must have played a major part in spreading the new rhythms across the country. He appeared in the London Hippodrome revue *Joyland*, toured with La Belle Leonora's Ragtime Orchestra (1916), and then with a group called the Syncopating Sextette (1917). Both of these bands consisted otherwise of British musicians. They had been preceded on to the halls by Joe Jordan's Syncopated Orchestra, led by the pianist who had been in London in 1905. This band included trumpeter Russell Smith, later the leader of Fletcher Henderson's trumpet section. The group appeared in the Hippodrome revue *Push and Go* in May 1915 and went on a short tour.[4] These perambulations around the country began to expose Afro-American musical developments to a much wider audience than could afford entry to exclusive London clubs. Attention focused on the drumming and some observers realized they were in the presence of interesting new styles.

Jordan had brought with him another young drummer, Hughes Pollard, billed as 'Black Lightning'. *The Stage* remarked:

> The top-liner of the combination is a trap-drummer, by name Black Lightning, who varies his work on the drum with the use of all sorts and conditions of contrivances arranged upon a huge horseshoe.... Black Lightning is destined to become a favourite with orchestras.[5]

Others were less impressed. It was said of Louis Mitchell that 'If this gentleman could be induced to moderate his transports he would not only be better appreciated but would give his fellow artists more chance of being heard'.[6] Many reviewers were put off by the volume of noise while acknowledging the artistry displayed, but the inconsistency of the responses underlines the absence of any established critical standards. The affinity with minstrelsy was evidently helpful to some.

> Jordan's Syncopated Orchestra at Newcastle's Empire Theatre are unquestionably one of the smartest combinations since minstrelsy was in its prime. They, number-ing ten, present an entertainment anything but antiquated, and ... sing and dance in a manner that entirely drives away dull care and compels one to be joyful.[7]

In November 1915 another high-class London venue, the Savoy Hotel, started to hold Dinner Dances featuring 'a Coon Band', which may at first have been merely a stylistic description. By August 1916 black drummer Alec Williams, who had made his European début at the 1900 Paris Exhibition, was helping to establish the reputation for avant-garde dance music that the Savoy retained through the 1920s.

> As a ragtime drummer, Mr. Williams is second to none. His tempo, rhythm, and executive ability are perfect, and he has the good sense never to play too loudly. He is a splendid entertainer also, and when he throws his sticks about and dexterously catches them he wears a broad smile which is highly infectious.[8]

That drummers of this school were inclined to be noisy, at least in comparison with the norms of the times, is readily believable if we are to take seriously a reference to Louis Mitchell 'operating upon cow-bells, motor-horns, tramcar-gongs, and other fearsome means of discord'.[9]

The band from Ciro's made a number of records during 1916 and 1917. Their reputation has not been assisted by the record company's choice of band name: Ciro's Club Coon Orchestra. They reveal a fine string band with a distinctively Afro-American approach and an extraordinary gift for adapting the most improbable material. 'My Mother's Rosary' (Columbia 641) is among their best efforts and vocalist Seth Jones handles the lyrics as if quite indifferent to their utter banality. Contemporary recording techniques unfortunately restricted drummers largely to woodblocks and cymbals. At this time, Tin Pan Alley was afflicted with one of its periodic crazes for cod-Hawaiian songs; the group was given some of these to record and they come out sounding like Afro-American string-band music too. It's no wonder, though, that contemporary reviewers were intrigued but confused.

New Orleans jazz arrived in Britain in April 1919 in the persons of the white Original Dixieland Jazz Band. Their robust blend of ragtime and march music seemed revolutionary, perhaps in part because it lacked those already familiar Afro-American characteristics whose absence has led later commentators to find their music somewhat shallow emotionally. Their publicity was certainly calculated to discourage any serious consideration of their music's artistic qualities. 'Jazz is the assassination, the murdering, the slaying of syncopation. . . . I even go so far as to confess we are musical anarchists', asserted leader Nick LaRocca.[10]

This is the last description anyone might have applied to the group of black musicians who arrived in June 1919. The Southern Syncopated Orchestra had been formed in the USA in December 1918, largely from musicians associated with the Clef Club, and had made an American tour earlier in 1919. The troupe of fifty performers was somewhat reduced for their opening in London at the Philharmonic Hall on 4 July 1919. The orchestra's principals were conductor Will Marion Cook and business manager George William Lattimore; control of the orchestra subsequently became the subject of litigation between these two in the English courts. As might be expected of a group of this size, the repertoire encompassed a wide range of Afro-American material, including spirituals, ragtime, plantation or 'coon' songs, and formal compositions such as those of Samuel Coleridge-Taylor. The orchestra's ranks included at least two apostles of the new jazz in trumpeter Arthur Briggs and, importantly, the New Orleans clarinettist Sidney Bechet, widely acknowledged as one of the music's greatest figures. They were thus able to bridge the gap between the familiar forms of Afro-American music and those which were just emerging from New Orleans on to the world stage.[11]

The orchestra was not an immediate success, but attendances steadily built up during the five months of the Philharmonic Hall engagement, perhaps assisted by the royal patronage reflected in their employment at a party for the royal household at Buckingham Palace on 9 August 1919. Their performances attracted the attention of a wide variety of commentators, among them Ernest Ansermet, conductor of L'Orchestre de la Suisse Romande, whose appreciation of Sidney Bechet has been hailed as the first critique of a jazz performance ever published. Most British reviewers treated the performances seriously.

> This negro folk music is quite an art-music of its own and is of course best when interpreted by those who truly love and understand the spirit of it as these thirty-six players do. There is richness of melody, diablerie, merriment and some pathos interwoven, but the unique entertainment is one music lovers should not miss as it serves to demonstrate how very far from its original sources nine-tenths of the ragtime we get howled at us has strayed.[12]

Concerns about authenticity would be a leading theme of later jazz criticism, though at this period they are likely to result from the increasing awareness of the importance of folk music, which had reached its climax in the first decade of the century. Many of those involved in this movement had been concerned to establish an ideological basis for distinguishing true folk music from the merely popular. Also observable are the effects of an inadequate critical vocabulary as reviewers struggled to convey the emotional effect of the performances:

> Mr Carroll Morgan in 'I Got A Robe' continues to score a personal triumph challenged only by the anonymous hero of the 'Battle of Jericho'. The epipolazic Mr Morgan carols like a confident skylark serenely 'all over God's heaven', while the slick inexorability with which, when 'Joshua commanded the children to shout, the walls came tumbling down', would draw tear after tear from the excruciated eye of Balbus.

Nor was Ansermet alone in noting that Sidney Bechet was a remarkable musician. An earlier review in the same publication, *The Cambridge Magazine*, pronounced:

> The slaves were uneducated – they were kept uneducated of set purpose, and they could naturally read no musical score. Having a great sense of rhythm they extemporized on any tunes, using subtle dissonances which are characteristic of them.... This sort of thing still subsists.... What can be done in this way is illustrated by Mr Sydney Bechet, who extemporizes a clarinette solo about 10 o'clock, and compels admiration, so true is his ear and so rhythmical and vital his conception.[13]

The author of these astute remarks is anonymous, but has a good claim to be regarded as Britain's first jazz critic!

After the end of the initial engagement at the Philharmonic Hall, the wage bill for such a large orchestra became insupportable, the musicians were not always paid, and the personnel underwent numerous changes. Will Marion Cook had returned to the USA and by November 1919 had been replaced as director by Egbert E. Thompson, 'The Black Sousa', a Sierra Leonian raised in Jamaica. When Cook returned in February 1920, he found the orchestra in disarray and his subsequent disputes with Lattimore led to rival groups performing simultaneously in Liverpool and Nottingham for a period in April 1920.

A small jazz group drawn from the orchestra's ranks performed at the Buckingham Palace garden party on 9 August 1919, and another such group played for dancing at the Portman Rooms in Baker Street later in the year. The most significant such group was the Jazz Kings, under the leadership of Benny Peyton, which opened at the Embassy Club in Bond Street on New Year's Eve 1919. The sidemen included Sidney Bechet and Haitian alto-saxophonist Fred Coxcito. From October 1920 the Jazz Kings were featured regularly at the Hammersmith Palais de Danse, probably London's leading dance hall, and often doubled at the same management's exclusive Rector's Club in Tottenham Court Road. Other bands involving personnel from the Southern Syncopated Orchestra were to be found around London's clubs and dance halls. Drummer Buddie Gilmore, another Clef Club alumnus who had joined the orchestra in September 1919, had bands at Ciro's in the winter of 1920–21 and at the Hammersmith Palais de Danse the following April. Another regular venue for black bands was the private Moody's Club in Tottenham Court Road.

So great was the demand of London's club-going set for 'authentic' Afro-American jazz that it far exceeded the supply. The ranks of the Southern Syncopated Orchestra itself were soon swelled with non-American members of the African diaspora. By the time that nine of the then thirty-two members were lost in the sinking of the SS *Rowan*, on which they were travelling between engagements in Glasgow and Dublin on the night of 8–9 October 1921, it included Trinidadian brothers Cyril and George Blake, Jamaican trumpeter Joe Smith, Sierra Leonian pianist Frank Lacton, and Nigerian banjoist Gay Bafunke Martins. Haitian flautist Bertin Salnave, recruited in Paris in 1919, had left shortly before, and conductor Egbert Thompson was the only player left from the Philharmonic Hall engagement. Sidney Bechet reportedly re-marked in later years that he had played with many black musicians in Europe who had no feeling for jazz.[14] Initially at least, many of these players' knowledge and experience of Afro-American music must have been little, if at all, in advance of their British contemporaries.

An example of a successful career in jazz by a British-born musician of African ancestry is Gordon Stretton's. Born in Liverpool on 5 June 1887, the son of a seaman and a local woman, he entered show business as a singer and clog-dancer in the Eight Lancashire Lads. In 1908 he was to be found singing with a visiting Jamaican choir. In 1916 he sang with two touring shows directed by Billy Dorsey from Louisville, Kentucky, who had come to Britain in 1915 with Joe Jordan. After that he took up drums to play jazz with Dorsey, playing for high society at Rector's and the Grafton Galleries, where the Prince of Wales was a regular customer. After a sojourn in Paris, where his Orchestre Syncopated Six recorded in April 1923, he spent the remainder of his long life in Argentina.

Unfortunately the recorded evidence for the bands of this era is extremely scanty. Benny Peyton's Jazz Kings are said to have recorded, but the results were not issued and do not appear to have survived. The largest body of relevant recordings was made by Vorzanger's Band, three Afro-Americans and three Englishmen who are often credited as the first racially mixed jazz group to record. The music is a curious mixture of jazz, ragtime and music-hall, and has considerable charm.

In the absence of recorded evidence it is difficult to interpret some claims made for contemporary musicians. For example, it was said of Ghanaian pianist Caleb Jonas Quaye, known professionally as Mope Desmond, that 'This Mop, an African, was the best blues player in England. The dancers used to stop in front of the band to take in the astonishing way he performed the real blues'.[15] These are remarkable claims to make for a Ghanaian, but the speaker, Bertin Depestre Salnave, was Haitian and we can only speculate on his competence to judge 'the real blues'!

Desmond was a member of the Five Musical Dragons, who played at Murray's Club and also included trumpeter Arthur Briggs. Members of the band were en route to Wolverhampton to play at a rugby-club dance on 21 January 1922 when they were involved in a freak railway accident at Blisworth in Northants and Desmond was killed. In general, however, the black small bands seem to have confined their activities very largely to London clubs, and possibly this limited social and geographical base contributed to the decline in their fortunes after 1922. Other factors may include a growing awareness of the superficially more sophisticated forms of syncopated dance music which white American musicians were synthesizing from jazz and light classical music. At any rate many of the more musically significant black performers from the London scene were soon spreading the jazz gospel on the Continent, most especially in Paris.

It is likely that they had been sensing growing racial intolerance in London. Black artists had continued to be involved in the general entertainment business and a number of black-cast shows had toured the variety circuits. Ubiquitous among them were companies organized by Will Garland under such period names as *Coloured Society* and *A Trip to Coontown*. At the end of 1922, Garland's company became the focus of attacks by the tabloid newspaper *John Bull*, alleging general immorality and undesirability. Trade union interests soon detected an opportunity for restrictive practice, and the Actors' Association directed a volley of scurrilous and racist allegations to the Home Office, which duly noted that they were without foundation.

At this time two entrepreneurs, Sir Alfred Butt and Charles B. Cochran, were planning the importation of black-cast companies from the USA. The ire of the trade unions was soon redirected against their efforts, with the strident assistance of crusading journalist Hannan Swaffer, whose efforts can rarely have been directed to a more ignoble end.

The resulting controversy provided the Musicians Union with an early opportunity to state their view that anything a black man could do a white man could do at least as well. An official told Swaffer:

> There are something like two thousand of our union out of work. Many of them are unemployed because of the introduction of American negro bands, now in favour with certain dance clubs. British musicians could play quite as well.[16]

Denial of the cultural uniqueness of Afro-American music would be central to the Musicians Union's policy in the coming years, but the government remained unconvinced. Despite the orchestrated protests, the companies which Butt and Cochran were seeking to import received work permits. The cast of *Plantation Days*, engaged to appear at the Empire Theatre in *The Rainbow*, were granted permits 'for six weeks only unless extended. This was a speciality turn for which Britons could not be substituted and the success of the item was likely to promote employment'.[17] Racist barracking greeted James P. Johnson's Orchestra at the opening of *The Rainbow* on 3 April 1923, but despite the hostility of critics harping on old themes – 'Mr. James Johnson and his company in *Plantation Days* ... let loose a little hell of noise and danced, stamped, yelled, shouted and saxaphoned [*sic*] until everybody was deafened and exhausted'[18] – the company survived their allotted six weeks, gaining sufficient royal patronage to attract notice. As well as Johnson, one of the seminal figures of Harlem stride piano, the band included New Orleanian bass player Wellman Braud, later a key figure in Duke Ellington's Orchestra, and reedman Darnell Howard.

By the time Cochran's imports arrived from Sam Salvin's Plantation Restaurant in New York City to open in *Dover Street to Dixie* on 31 May 1923, the controversy was dying down. Will Vodery's Plantation Orchestra, which accompanied this show, was nearer to a conventional theatre pit-orchestra. Records by Vodery's bands show considerable compromise with (presumably) audience expectation, though the music remains distinctively Afro-American in rhythmic character and solo work retains highly personal tonality, as in the muted trumpet-playing of Johnny Dunn, who was featured in London. Vodery's band also accompanied a later London show, *Blackbirds of 1926*. Both productions featured Florence Mills, whom Cochran said, 'had made her London reputation before her first song was ended'. She was heard by future bandleader and jazz critic Spike Hughes:

> I believe if I had shut my eyes while Florence Mills was singing I could not have told whether she was white or coloured, in short, she was a song-and-dance artist who might have come from either side of the Atlantic.[19]

Hughes's praise went to the band and to blues singer Edith Wilson, a much more idiomatic performer who was featured both in 1923 and 1926 and was the first blues artist of established repute to appear in Britain.

All these shows were anchored in a nostalgic view of the old South, as is evidenced by their plantation settings, but sought also to present an image of up-to-the-minute Harlem sophistication, sometimes with *risqué* overtones. One sketch in *Blackbirds of 1926* so offended self-appointed censors in Liverpool that it had to be amended.[20]

The London clubs had turned to importing 'acts' rather than bands, adopting a distinction which would eventually be imposed by law. In September 1925 the Piccadilly Club featured Sissle and Blake, the latter being the famous ragtime pianist Eubie Blake. Noble Sissle was a light popular vocalist, who later fronted a significant jazz big band. The ten recorded performances which are the legacy of this visit emphasize Sissle's singing, but Blake's piano solos were a regular feature of the act. 'My playing of jazz', said Eubie, 'seemed particularly astounding to the English musicians. They tried to classify it according to musical form, but failed.' The duo toured the halls, and also wrote songs for *Cochran's Revue*, before returning to the USA in the spring of 1926.[21]

Some of the British nationals who had worked in the London dance clubs joined the exodus to the Continent, others formed music-hall acts similar in character to the black acts of earlier years. Trombonist Ellis Jackson, an American who had come to Britain in 1907 with a minstrel troupe and had become a naturalized Briton, was one who took this route. Some touring revues carried small jazz groups with them; violinist George Mitchell Smith, a former member of both the Southern Syncopated Orchestra and the Jazz Kings, is found in 1926 in the Melody Mixers Band touring with a revue called *Still Going Some*. This band also included drummer Amos Howard, who had had his own act on the halls in the 1910s as 'The Droll Dancing Darkie'. This dispersal of Afro-American performers must have both broadened the opportunities for audiences to be exposed to their music and emphasized continuities with older and already familiar forms of Afro-American entertainment.

By the late 1920s British tastes were lagging behind musical developments in the USA. The most appreciated visitors in this period were closer stylistically to Florence Mills than Edith Wilson. One of the music-hall trade papers advised American artists not to sing 'blues', as British audiences did not appreciate them. When the leading blues and jazz singer Ethel Waters appeared at the London Palladium and the Kit Kat Club in 1929, the same paper commented that 'Ethel Waters had evidently not read our article on the British want of appreciation of blues. In her other numbers she touched high-water mark'.[22]

Some other visitors of this era probably didn't need the warning. Alberta Hunter, composer of 'Down Hearted Blues' and a singer of impeccable blues credentials on and off record, was actually billed as 'America's Foremost Blues Singer' at the Argyle Theatre, Birkenhead, in February 1928. None the less, she evidently toned down her performances for European audiences. Doubtless some of her work was heavily coloured by her background, but her performance as 'Queenie' in the London production of *Show Boat* (1928–9), her stint as a band singer with Jack Jackson's society dance orchestra at the Dorchester Hotel in 1934, and her appearance as 'Princess' in an all-black *Robinson Crusoe* at Christmas 1934, are equally typical of her public face.

Similar compromises were made by the few full bands which managed to play in Britain in the later 1920s. Leon Abbey brought his band to London to play at the Olympia Dance Hall, where they opened on 16 December 1927. 'It was one of my greatest disappointments,' he later recalled, 'but it turned out to be the foundation of my success. The band was very well rehearsed . . . the costumes were right . . . and we had the Grand Opening.' The next morning, Abbey was summoned to the proprietor's office: 'The way the boys carried themselves was fine . . . the uniforms were beautiful . . . BUT that screaming of the horns *isn't done heah!*' Special arrangements had been written for the engagement, 'But I went on the stand the following evening and didn't pass them out . . . just concentrated on melodies and popular tunes, and after that everyone was tickled to death.' The effect pleased one reviewer: 'wonderful rhythm and harmony but more restrained than the usual coloured entertainers' was the verdict. It is difficult to judge how far the changes merely eliminated unacceptably 'modern' effects and how far they compromised the music's essential character. In the case of another violinist visitor, Eddie South, 'The Dark Angel of the Violin', records reveal a carefully honed mixture of hot playing, swinging rhythm, and tasteful effects respecting the European distaste for loud noises without abandoning Afro-American idioms.[23]

Noble Sissle brought his French-based big band to tour the British variety halls in 1929, following in the footsteps of Sam Wooding's jazz and show band which had come in 1926. By the time Sissle's band returned for a season at Ciro's club in November and December 1930, union pressure to exclude foreign musicians had so intensified that protracted negotiations were needed to secure an agreement dependent on Billy Cotton's band playing for a similar period at the Paris Ciro's and on the engagement of an additional British band to play opposite Sissle's in London. Sissle's 1930 band included Arthur Briggs and trumpeter Tommy Ladnier. Records made in both years show a fine swinging band, but now seem to feature too much singing and too few solos. The Prince of Wales had requested Sissle's trip to Ciro's but after his departure the renewed demand for black music could be met only by employing a small band of black residents led by Ellis Jackson, who was soon 'poached' by Billy Cotton and spent the next twenty years as a trombonist and occasional tap-dancer in his show band.[24]

In the later 1920s a small specialist public for jazz gradually emerged, though its interests at first centred on the white avant-garde of the period, whose music now seems notable for substituting clever effects for feeling and swing. The now-acknowledged classics of black jazz were at first dismissed as old-fashioned or even inept, but in the early 1930s an awareness of jazz as distinctively Afro-American music began to emerge under the enthusiastic tutoring of such writers as Spike Hughes and John Hammond in the *Melody Maker*. The resulting demand for top-class authentic jazz brought visits by Louis Armstrong (July–October 1932 and July 1933 to July 1934), Duke Ellington's Orchestra (June–July 1933), and Cab Calloway's Orchestra (March–April 1934). The significance of these visits has been analysed in considerable detail elsewhere. Suffice it to note that Ellington's and Calloway's Sunday appearances at the Trocadero Cinema at the Elephant and Castle were the first jazz concerts in the modern sense to be staged in Britain.[25]

Though lionized by the *cognoscenti*, these musicians appeared under the auspices of the general entertainment industry, as their predecessors had done. The trade was wary rather than hostile, but the layperson was most often bewildered. Old concerns made themselves felt.

> Louis Armstrong ... plays the trumpet as though to put it to death by his own hands, an illusion heightened by the expiring shrieks the instrument occasionally yields.... It is all very elemental, Africa spoke.[26]

Tenor saxophonist Coleman Hawkins made an extensive tour as a featured soloist with the bands of Jack Hylton and Mrs Jack Hylton (Ennis Parkes) (March–December 1934). He seems to have made few concessions to entertainment values and to have been widely appreciated none the less. However, the attitude of the business is perhaps demonstrated by one fan's recollection that he and some friends were barred from Brighton Hippodrome after disrupting the show several nights running by demanding encores from Hawkins.[27]

This brief irruption of the greats soon came to a premature end. In March 1935 the Musicians Union at last persuaded the Ministry of Labour to cease the issue of work permits to American musicians. The ministry had been staunchly resisting pressure for many years and their reasons for collaborating in the imposition of this 'cultural iron curtain' at this juncture have never been entirely clear. The reasons that they had previously given for a more open policy had certainly lost no validity. The ban was to last more than twenty years but was never as complete as its proponents might have liked, since it applied only to 'musicians' and not to 'entertainers'.

The most important figure to push through this loophole in the 1930s was probably the renowned Harlem stride pianist Thomas 'Fats' Waller. He toured Britain twice (July–October 1938 and March–June 1939), and was exposed to audiences far removed in expectations and understanding from the jazz audience, who were often unimpressed by the resultant programming. Pianists were particularly easy to represent as variety acts and another jazz pianist, the under-rated Garland Wilson, was probably the most widely travelled of any Afro-American visitor. He first appeared in February 1932 as accompanist to singer and film actress Nina Mae McKinney, who was a competent bluesy jazz singer when she chose. This association ended in late 1934 and Garland retreated to Paris, where he was soon recruited by British bandleader Jack Payne. He toured with Payne's show band for a year and was frequently treated by reviewers as the show's star. A further British visit over the winter of 1936 –7 included a long residency at the Shim Sham Club in Wardour Street, one of a new breed of 'jam' clubs where improvised small-band swing music could be heard. Wilson's variety appearances are remembered by enthusiasts as sometimes disappointing, but not so his club gigs, and he was an enthusiastic sitter-in. He is even remembered touring local pubs between sets at the Brighton Hippodrome, commandeering any available piano. The appearance of another legend of jazz piano, Art Tatum, at Ciro's and the Paradise Club in 1938 in the guise of a variety act strains credulity, even if he did make two television appearances and appear as a guest on Arthur Askey and Richard Murdoch's comedy programme *Band Waggon*.[28]

The ban was circumvented in another way by alto-saxophonist Benny Carter. He came to Britain in March 1936 to act as arranger for Henry Hall's BBC Dance Orchestra. It was later said that he had been prevented from playing a note in public, but he was heard as a saxophonist at private sessions organized by the then popular local jazz societies called Rhythm Clubs. Eventually authorization was also given for him to perform at concerts for students, though at the London Hippodrome on 10 January 1937 he was provided with a full supporting cast of variety acts. The same concession was made in March 1939 when Coleman Hawkins returned to Britain to play a series of recitals promoted by music dealers and supposedly open only to bona fide musicians. It remains mysterious why the Musicians Union was prepared to depart from its declared policy in these cases. In May and June 1939 Hawkins again toured with the Jack Hylton show. Presumably the educational saxophone master had become a variety act again![29]

Black-cast shows could still be authorized and could bring their orchestras, provided that they played on stage and not in the orchestra pit. This procedure was followed in respect both of *Blackbirds of 1934* and *The Cotton Club Revue* (1937). The former brought to Britain a major jazz figure in trumpeter Valaida Snow, who was later able to appear widely as a variety act. She has suffered the eclipse which has been the invariable lot of women who had the temerity to play jazz on any instrument other than the piano. The many recordings she made in London in 1935–7 provide no excuse for continuing this neglect. *The Cotton Club Revue* was accompanied by Teddy Hill and his Orchestra, a star-studded aggregation including long-time Count Basie trombonist Dickie Wells and the future bebop trumpeter Dizzy Gillespie. Both shows delivered a good sprinkling of jazz alongside their comedy and dancing and were well received. No mention of Gillespie's playing has been found in contemporary sources, even though he recalled jamming with local musicians at the Nest Club.[30]

By the late 1930s the demand for Afro-American music, now perceived as a demand for 'authentic' jazz, had again exceeded the supply. The policies of the Musicians Union and the Ministry of Labour prevented any significant increase in the supply of Americans and once again the black community in Britain moved to fill the vacancies. Many of those involved had no previous experience of jazz but soon learned the music their public demanded. The extent to which relationships between the various musical idioms of the African diaspora facilitated this process has been little investigated. What is certain is that players like Jamaican trumpeter Leslie 'Jiver' Hutchinson (1907–59), Jamaican saxophonist Bertie King (1912–80s), Jamaican pianist Yorke De Souza (1913–86), Barbadian trumpeter Dave Wilkins (b. 1914), Trinidadian saxophonist David 'Baba' Williams (1916–41), and Trinidadian guitarist Lauderic Caton (b. 1910) were amongst the most idiomatic non-American jazz musicians ever to work in Britain. In 1936 Jamaican trumpeter Leslie Thompson and Guyanan dancer Ken Johnson organized a swing band called the Emperors of Jazz. After passing under Johnson's exclusive leadership in 1937, this band established itself through long residencies at the Old Florida Club in Bruton Mews (1936–8) and the Café de Paris in Coventry Street (1939–41) as one of the country's leading jazz groups. Its career came to an abrupt end on 8 March 1941 when the Café de Paris was blitzed and Johnson and Dave Williams were killed.[31] Johnson's band achieved wide notice through broadcasts and concert appearances, but most Afro-Caribbean and native black musicians worked mainly in West End night clubs and jam venues, where their vigorous and energetic music was much appreciated by enthusiasts. The ambience of the era was captured in December 1941 by live recordings of Cyril Blake's band at Jig's Club in Wardour Street, especially 'Cyril's Blues' (Regal-Zonophone MR3597), whose raw energy forms a fitting swansong to Britain's first jazz age.

Acknowledgements

Grateful thanks to Josephine Beaton, Morten Clausen, John H. Cowley, Jeffrey P. Green Rainer E. Lotz and Edward S. Walker for information incorporated and to the staff of the Public Record Office and the British Library for access to sources. Extracts from Crown Copyright Records in the Public Record Office cited in this chapter appear by permission.

SYNCOPATION

Sissle and Eubie Blake

OT M. DELL

fox trot was born and the other dances that have gyrated around that measure since its inception.

There are people who condemn this modern music. In syncopated melody they find only discord and a touch of the barbaric.

Those who are familiar with the works of the immortal Liszt will recognise that he made a very deliberate and general use of syncopation; indeed, it might be said that Liszt was responsible for the introduction of syncopated music.

It was a different kind of genius, the genius of the coloured people of the southern states of America, which provided the world with these new measures and, it must be confessed, revivified dancing in so doing.

One may very well ask what would have been the outlet for pent-up war emotions had there not been spirited dances to help officers, men, and the women of this country to dance away their troubles.

Even if for this alone, one can find justification for syncopated music and pay additional homage to those who introduced it.

Blake and Sissle have been pioneers of this new movement in music and to-day they are partners as in the old days.

Sissle and Blake

content with merely performing in this country. At the present moment Noble Sissle is engaged upon the life of Jim Europe, and in addition to that is at work upon a musical comedy which, with Blake's music, bids fair to have a production in the very near future.

Blake's music has been recognised as "up to the moment," and it will not be long before it is generally heard in Great Britain.

Extract from an appreciation of Noble Sissle and Eubie Blake by Draycot M. Dell in *Popular Music Weekly*, London, September 1925. *Collection: Paul Oliver*

4   London is the Place: Caribbean Music in the Context of Empire 1900–60*

JOHN COWLEY

The development of indigenous music in the English-speaking Caribbean is a complex subject. As a generalization, however, the most persistent evolutions are associated with either sacred or secular occasions, sometimes reflecting a combination of both. Usually such activities show some evidence of cross-fertilization stemming from adaptation to new circumstances by people of African, European, and other cultures involved in the world diaspora to the Americas.

In Jamaica, where the predominant European Christian influence has been Protestantism, the primary black sacred/secular celebration is known as 'Jonkunnu'. It has been held at Christmas for two centuries or more and is also held on 1 August, in commemoration of the day in 1838 when Apprenticeship was abolished and Emancipation from slavery finally achieved throughout the British Caribbean. Among other 'Protestant' islands, St Kitts-Nevis have their 'Christmas Sports' including mumming, Bermuda its 'Gombey' parades, while the Bahamas have adopted 'Jonkunnu' as the name for their Christmas festivities.

Caribbean-French sugar planters and their slaves, from Martinique and other French-speaking territories in the region, settled in Trinidad in the 1780s. They consolidated the European influence of Roman Catholicism in the island and thereby provided the focus for its most important sacred/secular event – Shrovetide Carnival. Christmas is also celebrated to a lesser extent. The history of both festivals has been traced from the time the British took the island from Spain in 1797. Shrovetide Carnivals are held also in Carriacou, Grenada, Dominica, St Lucia, St Vincent and Tobago.[1]

Music is a fundamental ingredient of these events – whether the primary acitivity is at Christmas, Carnival, or at another point in the calendar – and is organized to accompany street parades and other forms of communal or individual competitive activity, including recreational dances.

* Extracts from Crown Copyright Records in the Public Record Office appear by permission.

Festivals provide a focal point for performing different musical styles that have evolved separately in each of the islands of the Caribbean, sometimes just in the context of these types of carnivalesque, but more often than not also in relation to other social activities. They also integrate with common elements such as language and similar cultural evolutions, including migration of people from island to island, or elsewhere, in the course of international circumstances.

The history of black British Caribbean music, within this context of 'Empire', and the timespan 1900–60, can be divided roughly into two periods. The first period is represented by the close of the reign of Queen Victoria (on her death in 1901) and the end of the Second World War. The second ends immediately prior to the 1962 Independence of Jamaica and Trinidad, when Empire links were in crisis. I shall emphasize 'indigenous' music, its relationship to the Empire capital, London, and the employment of migrant musicians there. The word 'Empire' is used as this is how the British hierarchy perceived its overseas territories at this time and conditioned the way in which inhabitants lived there or in Britain itself.

By way of background, in the earlier period the principal musical region was the Eastern Caribbean, centred on Trinidad and including Guyana. Most documentary evidence available concerns Trinidad and the evolution of calypso as an important, but sometimes separate, ingredient of the island's multi-cultural Carnival tradition, founded on a strong African-American base. There are, however, data on other independent strands of West-Indian-developed music.

In the English-speaking area as a whole, British music from that of the social 'elite' to that of the 'folk' had considerable influence, including the 'mother country's' military repertoire, represented by black membership in the bands of the armed forces and the police. It must also be noted that, with the exception of some contemporary folklore material and data on the band of the British West India Regiment (whose headquarters were in the island), very little has been published on 'popular' music and musicians in the more northerly British territory of Jamaica during this first time span.[2]

Reports of topical themes in African-American songs range from the period of slavery to the present day and in all regions of the Americas where Blacks have settled. Calypso, which originated in Trinidad, is one of the most famous of this genre to have developed in the Caribbean. In many respects it grew from the hierarchical structure of the Carnival bands which, in masquerade, adopted the European nomenclature of Kings, Queens, Lords, Ladies and other measures of social status. For the black maskers, in a world turned upside down, these served to satirize the symbols of European power as well as to establish an African-American authority over them. A pattern of past African hierarchies in the masquerade traditions was probably maintained. Lead singers, or chant-wells, sang at the head of marching bands to responses sung in chorus by their members as they paraded competitively in Carnival. In line with band hierar-chy the songsters also adopted 'powerful' names as their soubriquets. Among numerous accretions their topical calypsos were based on earlier improvised songs for creole drum dances such as the belair and old kalenda (common in the

French-speaking Caribbean), the songs of stickfighting-kalenda bands, the bongo wake dance, and the paseo dance rhythm from Venezuela.

Calypso in Trinidad prior to the early 1900s was sung almost exclusively in French Creole, but a gradual change began around the turn of the century and some of the earliest printed 'calipsos' (note the initial spelling), published in the *Port of Spain Gazette* during the 1900 Carnival season, are almost wholly in English. They include panegyrics for the British Empire in the form of boasts of military prowess. One is ascribed to the White Rose masquerade band and, probably, was sung by its one time leader Henry Julian: Julian White Rose. His masquerade character and singing soubriquet at that time was the Iron Duke. The first calypsonian to record commercially (in Trinidad in 1914, for the US-based Victor Talking Machine Company), he provides an important early example of a musician and his commercial activities. So too does dance-band leader and pianist Lionel Belasco, who was recorded at this time and in the vanguard of Trinidad musicians who migrated to New York to make a career there, which included regular recording sessions (from 1915 onwards). His records were exported to Trinidad and Latin American countries.[3]

Migration has been a feature of English-speaking West Indian societies, both within the circum-Caribbean, and to North America and Europe, the principal conurbations being New York and London. Both were (and remain) centres of local and mass 'entertainment' and afforded jobs for migrating musicians in clubs, the theatre and, on occasion, recording for the gramophone, and radio broadcasts (after the latter's rise as a mass medium in the 1920s). There is documentary evidence from both metropolises of the participation of West Indian musicians in all these activities. Indigenous Caribbean music was one means by which they earned a living in New York from the 1920s and in London from the 1940s.

Centering on the 'Heart of Empire' (London) and concentrating on commercial activities there, I shall briefly explore metropolitan–Caribbean musical relationships. In this my purpose is not to look at concert styles, nor to provide a definitive study, but to pinpoint illustrations in context.

While 1900 is a convenient date for commencing discussion of musical developments in the Eastern Caribbean, the conclusion of the First World War (1918) and the consequent demobilization of black soldiers and sailors who fought for the Empire cause, provides a focal point for discussing West Indian music and musician in London. For example, in a 1946 *Melody Maker* article, Trinidad-born string-bass player and bandleader Gerald 'Al' Jennings refers to a band that he formed during his naval service which played on the cessation of hostilities, for wounded 'coloured' soldiers prior to their repatriation. West Indian and African musicians were involved in the popular black Southern Syncopated Orchestra that came to Britain in mid-1919, originally with a supposedly all-US American complement, and toured the country until 1921.[4]

Proportionately few Blacks lived in Britain at this time and migrants or visitors tended to find accommodation via family connections or, perhaps, occupational association. The latter was certainly true of the St Kitts-born pianist George Ruthland Clapham. He shared an address with the celebrated black-American reed-playing virtuoso Sidney Bechet (an original member of the Southern Syncopated Orchestra: see Chapter 3) at the time of the latter's deportation in 1922.[5]

Documentary material on the activities of black Caribbean musicians in London is scanty throughout the 1920s, brushes with the authorities excepted. The position of the capital as a major centre of commerce, including companies manufacturing gramophone records, led, however, to the release in 1927 of nine specialist records for an English-speaking West Indian clientele. These were so designated in the British Parlophone catalogue for that year. They were drawn from the Okeh West Indian series of Parlophone's New-York-based US affiliate, the General Phonograph Corporation. The Okeh records were exported to the West Indies and, in the absence of evidence to the contrary, it is assumed that purchasers of Parlophone's equivalent were local; their records were certainly released using numbers in a series in which other specialist British material was marketed.

Three US-based Caribbean performers were represented in this series: Slim Henderson (probably a vaudevillian); Sam Manning (a Trinidad-born actor and vaudevillian, later involved in musical production); and Cyril Monrose (a superbly idiomatic Trinidad violin player and bandleader). Henderson (recorded 1924) and Monrose (recorded 1925) were responsible for one release each; the seven others were by Manning (two recorded in 1924, the remainder in 1925).

Although I have been unable to hear all of these 78rpm issues it should be noted that 'Amba Cay La' (Under the House)' (made by Manning in 1924) is the first recording of a popular Trinidad Carnival 'leggo' sung in French Creole. 'Leggo' – meaning 'let yourself go' – is a primitive form of calypso sung during Shrovetide parades. 'The Bargee', recorded by Manning in 1925, describes the murder of an East Indian by a black ex-West Indian soldier in a dispute over a girl.

> Listen folks, listen carefully,
> While I tell you all a story,
> A story that end in tragedy – aah
>
> It's called a bargee, this
> Bargee in Hindustani,
> But in English it means a tragedy – mmm
>
> The girl, a telephone operator,
> Her lover a handsome ex-soldier
> The murderer of the East Indian – aah
>
> Soldier took his girl out motoring,
> The Indian took his cows out grazing
> When he saw the lovers swooning
> He started out interfering – aah

In the accompaniments the clarinet weaves round the melody and a *cuatro* player strums rapidly, occasionally knocking on his instrument.

Generally, the music represents the repertoire of the Eastern Caribbean, exceptions are Slim Henderson's 'My Jamaica' – a satirically sentimental song about Jamaica from the 'viewpoint' of a migrant to the USA; and Manning's 'Sly Mongoose' – with lyrics based firmly on the career of the black Jamaican prophet, Alexander Bedward.[6]

By virtue of their activities, two personalities dominate the West Indian musical scene in Britain in the period between 1930 and the Second World War. Both were from Guyana: clarinettist, bandleader, promoter and journalist Rudolph Dunbar (see also Chapter 1), and the dancer and bandleader Ken 'Snakehips' Johnson. They each led 'all coloured' dance bands which employed British West Indian musicians. The latter came from a variety of backgrounds, including the former band of the British West India Regiment, and police bands in Guyana and Trinidad. Dunbar and Johnson's main clienteles were Whites and, in general, their repertoires were drawn from the popular music of the day, which included black American jazz. *Melody Maker* reports indicate that both bands drew upon a pan-Caribbean personnel and directed their music towards an Empire audience.

Dunbar was no stranger to Britain, having first visited the country as a member of Will Vodery's Plantation Orchestra in the touring show *Blackbirds of 1926*, with whom he recorded. Based in France in the late 1920s he was a member of the band of black British musicians that the Paris-based black American jazz violinist Leon Abbey brought to London in 1930. This move was made to circumvent work permit restrictions on US black musicians, one of the factors underlying the employment of black British musicians at this time. Dunbar appears to have settled in Britain by mid-1931 and his band flourished in the period 1933–4. In December 1934 it made one issued recording accompanying the vocalist Gladys Keep (of Reading) singing two American jazz standards: 'Dinah' and 'St Louis Blues'.[7]

Late in June 1934 Sam Manning and Lionel Belasco arrived in Britain from New York and, by the beginning of August, Belasco and his Orchestra had recorded twelve titles for UK Decca's foreign series. Featuring 'Rumbas' and 'Valses' these were almost certainly aimed at the growing European market for Latin American music, which had been developing since the introduction of the 'sinful' tango in the first decade of the century. Led by Belasco playing piano, it is possible that members of Dunbar's band were the instrumentalists. Manning sang (in English) in four of these performances.

At some point Belasco returned to the USA, where he recorded again in September 1935. Manning, however, remained in Britain, touring initially with a show called *Harlem Nightbirds*, and stayed for several years. Probably because of his extensive and successful recording career in the USA and his 1927 British releases, he was able to negotiate a session with Parlophone in July 1935, leading his West Indian Rhythm Boys. These four sides have some claim to be the first recordings of idiomatic English-speaking Caribbean music in Britain. Two of the songs, 'Help Me to Fly Over Jordan' and 'No Hidin' Place', are classified as West Indian Negro spirituals. In these Manning sings lead to responses by a mixed chorus. A guitar is featured; it is played Hawaiian style in the latter. Of the other coupling, one title 'Sweet Willie' (a St Lucian biguine, about a wayward girl and her man) is sung by Manning, a re-creation of a song he had recorded for Okeh in 1925 (released here in 1927). As a novelty, the 1935 recording features rhythm and Hawaiian guitar accompaniment, with piano and percussion. This instrumentation is also featured on the other side of the record with, in addition, trumpet, violin and saxophone. Entitled 'Ara Dada Pasea', it is sung by Gus Newton (a percussionist who had played in Rudolph Dunbar's band), with a chorus influenced heavily by contemporary recordings of Hawaiian music. The violin, however, is played in a style associated with Trinidad. The title of the song seems to be connected with Rada, the name used collectively by New World African-Americans conscious of their Dahomian ancestry. The Venezuelan paseo is a dance tempo designated on many early calypso records that, as has been pointed out, was absorbed by the calypso itself.

In June 1936 Manning, Amy Ashwood Garvey (divorced first wife of Marcus Garvey, the former Jamaican leader of the United Negro Improvement Association), and Rudolph Dunbar started the Florence Mills Social Parlour in Carnaby Street, London, as an evening eating and live music venue at which both Manning and Dunbar performed. Neither, however, was involved in further recordings of black music in Britain before the Second World War.[8]

Two months earlier saw the formation of a band of black West Indian musicians under the leadership of Jamaican trumpeter Leslie Thompson, and Guyanese dancer Ken 'Snakehips' Johnson. Called initally the Emperors of Jazz, or Jamaican Emperors, it drew on a slowly increasing pool of black musicians from the Caribbean active in London during the 1930s. Thompson and Johnson parted company in 1937. Under the latter's leadership, however, the band was to sustain a much higher profile for black British jazz and dance band music in the United Kingdom until Johnson's untimely death (8 March 1941).

Johnson's band recorded in a newly launched 'Swing' series for British Decca in 1938, and again (with similar repertoire) for HMV in 1940. He was, however, fully aware of indigenous black Caribbean music, as can be seen by the programme of *Calypso and other West Indian Music* he presented in the BBC London regional service in 1939. This immediately followed the broadcast of the cricket test match between the West Indies and the MCC at Lords on 24 June. It featured gramophone records of Trinidad calypsos from September 1938 British Brunswick releases, drawn from what had become by then an extensive US Decca catalogue of this music. He also played contemporary US Decca issues themselves, and recordings of black Cuban and Martinique music made in Paris during the 1930s.[9]

Black Latin American music including rumba and other rhythms, was gaining popularity in Britain at this time and many of the English-speaking Caribbean musicians in London were versatile in these styles, in black American jazz, and in other dance band idioms. This is true of the West Indian membership of the 'All-Coloured' band led by Nigerian composer, organist and pianist Fela Sowande that played with the black American singer Adelaide Hall, who was resident in London from 1938. One member of this group was the Trinidad percussionist Edmundo Ross (later Ros), who was soon to build a career as London's premier Latin American music specialist (claiming to have come from Venezuela). Adelaide Hall's 'Empire' link was via her husband, a Trinidadian, Bert Hicks.[10]

With the outbreak of the Second World War, black West Indian musicians took a higher profile in London's clubland and so did their indigenous repertoires. From *Melody Maker* announcements and a wartime radio broadcast, calypsos, paseos, and West Indian folksongs are known to have been in the repertoire of the small band run at this time by Cyril Blake. He was a Trinidad-born guitarist, trumpeter and sometime vocalist, who was a veteran of the Southern Syncopated Orchestra, and of both the Dunbar and Johnson groups. He also played with the Cuban pianist, Don Marino Barreto, with whom Edmundo Ros had been associated. A band led by Blake, in which he played trumpet and provided the vocals, was featured in a celebrated 'live' recording session playing black American jazz in earthy fashion at Jig's Club, St Anne's Court, Wardour Street, London, in December 1941. The following year, he composed the topical calypsos for his BBC Forces wavelength broadcast of this Trinidad music on 14 June 1942, on which the singer was Gus Newton.[11]

Despite the success of Ken Johnson, general acceptance for black West Indian big bands in Britain was difficult to achieve. In 1944 the Jamaican-born trumpeter, and ex-British West India Regiment bandsman, Leslie 'Jiver' Hutchinson formed an 'All-Coloured Band' comprising the cream of London's black musicians. Like himself, many were former members of Ken Johnson's band. They recorded for Decca in July of that year, but their four jazz-orientated sides remain unissued. For fifteen years Hutchinson struggled to keep a band together and to make a living from his music.

At the commencement of the second period marked by the end of the Second World War, a recently demobbed Chief Petty Officer, the London-based Trinidadian 'Al' Jennings, brought an All Star Caribbean Orchestra from his homeland to Britain. Arriving at Southampton on 5 November 1945 his intention was to fulfil a role similar to that performed by his small group at the end of the First World War, but Jennings experienced difficulties similar to those encountered by Hutchinson in maintaining his band.[12]

On a different level of musical activity, Trinidad folk music, including calypso, was among a variety of topics covered in a BBC series devoted to *Travellers' Tales* from around the British Empire, broadcast between September 1943 and March 1945. Edric Connor, a folk music collector and trained baritone singer from Trinidad, and Learie Constantine, the famous Trinidad cricketer (and a calypso enthusiast) were contributors to the series; Constantine had been resident in Britain since the early 1930s, and Connor arrived in 1944 to study engineering. By late 1945 Connor had recorded two examples of black Trinidad folk music, in formal setting, for British Decca: 'The Lord's Prayer' based on a version used by the Shouters, or Spiritual Baptist Church, in Trinidad, and a carol 'The Virgin Mary Had a Baby Boy'; having published the music and words to both earlier in the year in a small collection of West Indian spirituals and folk songs.[13]

At the same time, a number of African musicians were performing in London, especially the group led by Ambrose Campbell, a Nigerian, which provided the accompaniment for the *Ballets Nègres*, organized by Jamaican dancer Berto Pasuka, with dancers from Britain, Africa and the Caribbean. Edric Connor performed a selection of his West Indian folk songs and a calypso during their appearance on BBC television on 24 June 1946.[14]

It is apparent that although London was a major centre for the production of gramophone records, very few recordings of indigenous black English-speaking Caribbean music, or, for that matter of dance band music played by black West Indian musicians, were made in Britain during the first period 1900–45. To some extent this is surprising in the light of the activities of those black musicians present in London. They did, however, represent a very small minority of the population. Unlike the position in British Africa, where indigenous recordings were made for export regularly by London-based companies from at least the 1920s, it is probable that commerical arrangements with US companies and, perhaps, a British lack of market perception led to this situation.

It was not until the arrival of the MV *Empire Windrush* at Tilbury on 21 June 1948, and with it the 'official' commencement of mass migration from the Caribbean to Britain, that there was a significant change in the West Indian musical complexion in the 'mother country': it signalled an expansion in the range of commercial activities. Of some seventeen individuals who described their occupation as artist, musician, singer or bandleader in the *Windrush* passenger list, two were the Trinidad calypsonians Lord Beginner (Egbert Moore) and Lord Kitchener (Aldwin Roberts). Also on board was the Trinidad vocalist Mona Baptiste, who had registered as a clerk. It was the presence of these authentic calypsonians together with the pool of musicians already available and, indirectly, the Empire dollar crisis, that led to the recording of indigenous British Caribbean music for export and local consumption.

Before examining this phenomenon it should be mentioned that two other Trinidad performers are known to have been in Britain in 1948: the calypsonian Lord Caresser (Rufus Callender) and bandleader Lionel Belasco (making a return visit). Belasco recorded a selection of instrumentals based on Caribbean rhythms for British Decca in October. It seems neither musician stayed in the country for a significant period.[15]

I shall summarize briefly the principal elements in the early history of English-speaking Caribbean music recorded in Britain. A key personality in this was the jazz critic, radio presenter and journalist Denis Preston who, as early as 22 July 1945, sponsored a Ragtime Concert at Toynbee Hall, East London, that included performances by the Guyanese reed-player and former Trinidad Police Bandsman Freddy Grant, with his West Indian Calypsonians (Grant had arrived in London in 1937). Preston was in New York from late July 1948, setting up London Records for the British Decca Record Company and was impressed by performances by authentic Trinidad calypsonians whom he had heard playing at locations on Lennox Avenue, in Harlem. On his return to Britain he found Lord Kitchener and Lord Beginner in residence and put the idea to EMI-Parlophone that there was a void in recording this music because of the dollar shortage in the sterling area, which had led to 'Empire' currency and trading restrictions with the USA. Between 1935 and 1945 US Decca (sold by their British owners during the war) had recorded calypsos regularly, either in New York or Trinidad, for West Indian export and for sales in the USA. After 1945, and before the sterling crisis in 1949, other American companies had taken up this trade.

The period of the Second World War in Trinidad was one of transition among calypsonians, with those who had established their reputations before that time being dubbed, using wartime military terminology, the 'Old Brigade' by the younger and up-and-coming new bloods, who called themselves the 'Young Brigade'. During Carnival the groups competed one against another singing their calypsos in 'tents' – locations whose construction had been based originally on folk buildings used for African-American ceremonies.

Lord Beginner was a leading representative of the Old Brigade, while Lord Kitchener was one of the prime members of the Young Brigade. It is useful to apply these distinctions when describing the group of Eastern Caribbean migrants led by Cyril Blake and organized by Denis Preston for his first calypso session in the United Kingdom, which took place at EMI's north-west London studios, Abbey Road, on 30 January 1950. It was fully reported both in the *Melody Maker* (London) and the *Trinidad Guardian* (Port of Spain). In addition to Beginner (who began his singing career in 1927), four other members of this band represented the 'Old Brigade'. All of them had migrated to Britain before the war: Cyril Blake himself (guitar), conga-drum-player 'Dreamer' (Reuben François), septuganarian Brylo Ford (*cuatro* – a small four-string guitar) and clarinettist Freddy Grant. Their average age was fifty-one. Ford (string bass) and Grant had participated in Blake's Jig's Club session in 1941. Alongside Kitchener (who started singing in Arima in 1938 and moved to the capital, Port of Spain, in 1944) the other two 'Young Brigade' performers (average age thirty) were Neville Boucarut (bass) and Fitzroy Coleman (guitar). Both had arrived here in 1945 with 'Al' Jennings' All-Star Caribbean Orchestra. .

With a preponderance of older musicians familiar with the music popular in Trinidad earlier in the century it is not surprising that the string band styles from that period were echoed in the accompaniment to these recordings, and to those in two subsequent Parlophone sessions, held in March, in which Preston also used a band led by Cyril Blake.

Ten titles, including two instrumental, were recorded at these three sessions, Parlophone releasing eight of them in four 78rpm records. One instrumental was issued, a string band March Calypso (for Carnival parades) entitled 'Iere' – the Native American name for Trinidad. The other instrumental 'Glendeena' was a Castilliane – a popular form of 'fast waltz' which, like the string-band style itself, had reached Trinidad from nearby Venezuela. A topical commentary by Fitzroy Coleman, 'The French President Visit Great Britain', that recorded the state visit of M. Vincent Auriol on 7 March, was unissued. Lord Beginner was the principal vocalist, maintaining a stylistic continuity with the past by singing topical calypsos about political events: 'The Dollar and the Pound' on the sterling crisis, and in 'General Election' an outsider's view of the events of 23 February. He also commented on personal relations in 'I Will Die a Bachelor' and in 'Housewives' on conditions in a post-war Britain where goods were still rationed. Brylo Ford (using the calypso soubriquet of Julian White Rose – the Iron Duke) sang a version of a pre-war calypso by King Radio 'Man Smart and Woman Smarter'. Kitchener, however, in more modern style, made a direct observation on his experience as migrant in London; describing the confusing novelty of travelling on 'The Underground Train':

> Ah-ah never me again, to go back on that Underground train
> Never me again, to go back on that Underground train.
> I took the train to Lancaster Gate,
> And the trouble that I met, I am going to relate,
> Well, friends, I had to bawl to a policeman,
> When I lost my way in the tube station, – so boys,
> > *I'm going to walk the journey and avoid the misery, not even a taxi,*
> > *I'm going to walk the journey and avoid the misery, not even a taxi*

> Ah-ah my first misery, is when I embark at Piccadilly,
> I went down below, I stand up in the crowd, don't know where to go,
> I decided to follow a young lady,
> Well I nearly met with my destiny,
> That night was bad luck for Kitchener,
> I fall down the escalator – so boys,
> > *I'm going to walk the journey and avoid the misery, not even a taxi*
> > *I'm going to walk the journey and avoid the misery, not even a taxi*

He also sang of his plans to escape from 'Nora' and go back to Trinidad to 'hear the steelband beating in John John' (Plaisance Road in Port of Spain).[16]

'Nora' was a huge success, both in the Caribbean and English-speaking West Africa. British involvement in the recording of indigenous West Indian music had commenced with a sparkle. This commercial viability assured future recordings by Parlophone and others, in particular, the newly formed specialist company Melodisc Records Ltd. The latter, an Anglo-American affiliation with French associations, began trading in late August 1949 and was registered at Companies House on 21 January 1950.[17]

From the evidence available, Preston supervised all the 'calypso' recordings for Parlophone and the early sessions for Melodisc. His first Melodisc session followed soon after the West Indian test match cricket success over the MCC at Lords on 29 June 1950. This comprised four recordings of Trinidad traditional music, including Lord Beginner's hugely successful 'Victory Test Match' – 'cricket lovely cricket' – commemorating this famous West Indian defeat of the MCC and symbolically the 'mother country' itself. Beginner also sang 'Straight Hair Girl' describing a contemporary fashion for hair-dyeing and straightening among black women.

As well as calypsos, there were two kalendas – stickfighting songs to accompany, and describe events or sentiments in what, by the 1880s, had become almost a form of ritual combat among black Trinidadians, especially at the time of Carnival and other seasonal occasions. Chanted in African call-and-response-fashion, with a lead singer and chorus, lyrics dating from the nineteenth and early twentieth centuries were usually composed in French Creole, as in these two songs. Like early calypso, with which they are associated, this music retains something of the Creole French-American as well as the Creole African-American influence in the cosmopolitan history of Trinidad.

Performing with the Calypso Rhythm Kings, Beginner took the lead in 'Sergeant Brown (Lè Rèzon Mé)', and Brylo Ford (as le Duc) sang the part of the caller in 'Boul' Vé-Sé'. The latter, with its line 'Fitzy caree, Myler reve', recalls a celebrated encounter between Eugene Myler and Fitzy Banray, which Myler (noted in a 1905 newspaper as 'Head stickfighter of Trinidad') won with one blow. The accompaniment, by the Calypso Rhythm Kings, imitates the rhythms of the tamboo-bamboo stamping tubes that in the twentieth century usually accompanied this music. On aural identification the musicians were Freddy Grant (clarinet), Brylo Ford (string bass), Fitzroy Coleman (guitar), and a percussionist playing bottle and spoon.[18]

A second session supervised by Denis Preston for Melodisc was recorded in about September 1950; it featured two more calypsos from Lord Beginner and two traditional Jamaican folksongs performed by the Jamaican dialect champion and writer, Louise Bennett. One, entitled 'Bongo Man' (also known as 'Wheel and Turn Me'), was described as a Christmas song and is thereby associated with the Jonkunnu masquerade held in Jamaica at this season. The other was a Jamaican song of long standing, 'Linstead Market', which had been printed as early as 1907 in Walter Jekyll's *Jamaican Song and Story*. The backing to this coupling included Leslie 'Jiver' Hutchinson (trumpet), Freddy Grant (clarinet) and Norbert Payson (tenor saxophone) – another ex-member of the 'Al' Jennings' Orchestra.[19]

Louise Bennett recorded a further session at about the same time for the label Tri-Jam-Bar, with Leslie 'Jiver' Hutchinson's West Indian Orchestra in accompaniment. It comprised four more Jamaican folk songs: 'Cudelia Brown', 'Matty Rag' and 'Hog Eeena De Cocoa', 'Dis Long Time Gal'. Together with her Melodisc recordings, these appear to be the first releases of authentic black music from Jamaica made in Britain for sale both here and in that island.

Evidently, Preston supervised one other session for Melodisc in the latter part of 1950, an instrumental version of the leggo 'Caroline', performed by the Trinidad Steel Band, which may be the first commercial recording to feature exclusively this important twentieth-century instrument. Involved in the production was Boscoe Holder who, with his wife Sheila Clarke, came to Britain from Trinidad in April 1950 with their dancing troupe and a set of steel drums. All were featured in the Holder's Creole miscellany *Bal Creole* broadcast by BBC television on 30 June 1950.[20]

Taken as a whole, these 1950 recordings can be used as a general indication of the way in which British recording of West Indian music developed in the first five years of the decade. The emphasis was on Trinidad styles, with calypso to the fore, its topicality indicated in themes of migration, politics and personal relations. Sometimes new recordings were made of songs that can be traced to previous versions, mainly before the Second World War, and there were occasional glimpses of other aspects of the island's musical heritage.

In contrast, only a small proportion of the singers who recorded in Britain at this time were from Jamaica. They tended to perform songs from that island's traditional repertoire, rather than new material in the fashion of the Trinidadians. Later developments broadened the base of the musical styles recorded but, in essence, left intact its core components.

While recordings in 1950 set the scene for the subsequent development of English-speaking Caribbean music in Britain, 1951 was the year of its greatest surge, sparked probably by the advent of the Festival of Britain and the internationalist spirit of the times.

In this respect 'Festival of Britain' is the title and subject of one of the songs that Kitchener featured in his first session for Melodisc, held in about January or February 1951. It was coupled with 'London is the Place for Me', a song he had composed during his passage on the *Windrush* and performed for a newsreel film on his arrival at Tilbury on 21 June 1948. The other two titles from this session were 'Kitch's Cricket Calypso' in praise of the West Indies' clinching the test match rubber with England the previous year, and 'Kitch's Be Bop Calypso' which praises many of the stars of that new wave of black American jazz. Most be bop performers recorded for US Savoy, with whom Melodisc had a leasing arrangement via their American director Emil Shalit.

Departure from the norm of Denis Preston's previous calypso productions was signalled by his use of a more varied musical combination. This included the Jamaicans Bertie King (clarinet/alto-saxophone) and Clinton Maxwell (drums), as well as Freddy Grant (clarinet/tenor-saxophone), Neville Boucarut (string bass), Fitzory Coleman (guitar) and the Guyanese pianist Mike McKenzie. Like Grant, both King and Maxwell had participated in the pre-war black music scene in London, the latter two having played together in Jamaica before migrating to Britain.[21]

Variety of repertoire and instrumentation blossomed as the year progressed. Preston recorded further calypsos, two Barbados-Jamaican competitive comic dialogues, two castillianes, Martinique biguines, more Jamaican folk songs, Cuban music, and early French Creole calypsos for Melodisc; he also recorded calypsos for Parlophone. A feature of some of these sessions was the use of African percussionists – such as Billy Sholanke's conga drum playing in Mona Baptiste's version of Nat 'King' Cole's 'Calypso Blues'. Preston also supervised the first Melodisc recordings by Ambrose Campbell's West African Rhythm Brothers at this time.

All this activity, however, must be seen alongside what was, for Trinidad, the most significant musical event of the year: the successful sponsorship of the Trinidad All Steel Percussion Orchestra (TASPO) for the Festival of Britain celebrations at the South Bank in London. Key instrumentalists were selected from seventy steel bands in Trinidad. They were trained and conducted by Lieutenant N. Joseph Griffith of the St Lucia Police, who had served previously in the Trinidad Police Band. Including Griffith, eleven musicians reached

London where they made their début at the Festival on 26 July 1951. Many of the important concert events in their ten-week stay were organized by Edric Connor. With a repertoire of calypsos, sambas, mambos, waltzes, marches and occasional adaptation of the 'classics', they were a sensation. This acceptance in the 'mother country' led to greatly improved social recognition for steelbands in Trinidad and the Caribbean as a whole. TASPO recorded at least two couplings for Danceland which with four other titles were later re-released by Vogue as by the Trinidad All Steel Percussion Band. One band member, Sterling Bettancourt (of 'Crossfire', St James, Port of Spain), stayed in Britain to train as a Linotype operator and subsequently made recordings here.[22]

At the same time as funds were raised in Trinidad for TASPO attempts were made to obtain the patronage necessary to send four calypsonians as representative singers for the Festival of Britain. In the event this was unsuccessful, but one veteran calypsonian eventually travelled to London: the Roaring Lion (Hubert Raphael Charles/Rafael de Leon). He arrived at Southampton on 25 August, and appeared at the Festival with TASPO on 3 September. Within a week he had been recorded by Denis Preston for Melodisc, and by early October also for Parlophone.[23]

One further 1951 session organized by Preston is worthy of special mention. Renowned jazz reed-player Bertie King, a veteran of Ken Johnson's band, cut a 'farewell' session on 19 October, just before his first return trip to Jamaica since arriving in Britain in 1935. Included were versions of two Jamaican folksongs 'Sweetie Charlie' and 'Sly Mongoose', with vocals by Tony Johnson, another Jamaican. Both were described as mentos – generic name for a style of dance and topical song in the island.

According to a *Melody Maker* report, King was to collect material for Melodisc's West Indian catalogue during his four-month engagement leading a seven-piece band at the Hotel Casablanca, Montego Bay. At least one coupling probably resulted from this arrangement: 'Don't Fence Her In' and 'Glamour Girl' by the Ticklers with vocal by Harold Richardson (Melodisc 1214 – released in Britain in March 1952). This was recorded and issued originally by the Kingston, Jamaica-based Stanley Motta Ltd, on their Motta Recording Studio label. Almost certainly these were the first location recordings of Jamaican music to be issued in Britain for the home market.[24]

The year 1952 also saw a series of experimental recordings produced by Denis Preston for Parlophone that combined British disciples of New Orleans Creole Jazz, led by trumpeter Humphrey Lyttelton, with a West Indian rhythm section, led by Freddy Grant. These recordings, by the Grant-Lyttelton Paseo Jazz Band, favoured a North American repertoire. There were two exceptions, however: 'Fat Tuesday' – another name for Mardi Gras in New Orleans – was based on a tune 'dug up from the recesses of [Freddy Grant's] memory'; and 'Mike's Tangana' was written by Mike McKenzie in a way that fused black Latin American and North American styles. A touring show was organized to feature this music and its musicians. Included in the package were three West Indian singers George Browne (a Trinidadian, known initially as Young Tiger),

Tony Johnson, and the Guyanese 'tenor who makes no error' Bill Rogers (Augustus Hinds).[25]

Rogers, like Lion and Beginner, was a veteran of Caribbean music recording, having first appeared in RCA Bluebird's West Indian series in 1934. He called his calypso-like style Shanto, and remade some of his earlier material in two sessions cut for Preston in July; one for Parlophone, the other for Melodisc. These included two of his most famous songs 'Weed Woman' and 'B.G. Bargee'.

This, however, was Preston's last accredited 'calypso' record supervision for Melodisc. A disagreement between Emil Shalit (then living in Reading, Pennsylvania) and his British partner Jack Chilkes came to a head earlier in the year and legal action ensued. Chilkes began working for another small British record company, Polygon, and in November 1952 they launched the Lyragon label for the West Indian/West African market. Lyragon used some material that had almost certainly been destined for Melodisc, including recordings by Kitchener (with whom Melodisc had a UK contract).

Lyragon issued a steady stream of releases throughout 1953. One, 'Calypso Medley No.1', played on the ping pong steel drum by Sterling Bettancourt, provides a useful sample of the status of West Indian music in Britain and its popular dissemination at the time of its publication in May.

The first side of this two part record features the melodies of 'Ugly Woman' (recorded by the Lion in London in 1951, but also at his first recording session, in New York, in 1934); 'Nora' (Kitchener's 1950 hit); and 'Brown Skin Gal' (recorded in Trinidad in 1946–7 by King Radio, and in London by Edmundo Ros in 1949). Side two has melodies of 'Rum and Coca-Cola' (the Lord Invader calypso on which was based a 1944 US hit by the Andrews Sisters); 'Everybody Loves Saturday Night' (a West African Highlife, the earliest traced recording of which was made in Lagos by Akanbi Wright in 1942); and 'Anacaona' (a 1935 New York title by Beginner, released in Britain in 1938). The inclusion of the Highlife emphasizes the popularity of London-recorded calypsos in West Africa.

Although this medley stresses continuity with the past, 1953 was a period of change in recording West Indian music in Britain. By April two key reed-playing musicians had left London, Freddy Grant for New York in that month, and Bertie King for Jamaica in September 1952 (he returned in 1954). In June, Emil Shalit was successful in his lawsuit against Jack Chilkes but it was not until October that Melodisc began recording calypsos again, having clearly come to an arrangement with Denis Preston regarding the latter's master recordings. There was a change, too, in musical direction. While personal relations (sometimes in scatalogical fashion) were a feature of these recordings from the outset, Melodisc's new policy was to place much greater emphasis on this aspect of the calypsonian's repertoire.[26]

A new Jamaican performer appeared in Melodisc's lists at this time: Eric Hayden, whose version of the bawdy 'Giver Her the No.1' gave further distribution to a song recorded originally in 1946 by the La Motta Brothers in

New York. There were also recordings leased from the USA, such as the very popular 'Last Train to San Fernando' by the Duke of Iron (Cecil Anderson), a Trinidadian singer of calypsos who had been based in New York from the late 1930s.

Mention must be made of three more Trinidad calypsonians who came to Britain: the Mighty Terror (Fitzgerald Henry) in 1954; and Lord Invader (Rupert Grant) and Young Kitchener (probably L. Joseph) in 1956. All three recorded for Melodisc, and the former two for Nixa, a new label launched in 1956, for whom Denis Preston produced recordings of jazz, calypso and other styles.

The year 1956, however, signalled the end of the recording of calypso in Britain for the West Indies. The success of the Mighty Sparrow (Slinger Francisco) in winning the Carnival calypso competition that year heralded a new era for calypsos recorded on location in the West Indies. It paralleled the political rise of the Peoples National Movement in Trinidad and the imminent formation of what became an unsuccessful Federation of British West Indian Territories. EMI pressed some of Sparrow's earliest recordings for the Kay label (run by the Christopher Recording Service in Trinidad) and in 1957 launched their own DPD export series of Guyanese-recorded calypsos on Parlophone. Some West Indian recordings, including calypsos, continued to be made in Britain, however, principally for the home market, or for West Africa, such as Kitchener's specially commissioned 'Birth of Ghana'.[27]

At some point in the mid-to-late 1950s, circumstantial evidence suggests Emil Shalit set up a recording studio in Jamaica run by the Caribbean Recording Co. Ltd. He appears to have launched the Caribou and Kalypso labels there, as well as distributing them in Britain. Starlite (a subsidiary of the British label, Esquire) also leased material from Jamaican sources in this period.

Finally, it is worth drawing attention to one Starlite session recorded in Britain in 1960 by the Jamaican singer Azie Lawrence; all four songs he recorded were credited to (Sam) Manning and his Antilliana Music publishing house. It seems fitting that this Trinidadian pioneer of West Indian music recording both in the USA and Britain should conclude this résumé of London-based English-speaking West Indian musical activity. Lawrence's origin in Jamaica anticipated the rise in Britain of ska, blue beat and other Jamaican-derived popular styles of the 1960s. It is significant, however, that the means to distribute such recordings in Britain were already in place.[28]

This short survey of music played by black Caribbeans in Britain, from the turn of the century to 1960, gives a general indication of their relationship with their 'mother country' (using the phraseology of the time). By virtue of their birth, until the break-up of the Empire and the UK Immigration Act, all were British subjects and free to travel within the world-wide bounds of British territories. This also gave them easy access to the USA that was curtailed only by the McCarran-Walter Immigration Act of 1952. Many instrumental musicians among this group, especially those who arrived before 1945, received their training via British institutions, principally police bands in the Caribbean, and the British Army's musical training establishment at Kneller Hall, Whitton, in Britain. In many respects these older musicians were representative of the Empire culture into which they were born, and in which they made their living. In this they parallel the Old Brigade calypsonians in Trinidad, whose repertoire evolved in the same period under similar circumstances. The upheaval of the Second World War with, for example, the introduction of US military forces in the West Indies (Trinidad in particular), altered the musical landscape in these colonies and later in Britain itself. Younger musicians adapted to this different perspective.

Something of the change can be discerned from the repertoire of the calypsonians who recorded in Britain after the Second World War: Lord Beginner, the Lion, and Lord Invader being identified with the Old Brigade (who had risen to fame in Trinidad prior to the War) and Lord Kitchener, the Mighty Terror, and Young Kitchener with subsequent Young Brigade developments.

Direct observation on international politics, critical or otherwise, was the remit of the Old Brigade exemplified by Beginner's 1951 recording encouraging 'Federation' among the British West Indian colonies, and Lion's 1952 commentary on procrastination among the politicians in his 'West Indies Get Together'. In contrast, Kitchener's 1957 recording in praise of the short-lived 'Federation' does not have such political conviction.[29]

For the representatives in Britain of the Young Brigade the issues had changed, in general their commentaries were directed at more readily identifiable local issues, such as the problems of migration (including racial discrimination). Exceptions, where Old and Young Brigades came together, were in the treatment of black success in sport, which symbolized integrity for Blacks in relation to Whites, and identification with Africa. The latter had been an important component in calypso commentaries from the 1930s, when Mussolini invaded Ethiopia/Abyssinia. In this vein Terror's 'The Emperor of Africa' (recorded in 1954) relates his wish to go to Ethiopia and visit its Emperor (Haile Selassie) and escape from racial discrimination in Britain.

> Ah, lovely Africa, lovely Africa,
> Please send for Terror,
> I want to have a good talk with the Emperor,
> I want to go to *lovely Africa*, Mama,
> > *lovely Africa*,
> Please send for Terror,
> I want to have a good talk with the Emperor, – Mama.

> I dreamt him last night, so to see him is my delight,
> I would feel as a man
> To be in Africa and finish with Great Britain,
> I want to go to *lovely Africa*,
> > *lovely Africa*, [etc]

> Ah, I want my tribe markings,
> Doing such a thing is no sky lark,
> For in the white man's land, there is too much racial discrimination
> I want to go to *lovely Africa*, [etc]

More generally British West Africa (like the West Indies, moving towards independence) was the subject of such songs – Kitchener's 'Africa My Home' from 1952, Invader's broader-based 'I'm Going Back to Africa' from 1956 (with a melody taken from a stickfighting kalenda), and the Tobagonian Lord Ivanhoe's 'Africa Here I Come' (celebrating Ghana's Independence and expressing sentiments similar to Invader) from 1958.

In Trinidad, especially after the rise of Sparrow, the emphasis shifted from the general to more particular commentary on local events. The Empire, and the Commonwealth that began to replace it, faded into the background as more urgent issues based in the West Indies became the thrust of the topical repertoires for the popular calypsonians of the day.

By the time of Independence in Trinidad and Jamaica in 1962, the resident Old and Young Brigade calypsonians had begun to leave Britain and settle in Trinidad again. It seems the Mighty Terror was last to leave and, symbolically, he won the crown as King of Calypso for 1966 singing 'Last Year's Happiness', celebrating his return to Trinidad for Carnival in the previous year. With the rise of the street Carnival in Notting Hill at the same time, this heralded the end of an era and the beginning of another for West Indian music in Britain.[30]

Appendix: List of records, by label and issue number, to which direct reference has been made

Arco (USA)

| 1209 | *Give Her Number One/* | |
| | *I Wanna Settle Down* | La Motta Brothers |

Danceland (UK)

DL 0011	*Allies Quick Step/*	
	Papito	TASPO
DL 0012	*Coolie Man's House a Fire/*	
	Go Away Gal	TASPO

Decca (UK)

| F 8531 | *The Lord's Prayer/* | |
| | *The Virgin Mary Had a Baby Boy* | Edric Connor |

Lyragon (UK)

J 704	*West Indies Get Together*	Lion
	Sons and Daughters of Africa	Beginner
J 712	*Calypso Medley No.1*	
	(both sides of record)	Sterling Bettancourt

Melodisc (UK)

1133	*Victory Test Match/*	
	Sergeant Brown (Lè Rèzon Mé)	Beginner
1134	*Straight Hair Girl*	Beginner
	Boul' Vé-Sé	Le Duc
		₌(Brylo Ford)

1139	*Linstead Market/*	
	Bongo Man	Louise Bennett
1162	*Kitch's Cricket Calypso/*	
	Kitch's Be Bop Calypso	Kitchener
1163	*Festival of Britain/*	
	London is the Place for Me	Kitchener
1181	*Calypso Blues/*	
	Ba Mwe Un Ti Bo'	Mona Baptiste
1185	*Caroline*	Trinidad Steel Band
	Six String Calypso	Fitzroy Coleman
1198	*Sweetie Charlie/*	
	Donkey City	Bertie King
1208	*Africa My Home/*	
	My Landlady	Kitchener
1214	*Glamour Girl/*	
	Don't Fence Her In	The Ticklers
1230	*B.G. Bargee/*	
	Nice Woman, Ugly Man	Bill Rogers
1231	*Imogene/*	
	Sly Mongoose	Bertie King
1256	*Give Her the No.1/*	
	Montego Bay	Eric Hayden
1316	*Big Bamboo/*	
	Last Train to San Fernando	Duke of Iron
1319	*The Emperor of Africa/*	
	Hydrogen Bomb	Terror
1390	*Birth of Ghana/*	
	Kitch's Mambo Calypso	Kitchener
1430	*Federation/*	
	Alphonso in Town	Kitchener

MNE (Trinidad) (in long-playing record)
| 001 | *Last Year's Happiness* | Terror |

MRS (Jamaica)
| 08 | *Glamour Girl/* | |
| | *Don't Fence Her In* | The Ticklers |

Nixa (UK) (in extended play records)
| NEP 24038 | *I'm Going Back to Africa* | Invader |
| NEP 24087 | *Africa Here I Come* | Ivanhoe |

Parlophone (UK)
E 4109	*Help Me to Fly Over Jordan/*	
	No Hidin' Place	Sam Manning
E4110	*Sweet Willie*	Sam Manning
	Ara Dada (Pasea)	Gus Newton
R 3850	*The Bargee/*	
	Mabel (See what you've done)	Sam Manning
R 3851	*Sweet Willie/*	
	Camilla (When you go please don't come back)	Sam Manning

R 3853	*Susan Monkey Walk/*	
	Amba Cay La' (Under the House)	Sam Manning
R 3854	*Sly Mongoose/*	
	Brown Boy	Sam Manning
R 3857	*Goofer Dust John/*	
	My Jamaica	Slim Henderson
R 3543	*Friendless Blues/*	
(new series)	*Fat Tuesday*	Grant-Lyttelton
		Paseo Jazz Band
R 3587	*London Blues/*	
(new series)	*Mike's Tangana*	Grant-Lyttelton
		Paseo Jazz Band
MP 102	*Nora*	Kitchener
	The Dollar and the Pound	Beginner
MP 103	*The Underground Train*	Kitchener
	I Will Die a Bachelor	Beginner
MP 104	*Housewives/*	
	General Election	Beginner
MP 109	*Man Smart and Woman Smarter*	Iron Duke
		(Brylo Ford)
	Iere	Cyril Blake
MP 112	*Federation/*	
	Rum More Rum	Beginner
MP 118	*Weed Woman/*	
	Hungry Man from Clapham	Bill Rogers

Regal-Zonophone (UK)

| MR 1531 | *Dinah/* | |
| | *St Louis Blues* | Gladys Keep |

Starlite (UK)

45–022	*West Indians in England/*	
	Jump Up	Azie Lawrence
45–041	*Love in Every Land/*	
	No Dice	Azie Lawrence

Tri-Jam-Bar (UK)

AB 101	*Cudelia Brown/*	
	Matty Rag	Louise Bennett
AB 102	*Hog Eena De Cocoa/*	
	Dis Long Time Gal	Louise Bennett

Vogue (France/UK)

V 9017	*Mango Walk/*	
	Take Me	TASP Band
V 9018	*Ramadin/*	
	Johnny	TASP Band
V 9019	*Papito/*	
	Allies Quick Step	TASP Band
V 9020	*Go 'Way Girl/*	
	Coolie Man's House	TASP Band

PART TWO

From the 1950s to the Present

MUSIC

DANCE

DEMBO KONTE & KAUSU KUYATEH
Traditional Kora music from West Africa

Dembo & Kausu are 2 master musician-singers from Gambia, and direct descendants in a tradition of music which has passed from father to son over a period of 600 years. The Kora is a 21 stringed harp-lute with the captivating sound of a celtic-harp, and is played with rhythm, delicate ornamentation & occasional improvisation. Presented with the assistance of Visiting Arts.

Fri. April 24 8 p.m. £2.50

NAHID SIDDIQUI and her musicians

Kathak is the classical dance style of Northern India: a form in which gesture, movement, posture & pace are determined by a constant flow of rhythm & pattern, and the close rapport between dancer & drummer. Nahid Siddiqui is the leading exponent of this ancient art, resident in the U.K. *"Every inch a piece of visual poetry"* Hindustan Times.

Sat. July 4 8 p.m. £3.25 F.P. £2.75

BEAU TEMPS SUR LA PROVINCE

Beautiful and haunting melodies, drawn from the traditions of central France played by this marvellous Lyonnais trio playing fiddle, bechomet, bourbonais pipes, hurdy-gurdy, melodeon and voices; returning for their second English tour, by popular demand.

Sat. May 30 8 p.m. £2.50

ADZIDO
PAN AFRICAN DANCE ENSEMBLE

A dazzling tapestry of dances from across the great African Continent expressing the strength, beauty & unity of traditional African culture. Performed by this magnificent troupe of 28 dancers & drummers who are the biggest & the best African dance company working in Britain today. Entertainment for all the family. Co-promoted with Stroud District Council **At the Subscription Rooms, Stroud.**

Friday July 24 8 p.m. £3.50 concs £2

African and South Asian musicians and dancers were among the performers in a festival of arts presented by PREMA, Uley, Gloucestershire, 1987. *Collection: Paul Oliver*

Introduction

PAUL OLIVER

For everyone who was there at the Winter Garden Theatre, Drury Lane, the events of Sunday 13 November 1949 must be engraved in their memories; they certainly are in mine. The occasion was a jazz concert given by Humphrey Lyttelton and his band, but for the capacity audience it was alive with the anticipation of an altogether more sensational sound. On stage the Lyttelton band, with the leader playing trumpet, Wally Fawkes clarinet, Keith Christie trombone, and George Webb on piano, put in a somewhat uncertain opening set. They had reason to be anxious. Virtually every jazz enthusiast in the audience had seen a circular distributed to London Jazz Club members by James Asman that the legendary – one can use the term advisedly – jazz musician Sidney Bechet would be in the audience. After the fourth number, 'Royal Garden Blues', the spotlight shone on the royal box and the rounded but dignified figure of a man, gravely smiling. He stood to the roar of the audience and the introduction of the compere, Rex Harris. The chorus of entreaties to play for us were quickly rewarded as he left the box.

Forty years after I can still recall the chilling of my flesh as the first notes of Béchet's soprano sax seemed to pierce the tabs before he came into view; he was playing 'Weary Blues' with a breadth of tone and a sweep in his phrasing that left me gasping. It left the Lyttelton band in a state of nerves too, and I recall Wally Fawkes tearing at his hair and attempting to escape by climbing the stage curtains, only half in jest. The rest of the concert was a one-man show; the band played respectfully in support of the leader, and if George Webb was caught out more than once by his inability to match Bechet's sequences, it threw into relief the sheer mastery of the New Orleans musician's inventive flow of ideas. We heard no one but Sidney Bechet and talked about nothing else on the way home. One of the gods had descended from Olympus, and for a brief hour had shared his gifts among ordinary mortals.

Black gods, white worshippers

During the 1950s, black communities were established in Britain that were to be the hosts to many musical forms, but they were consolidated at a time when visits by overseas musicians were virtually non-existent. Due to the implementation of the Musicians Union (MU) ban, which had been imposed in 1935, for over twenty years no bands were admitted to Britain. The MU ban was supported by the Ministry of Labour and backed by the force of law, with the ministry refusing to grant work permits for musicians from the USA until the American Federation of Musicians reciprocated and British musicians were employed there. Individual musicians could appear only as variety artists, and it was under this guise that Duke Ellington toured with his violinist Ray Nance in 1948.[1] But the appearance of Sidney Bechet with Humphrey Lyttelton's jazz band and of the saxophonist Coleman Hawkins a few months later led to the indictment and conviction of the promoters, who were seen as martyrs to the jazz cause by followers of the music. By denying American bands entry an important stimulus to music-making in Britain was denied, but the MU ban was as inflexibly applied as it was stupidly imposed.[2]

Undoubtedly the MU position was somewhat dented by the case, and the publicity in the music press that it generated. It was probably an influence on the MU's eventual rescinding of the ban, though it took several years for this to come about. When finally in 1956 the iron curtain was raised, black American jazz musicians figured prominently among the first visitors. Within the first couple of years the Count Basie Orchestra came twice, the Louis Armstrong All-Stars, the Lionel Hampton band, the Modern Jazz Quartet all toured, while Earl Hines teamed with Jack Teagarden to lead a mixed 'All Stars' band. For devotees of New Orleans jazz the tour by George Lewis was on a par with Bechet's appearance as living evidence of the 'authenticity' of the music, while enthusiasts of modern jazz were joyous over the appearance at a former cinema, the Gaumont State, Kilburn, in May 1958 of 'Jazz at the Philharmonic' with Dizzy Gillespie, Coleman Hawkins, Lester Young, Oscar Peterson, Roy Eldridge and Ella Fitzgerald.

Nevertheless, the presentation of many of their idols was inadequate and the performances of musicians who had been evaluated on their records, often of decades before, disappointed some audiences. 'Idols' is not too loose a term; jazz supporters worshipped American musicians, though from afar. When they heard them in concert the gap between the imagined perfection of distant gods and the reality was sometimes difficult to bridge. But adulation blunted criticism and partisan positions were reinforced. Seen from this distance the prejudices of enthusiasts for different kinds of jazz seem absurd; their advocates wrote like prophets of a new religion. The jazz sects lined in opposition; hot against cool, traditional against modern, black against white – with the majority in favour of black jazz from New Orleans.[3]

In imitation of their idols many young white British musicians formed jazz bands in the late 1940s while the ban was rigidly imposed, deriving their repertoires from collector's record issues. It was mimicry but it was 'sincere', and in the obsessional cult of New Orleans jazz, 'sincerity' and 'authenticity' were much valued. On the bandstand they affected the working clothes of the rediscovered veterans, and off it they spoke the jargon of jazz picked up from the glossary in Mezz Mezzrow's autobiography *Really the Blues*.[4]

Countless fans have followed the pilgrim's way to the hallowed grounds of New Orleans since the merchant seaman trumpet player Ken Colyer jumped ship to play there. His exploit (and brief spell in jail) took on heroic dimensions. For many, jazz had become a symbol of the irrepressible creative spirit of Blacks in the face of racial and economic oppression. Norman Mailer's 'white Negro' was reborn a thousand times among the jazz lovers who identified with their black musical heroes, for whom jazz was also a symbol of revolt: revolt against the values of their parents, against war, against 'commercialism'.

Given these symbolic attributes it was almost inevitable that New Orleans jazz – or what passed for it – was adopted politically. George Webb's Dixielanders began by playing in the Red Barn at Bexleyheath but it soon became the official band of the Challenge Jazz Club organized by the Young Communists, playing concerts in Holborn. The Aldermaston 'Ban the Bomb' marchers stepped to the parade jazz of a New-Orleans-style marching band beneath the black flag of Anarchism; later, many a Liberal or Young Conservatives hop was danced to the music of a 'trad jazz' band. To the communists the ensemble improvisation of the traditional band symbolized the sharing of responsibility and skills of collective creativity without individualism; to the anarchists the traditional line-up meant freedom of expression and the loose, unshackled federalism of 'head' arrangements; to liberals the music spoke of responsibility and selflessness; to conservatives, the strength and continuity of traditions ensured the basis for the individual enterprise of front-line soloists. In other words, jazz symbolized what its proponents chose to find in it that supported their own aims and ideologies, but for each coterie it provided the security of identification with a specialized group. But they and their successors, including the publishers of the Jazz Sociological Society (ideologically anarchist) and Jazz Appreciation Society (communist) booklets, prepared the way for the growing public for black music in the post-war years.[5]

It was a public which was divided between the record collectors, the critics and 'serious' students of the music, the musicians who endeavoured to replicate it, the listening audiences and the club dancers. They overlapped of course, but nevertheless these divisions overlaid the fragmentation of jazz music itself into different and sometimes mutually hostile sects. In broad terms, much the same account could be written of cool jazz, blues, or rock and roll. Successive phases and types of popular music had their dedicated followers, who enjoyed the cult status, spoke the specialized jargon, wore the clothes and bore the accoutrements of their respective subcultures.

While most, if not all, were musics intended for dancing, they were as frequently presented as performances for listening audiences, in clubs as well as concerts. Most of the genres had their passionate advocates. Typically, in the news-sheets and limited circulation magazines by which the followers of one musical cult or another kept in touch with events, and with each other, there was anger at the policies of the larger booking agencies, the press, the BBC and the major record companies for their failure to recognize the size and virtues of the respective genres. Evangelizing, proselytizing, seeking converts to the musical faith were part of the experience. Yet when a genre was popularized and the audience did expand, when access to the musical press, to radio, recording or eventually television was won, many felt the loss of the sense of in-group identity and solidarity against a hostile and insensitive public which membership of the musical coterie had offered. They resented the 'commercialism' of 'their' music and the popularization of the trad jazz boom, and seldom recognized the contradictions in their response.

During the 1950s black music in Britain had gained considerable audiences. Far from being merely entertained by it, they had come to exalt it in one or more of its manifestations. American jazz, blues, rock and gospel artists acquired an almost mythical status, and their concert appearances and tours provoked, as we have seen, complex emotional responses, as their performances and their personalities were matched against the idealizations of their admirers. The symbolic attributes of black music were not set aside, but were modified in the process of adjustment to the changes that had taken place in the musical forms between record collecting and live appearances. Ironically, while denying entry to American musicians the Musicians Union ban may even have assisted to a certain extent, in the creation of an audience for black musicians, by helping generate a demand for them.

But it was an *audience*; it did not create many opportunities for British black musicians. Versatile musicians such as trumpeter Leslie Hutchinson, saxophonist Bertie King, Coleridge Goode, the bass player, and drummer Ray Ellington were employed, if intermittently, by being adaptable. If it was black music, it was black music played – concerts and club dates by visiting jazzmen apart – by white musicians. There were other anomalies, such as the fact that calypso, introduced to Britain by black immigrants from Trinidad (as John Cowley has recounted in Chapter 4) was scarcely acknowledged in the jazz press, which was deaf to the black music in its midst; and most notably, that the concert audiences for black jazz, blues and even rock and roll performances were almost exclusively white.

The long hiatus brought about by the MU ban was important not for the incongruity of British Whites adopting and playing the music of American Blacks but for the preparation that it afforded for the black music in Britain that was to come. In the much-documented post-1950s era of rock and pop, black music was a source of continual inspiration. Many of the major British pop groups had cut their eye-teeth playing in blues-based skiffle bands and turned to black R and B artists for new rhythms and repertoires. But the fount of musical ideas was still American; it was some time before the full impact was felt of the musical forms that were developing within the growing black population of Britain.

Blacks in Britain

Since Kenneth Little's pioneering work *Negroes in Britain* appeared in 1947 a considerable body of literature on the subject of Blacks and Asians in the United Kingdom has been published.[6] Many studies were written in the 1960s when the scale, nature and impact of immigration from the Commonwealth countries was better known. The contentious Commonwealth Immigrants Act, first announced by Mr R.A.B. Butler in 1961 and implemented the following year, had at least the effect of making available statistics on the numbers of immigrants from the various countries of the Commonwealth, the outflow of those embarking from Britain, the net gains in population, and so on. Until that time no figures were accessible.

Where did the immigrants come from, in what numbers and in what proportions? In the 1950s the annual net immigration from the 'New Commonwealth' countries that had gained independence since 1945 was consistently less than 50,000. In 1955, when the total was some 42,700, three-fifths came from the West Indies, one in seven from India and only 1,850 from Pakistan. In 1959 the numbers were approximately halved, but anticipation of the new legislation had the effect of increasing the flow of immigrants in 1961, with 66,000 from the West Indies, 23,750 from India, and over 25,000 from Pakistan, where domestic issues had played a considerable part in changing the balance. By 1968 the total number of immigrants for the year was 66,700, but of these fewer than 5,000 were from the West Indies, 15,000 from Pakistan and 28,000 from India.[7]

Yet, adding up the numbers of immigrants over the years does not give a reliable indication of the black population as a whole: for a start, it does not account for the black population already resident in this country. But accepting this, the figures are still difficult to interpret. For instance, the Commonwealth immigrants living in Britain at the time of the 1966 census included a high proportion of students, often with their families, many of whom returned to their countries of origin soon after. Or again, children born in Britain of black families, estimated at the time as close on 20 per cent of the total black population would not have been enumerated as immigrants but would have appeared within the overall census figures as UK-born residents. There are other factors that affect the figures: for example, by 1970 the total number of immigrants from India may have included as many as 100,000 Whites who had been born there, but who settled in Britain after independence. With these and many other modifiers borne in mind it was estimated that in 1970 the black population was in the order of 1.2 million, or some 2 per cent of the total for the nation.[8]

Political events outside Britain contributed to the inflow of immigrants. Significant among these was the partition of Pakistan and India, and the later emergence in 1971 of Bangladesh as an independent state. In the late 1970s it was estimated that some 60,000 Bangladeshis were living in Britain; there were rather more Pakistanis, perhaps 80,000. The independence of Kenya in 1963 and the subsequent 'Kenyanization' policy in 1967 meant that non-citizens could obtain only temporary employment. Some of the 90,000 Kenyan Asians with British passports chose to come to Britain: around 8,000 a year until the so-called 'flood' (of 8,000 in eight months) which ultimately precipitated the 1968 Immigrants Bill introduced by a Labour government. The expulsion of Asians from Uganda by General Amin in 1972 added to the modest influx of East African Asians, many of whom were dispersed in different parts of the British Isles, including Scotland, though they soon moved south.[9]

Concentrations of citizens of West Indian, South-West Asian and African extraction – the sector of the population which is now termed, however inappropriately, 'black' – may be found in various parts of the country. Almost all are urban or suburban dwellers and the greatest numbers are located in the south-east, especially London and its suburbs, and in the West Midlands. Bradford, Brixton, Cardiff, Glasgow, Handsworth, Hackney, Leeds, Leicester, Manchester, Notting Hill, Sheffield, Southall, Toxteth and Wolverhampton are among the cities or sectors where the proportion of the black population became significant. Reasons for settlement in specific areas were predominantly related to the availability of work, which sometimes favoured specific groups: for example, Woolf's rubber factory at Southall, which employed Sikhs. Localized concentrations of particular ethnic minorities attracted people of the same origin – Jamaicans to the St Paul's area of Bristol, for instance. Facilities catering for specific interests, often owned and managed by immigrants or their descendants, were another magnet; by 1967 some twenty-five wholesale stores and a hundred retail grocers served the needs of Glasgow's 7,000 Pakistani community. By the 1960s black enclaves were firmly established in cities throughout Britain.[10]

With the ethnic concentrations came many of the problems and ills to which British black communities have been persistently subjected: substandard housing, overcrowding, health risks, poor working conditions, high unemployment, criminal exploitation, conflict with other communities, racial enmities, police harrassment, discriminatory practices, colour prejudice, Powellism. Against the repressive and often humiliating conditions Blacks coped and conquered, often gaining strength and dignity through the support of their own institutions: mosques, temples, churches, schools, youth clubs, political groups, carnival committees, community centres, even cinemas. In many of these music played an important part, providing opportunities for creative expression and outlets for repressed passions. But the significance of music in consolidating ethnic identity is seldom given more than a passing reference in the literature of the black experience.[11]

Black music in modern Britain

No discussion of black music in Britain can be separated from the social contexts of the genres. There is not one music but many, just as the sources of immigrants, the countries of origin, their faiths and their musical inheritances are also diverse. Under the conditions that they experienced in Britain, including those of contiguity with other black groups, and the social, economic and environmental pressures with which they had to come to terms, many of the musical forms flourished, but in a changed state. Younger generations of Blacks, including the increasing proportion who were born and raised in Britain were inevitably facing crises of identity, as they grew up in a country of which they were legally a part, but where so many were disadvantaged.

The chapters in Part Two examine some of the complexities of Afro-Caribbean and South-West Asian musical forms as they have been sustained or have evolved in Britain. Of the various manifestations of the black experience in the British Isles perhaps the longest history has been that of Africans. In spite of this, the African presence in the post-war years has been neither as evident, nor as territorially defined as have been the presence of West Indian and Asian groups. Chris Stapleton (Chapter 5) shows that Africans have made a contribution to British black music for centuries, though often in circumstances which gave relatively minor opportunities for the expression of their inherent skills and traditions. Recognition of these came only with the popularity of high-life and Afro-rock in the 1960s. While a number of African musicians formed bands in Britain, African music, even in the 1980s, has been marked more by the number of visiting groups than for their base within the African community in these islands.

For many West Indians and their descendants, especially among the members of the Rastafarian millenarian cult, Africa represented a symbol of their origins, and the music and culture of Africa was idealized as they dreamed of a return to the Promised Land of Ethiopia. Rastafarian musicians used African rhythm, syncopation and call-and-response patterns to 'deepen the Dread' in their music.[12] Yet this music has received more attention than most black genres in Britain, with many of the more deliberately palatable recordings making the charts. But, as Anthony Marks shows in his overview of the past twenty-five years (Chapter 6), black idioms like American 'soul' and Jamaican 'ska' had meaning too for many young Whites. If, for some, music offered a meeting-ground for some of Britain's black and white youth in playing or in dancing, for others it pointed a way towards professional music-making with perhaps the prospect of club dates, tours and recording. The 1980s witnessed a period of considerable, if at times frankly commercial, musical exchange.

Whether this is yet another manifestation of the exploitation of black idioms by Whites, or whether it represents a more profound and significant cultural meeting-ground, it may still be too early to judge. The implications of the growing popularity of the steelbands, however, with both black and white young performers learning under the tutelage of West Indian musicians, are assessed by Thomas Chatburn (Chapter 7). After outlining the origins of the 'pan' movement in Trinidad he discusses the processes whereby they learn to play complex pieces, and indicates their potential for innovation in musical education.

Some forms of music have stayed with the ethnic communities from which they sprang, and though they have had a measure of wider exposure, flourish best within them. Such is the case with Bhangra, a secularized form of festival music, popular among Punjabis who constitute the largest sector of south Asian cultures in Britain. In a shared chapter Sabita Banerji explains not only its cultural background but also how its nature has changed with adoption by other immigrant groups, development following the rise of Indi-pop, and creative eclecticism with commerical promotion. Considering this process, anthropologist Gerd Baumann examines the conflicts of values when community roles and loyalties confront Bhangra musicians intent on professionalization (Chapter 8).

Among the British groups of South Asian origin are several with Khalifa musicians, members of a minority Muslim sect who stemmed from Gujarat, though sometimes by way of East Africa. An ethnomusicologist, John Baily, explains some of the religious issues that affect music-making among Muslims who came from Pakistan to Bradford (Chapter 9). Though they are becoming de-professionalized they still continue to be performers of *ghazals* and *qawwālis*. Baily's essay, like other chapters in Part Two, brings this review of aspects of black music in Britain to the present, through the narrower focus of a specific case study.

5 African Connections: London's Hidden Music Scene

CHRIS STAPLETON

African musicians have been living and working in Britain for centuries. For long periods their work has constituted a virtual underground: providing a possible source of identity and cohesion inside the African community, but little known beyond that. At other periods, it has leapt into a wider prominence, reaching well beyond the community network.

In the 1980s African music has found a growing audience with white British listeners. There is an air of 'discovery'. But history puts this into perspective, showing a continuous musical presence as Africans worked, studied and struggled for their freedom at the centre of the Empire.

We have only tantalizing glimpses of the first African musicians to play in the British Isles: the African drummer, probably seized from Portuguese slavers, who played at the court of King James IV of Scotland in the sixteenth century; the black trumpeter who worked for Henry VII and Henry VIII; the drummers and dancers with whom Elizabeth I, despite her efforts to repatriate black people, was portrayed. Black performers took part in London pageants: a performance from 1673 included a band playing pipes, tongs, a key, a gridiron and a salt box to recreate the sound of West Africa.[1]

Later, there were the 'black hops' – mentioned by Michael Pickering (Chapter 1): London dances set up by black musicians in the late eighteenth century – and the fashion for 'Turkish' military music that gave European bands new, emphatic instruments, among them large bass drums, tambourines and cymbals. In Britain the musicians, who attracted large and excited crowds, were never Turkish. They were African or of African descent.

If Britain's unholy dealings in the slave trade brought African people to Britain in the first place, others would soon follow. By the end of the nineteenth century, the former slave ports of Bristol, Liverpool and Cardiff had African communities, made up of seamen and civilians. London, the main area covered by this chapter, attracted a smilar mixture, with students, professional people and politicians forming a small but active community.

Visitors came and went. A South African choir formed in 1892, made up of

Zulu singers specializing in ballads, Zulu songs and glee songs, came to Britain where several of the members left to find work in London's music halls.

As in the eighteenth century, African military musicians made an impact. In 1897 fifteen members of the Sierra Leone Frontier Police came to London for Queen Victoria's diamond jubilee celebrations. Their bugler, 'Little Tom', won first prize for bugling. Five years later, further colonial troops came to Britain for the coronation of Edward VII. This was a time of great imperial shows and exhibitions: with the Great Exhibition of 1851 leading the way, followed by the International Exhibition of 1872, the Colonial and Indian Exhibition in 1886, and in 1899 the Greater Britain Exhibition, which brought displays of machinery, agricultural produce and other colonial goods to Earls Court.

The Greater Britain Exhibition also brought a group of black South Africans to take part in a sideshow entitled 'Savage South Africa'. If colonial goods were received as exotic novelties, so much more were the people themselves. The troupe was put together by South African entrepreneur Frank Fillis and shipped to Britain, along with a cargo of South African animals.

Once in London, the South Africans appeared twice a day at the Empress Theatre and spent the rest of their time making beads and bangles, grinding corn and brewing beer, staging war dances and other ceremonies, at a specially constructed 'Kaffir kraal' at the main exhibition. Here they attracted considerable public attention – including that of MP H.M. Stanley, who wrote to *South Africa* magazine on 3 June 1899:

> Your 'savages' are real African natives, their dresses and dances, equipments and actions, are also very real, and when I heard their songs I almost fancied myself among the Mazamboni near Lake Albert once again.[2]

What of their performance? On 13 May a *South Africa* reporter joined the stream of people moving towards the Empress Theatre:

> Suddenly a peculiar dirge-like chant was heard in the direction of the Queen's Palace and there was a general rush towards the great staircase leading from the Imperial Court to discover the cause of the mysterious sound. The crowd had not long to wait. In a few minutes, a mass of waving white plumes and weird war bonnets was seen advancing across the long passage-way, and then 'Savage South Africa', simply attired in bangles, bracelets, and loin cloths, burst with many a wild whoop into the midst of our full-dress civilisation.[3]

The following performance offered a spectrum of music and dance – including Matabele, Swazi and Basuto war dances, a representation of the Matabele war, complete with Maxim guns, Basuto pony races – and a Dutch family setting up camp in an area populated by live springboks and wildebeeste.

For Africans actually based in Britain, music had less to do with wild animals and the lure of the 'exotic', than with the struggle for a sense of identity, to keep their own voice alive in a tough environment. Often, the voice went unheard. Many Africans lost their lives fighting for the Allies in the First World War – but such was public ignorance of this fact that in 1919 the black community staged concerts and lectures explaining Africa's part in the hostilities.

Political and social organizations and the Church were the pillars of African life in Britain. In 1918 the African Progress Union was one of five societies set up by coloured people. At the inaugural meeting Frank Lacton, from Sierra Leone, played the piano between speeches. Lacton also worked with the Southern Syncopated Orchestra, which was based in London from 1919 (as Howard Rye has recorded in Chapter 3). Playing ragtime, minstrel songs and popular dance numbers, the orchestra became the focus for a network of London-based Africans – at different stages its membership included Lacton, William Ofori from the Gold Coast and Nigerian singer Akinlawon Olumuyiwa, who took the name Fred Archer.[4]

One of Britain's most famous composers throughout this period was Samuel Coleridge-Taylor, the son of a Sierra Leonean doctor, whose orchestral compositions blended African and black music into the western classical tradition. His compositions included *Four African Dances, Symphonic Variations on an African Air*, and *The Fairy Ballads*, the words written by a young West African, Kathleen Easmon (for others, see Chapter 2). His most famous work, *Hiawatha's Wedding Feast*, received a triumphant first performance in London in 1898 but, despite regular performances over the years, made little money for the composer.

Coleridge-Taylor also took part in the wider struggle for African rights. He supported the Pan-African movement, and organized the musical programme for a London Pan-African conference in 1900.

Britain's African community was in the vanguard of the fight against colonialism. In London, its members could organize, press their case, and make themselves heard. And as Africans came to Britain to protest at the way they were being treated – and to call for basic reforms – music became a part of their resistance.

One of the great nationalists was Sol Plaatje, the first secretary of the African National Congress, who first came to Britain in 1914 to fight the iniquitous Natives' Land Act of 1913. He returned in 1919, to ask the British government to give the vote to South Africa's Blacks, and made a third visit in 1922.

In South Africa Plaatje had sung with the Wesleyan Native Church Choir and Philharmonic Society at concerts whose programmes covered Negro spirituals, popular European songs and Xhosa pieces such as 'The Bushman Chorus' and 'Intlaba Nkosi'.

Britain provided further scope for Plaatje's talents. As Brian Willan points out in his biography, the South African joined the network of black artists connected with the Southern Syncopated Orchestra.[5] In 1919 he became a friend of the manager, George Lattimore, and watched the orchestra play at an Albert Hall peace dance in 1919. In 1920 the Southern Syncopaters played at a benefit for the newly formed South African Bantu Brotherhood Committee, at which delegates from the National Congress of British West Africa – in London to demand a greater say in the running of the British colonies – were also present.

Some of Plaatje's energies went into raising money to bring out a Brotherhood hymn book, but progress was slow. A ray of hope came in 1923, when George Lattimore asked him to arrange entertainment to go with a film of African wildlife called *The Cradle of the World*.

During the interval Plaatje led a South African troupe through a series of South African songs and war dances. The fact that Plaatje, a champion of progress in South Africa, should have appeared on stage dressed in 'native' costume, seems ironical: as Willan notes, one of his aims was to enlighten the world about modern Africa. But here he was, in Britain and out of pocket, confirming its prejudices in a scenario that smacked of 'Savage South Africa'.

But Plaatje was not alone: the problem of fighting the crude, usually racist stereotype of 'primitive' Africa, is one that has faced most of its musicians seeking to make their way in Britain.

African musicians were quick to take advantage of Britain's fledgling music industry. Some of the earliest British releases came from the Gramophone Company which, in 1905, released a record of Congo pygmy music; by the mid-1920s the Reverend J.J. Ransome-Kuti, father of the Nigerian singer Fela Kuti, was recording Yoruba songs to piano accompaniment. In 1923 Plaatje himself made three records featuring hymns, traditional songs and a version of the 'Kaffir Wedding Song' for the Gramophone Company's Zonophone label. One of the discs included a version of 'Nkosi Sikelel' iAfrika', adopted as the South African black national anthem and one of the great songs of black resistance. This is possibly its first appearance on record; interestingly, no mention of the song appears on the label.

Other musicians followed Plaatje's example: using Britain both as a place to record – paradoxically as a way of reaching greater numbers of listeners at home – and as a base for live performances. In those days, some Africans recorded in the west but the bulk of the recording industry was run by western companies who recorded in Africa, manufactured the records at home, and then exported them back to Africa. In this way the companies followed the usual route of colonial commerce; processing 'raw materials' and selling them back to the colonial subjects at prices decided in the west. A local industry first appeared in South Africa. The recording industry picked up on many of the sounds that were being freshly created in Africa. One of the leading West Africans was Kwame Asare, or Sam, an acoustic guitarist whose skilful blend of traditional sounds and finger-picking styles derived in part from the music of seamen from coastal West Africa, opened a new chapter in the music that became known as 'high-life'. Recorded in Britain in the mid-1920s, he was followed in 1926 by Griffiths Motsieola (the South African musican, later a leading talent scout for the Gallo record company), the Kumasi Trio from Ghana, in 1931, and the ten-strong Zulu Singers. Maud Cuney-Hare noted the rising prestige of African music in her book *Negro Musicians and their Music*:[6]

Today we find African song creeping from its native hearth and arousing curiosity and interest in the concert hall.

As evidence, she cites 'a concert of Bantu songs and rhythms given by the natives named Montsieola [*sic*], Duba and Marimbela' in 1932 and a stage show put on by the Ghanaian trio and the Zulu singers, under the direction of Reuben Caluza:

A mixed double quartette of the singers gave concerts before large audiences. The gifted native director, R.T. Caluza, had arranged African songs with piano accompaniments. In his collection of 100 melodies are found warm funeral and dance songs. The programme songs were sung in four-part harmony to an accompaniment of drum and tambourine.

In the same way that African politicians pressed their case for political independence, so African musicians pressed for a better public understanding of their culture. In 1933 Ekundayo Phillips, organist of Lagos cathedral, who was then living and working in London, gave a recital in Penge during which he discussed West African music, launched into European and African melodies on the organ, and played several African records including a collection of African songs he had recorded with an English choir. The same year, at a lecture in London on the music of the Mende people of Sierra Leone, seven Mende musicians gave a programme of songs, dances and percussion music.

African music found its way intermittently before a wider public. In 1934 the Edinburgh Wireless Singers performed songs by the Ghanaian composer E. Amu. The following year a performance of *Robinson Crusoe* at Lewisham Hippodrome included drumming from George Lanner from Accra, accompanied by Fred Morgan from Freetown and J.W. Odul from Nigeria. The *West African Review* responded optimistically:[7]

Africans from overseas – from the British West Indies and British West Africa – how the sight of them lifted one from bricks and mortar to lands of ancient ways and an old, old life. . . . All a show, but also a symbol and portent of that time . . . when race and race will make harmony and not discord, when every nation offering its quota of talent will make up the final and permanent apotheosis and peace and goodwill for all of us.

One of the towering performers of the age was Paul Robeson, whose work as an actor and singer was underpinned by a strong commitment to the freedom of black people. For Britain's African community, Robeson became a respected figure while his films, *Sanders of the River* (made in 1934 and also featuring Jomo Kenyatta) and *King Solomon's Mines* (1937), brought the continent and its culture to a mainstream audience.

The former, filmed partly in Uganda and the Belgian Congo, partly in Britain, with a cast of 200 extras drawn from the black communities of Cardiff and Liverpool, included a soundtrack of 'African' songs, written by Mischa Spoliansky, of which 'Congo Lullaby', 'Canoe Song' and others appeared on HMV records. *Kind Solomon's Mines* included a war dance sequence from Johannes Matsa, who had been talent-scouted while singing at a concert in South Africa.

Robeson's political views caught the mood of those Africans in Britain who viewed with alarm the struggles facing black people throughout the world. In 1933 a group of African and Afro-American artists gave a benefit concert at London's Phoenix Theatre in aid of the Scottsboro boys, who had been imprisoned in Alabama. Two years later, African residents held prayer meetings in aid of Abyssinia. Among the musicians taking part was Roland C. Nathaniels, a Ghanaian composer who had recorded a number of traditional songs, western dance band tunes and high-life songs for HMV.

The community drew strength from a number of organizations. They included the Church, local societies, and student and community bodies including the League of Coloured Peoples, the West African Students Union and the Gold Coast Students Union. Celebrations such as the annual 'All Africa Day', inaugurated in west London in 1925, helped draw the community together.

Discussion and debate focused on the issues of the day. The League of Coloured Peoples meetings examined racism: 'The world has become a neighbourhood, it has not yet become a brotherhood', said one speaker. The West African Students Union (WASU) took on similar topics – world politics, the pitfalls of western civilization – its north London headquarters being the scene of debates, meetings and social functions. In 1934 a dinner and dance featured 'African folklore and songs'; the following year Paul Robeson was installed as patron and leader of WASU while a 'ceremonial African air was sung lustily by all present in a ring formed with Mr and Mrs Paul Robeson in the centre'.

Fela Sowande, the Nigerian composer, became a leading member of the community, playing piano and organ at numerous functions. Sowande had come to London around 1935 studying first engineering then music. Although a gifted classical composer he also studied jazz, forming his own seven-piece band and playing Hammond organ at a West End nightclub run by Adelaide Hall. Sowande was not the only African musician to immerse himself in the popular dance scene: Augustus Quaye, known as Cab Kaye, a Ghanaian Jazz pianist, came to Britain in 1935. As a singer with Billy Cotton's band, he appeared at the London Palladium and later worked with Ted Heath, Eric Delaney, Vic Lewis and Edmundo Ros.

Although the West African Students Union would occasionally hire mainstream dance bands like E. Child's the Six Spirits of Swing, more often than not it relied on its own resources. Anniversary celebrations provided a strong focus: in 1934 a service at St Martin-in-the-Fields included African native airs, boisterous traditional melodies and harmonies, given western shape by the accompanying organ or piano. The following year's celebrations, to mark its tenth year, included a dance to the radio, speeches, and music and prayers again at St Martin-in-the-Fields. The *West African Review* reporter was moved to comment

Few who heard it will forget the fervour of the singing in the African melody Enyin Araiye, e la tun aiye se (Ye Powers of the earth, Bring permanent peace in our time).[8]

Paul Robeson joined the celebrations in 1936, an event which sheds further light on the music played at that period. The year before, he was serenaded by a piano player. Now the students provided a full Nigerian greeting with a *sakara* band: a deep, authentically Nigerian sound featuring drummers, singers and a *goje* or fiddle player. Robeson was met at the door of the student hostel and escorted in with African drumming and singing ... the sakara, a fascinating African orchestra, with its characteristic singing and dancing, was the next item, and the lady members danced rhythmically before their guests.[9]

The following year London celebrated the coronation of King George VI. West African student celebrations included a dance with an orchestra led by Mr O.A. Adeyin and a reception for the Alake of Abeokuta, a Nigerian dignitary, who was also entertained by the sakara band. The Royal West African Frontier Force took part in the march-past through central London.

From the late 1930s the numbers of African musicians coming to Britain seem to have increased; many were merchant seamen, who chose that profession as a way of widening their horizons and of finding a foothold in what was both the centre of 'Empire' and a pillar of the world's recording industry. From London, news of black musicians working the drinking dens of Soho and the presence of established black dance bands, such as that belonging to Ken 'Snakehips' Johnson, doubtless provided further incentive. In addition, many African countries shared Europe's fascination with Latin American dance music – HMV's Latin records were first sold on the West Coast in the early 1930s – and London offered possible employment via a scattering of bands playing rumba and other Latin American dance music. Edmundo Ros ran one of the best known, and employed a number of African musicians.

Among the new arrivals were Ola Johnson, a conga player who came to Britain in 1938; Emmanuel Ade, a tailor and percussionist; Brewster Hughes, a guitarist who came over as a seaman in 1939; Ginger Johnson, a merchant seaman who started playing with Edmundo Ros's band after the war; Ambrose Campbell, a Nigerian high-life artist who founded his West African Rhythm Brothers in 1946, along with a fellow Nigerian percussionist Ade Bashorun; Guy Warren, a Ghanaian drummer who played with Kenny Graham's Afro-Cubists; and Jimmy Scott, a percussionist from Nigeria.

For many, the prospect of new horizons went hand in hand with a wish to give African culture a wider exposure: possibly break new ground in the performing arts. In 1946 Ambrose Campbell took part in the *Ballets Nègres*, a show whose predominantly black cast brought, in the words of the *West African Review*, 'a new idiom, a Negro idiom' to the English stage.[10] *Ballets Nègres* featured West Indian and African dances – among them market scenes and a depiction of the clash between African religion and the west – performed to an African percussion, piano and acoustic guitar backing. Tellingly the *Review* also described the ballet as a 'novelty' – an indication of the level at which African music has traditionally found acceptance in the west.

Radio and television played its part in giving African music wider exposure. In 1946 a BBC radio programme *Around the World* featured Samadu Jackson and his drummers, who played 'Everybody Loves Saturday Night', a great favourite in West Africa. The following year, Ade Olujuwa and his West African Dunia Orchestra, with dancer Raphaele Lerougue, two acoustic guitarists and percussion players, appeared on BBC television.

But the greatest eye-opener, as in the eighteenth century, came from military musicians, with a lengthy tour in 1946 from the Band of the Gold Coast Police. Like many top African police and army brass bands, the Gold Coasters combined military numbers with light classics and African pieces, stretching from high-life, the urban dance band music that enjoyed enormous popularity across West Africa in the 1940s and 1950s, to traditional xylophone music. Throughout its stay, the band played concerts at Hastings, Folkestone, and two concerts at Hammersmith Palais. A total of 18,000 saw them perform in Leicester. For their farewell concert they played a dance at the WASU hostel, while at the HMV studios they recorded a selection of tracks including 'Everybody Loves Saturday Night'.

Over the next decades the new arrivals brought a variety of musical styles. From West Africa came high-life music in two forms – either a guitar-based sound, heavy with proverbial wisdom, plaintive singing and minor chords, or a breezier major key format, with a brass section playing jazz and dance-floor licks over different rhythms. Nigerian musicians brought *sakara*, powered by talking drums, *goje* fiddle and *agidigbo*, or 'hand piano', and juju music, which set guitar and plainsong harmonies above talking drums and other percussion. From South Africa came the explosive sounds of jazz from the townships and, by the late 1950s, *kwela,* a form of indigenized American jazz with an infectious beat and piping pennywhistles.

The popularity of the London-based bands continued, boosted by records made for the London-based Melodisc label whose roster included Ambrose Campbell's West African Rhythm Brothers and Ginger Johnson's band. Kenny Graham's Afro-Cubists recorded for Esquire from 1951 onwards, and featured a number of African artists including Ginger Johnson and Billy Olu Shalanke on congas.

Campbell's name and fame continued through the 1940s and 1950s as he played a double role: adding a new life to a British music scene in the post-war years and sustaining the African community in an often bleak environment. As in 1919, Britain in 1948 was hit by anti-black riots, and black people were set upon and beaten up in numerous incidents in 1956. The appeal of the band was strong: writing in 1954, a journalist in *West African Review* commented

> Evidently when times are good, the band is a full-time occupation. During the early years of the summer, however, they find other part-time employment. I must say their music made me quite nostalgic for Nigeria and as I left I heard them playing Fire Fire it reminded me very much of the days when walking in the garden of the Island Club in Lagos I heard Bobby Benson playing the very same wonderful tune.[11]

Campbell's popularity coincided with the setting up of African clubs in London. The new scene marked a shift in the presentation of African music, perhaps a new self-confidence, as African businessmen along with students and politicians – who now came to Britain in greater numbers than ever before – enjoyed their music in the heart of the West End.

Ade Bashorun, bongo player with the West African Rhythm Brothers, recalls the vitality of the 1940s and 1950s:

We were playing every night; either at town halls, festivals or the clubs in Soho, like the Abalabi and the Club d'Afrique. The Rhythm Brothers were doing the typical African music: we didn't want to follow the Latin style, like Edmundo Ros. The business side wasn't so good, however. Most of the time we played for 'chicken change'.[12]

The vitality of the scene attracted white commentators: in his 1957 essay, 'City After Dark', Colin MacInnes, author of *City of Spades* and *Absolute Beginners*, described his fascination with such clubs as the Myrtle Bank, the West-End-Rendezvous Club, the Sunset Club and others in Brixton, Whitechapel and Paddington. But his favourite remained the Abalabi in Wardour Street.

The Abalabi has long been the most authentic African club in London . . . a rarity, since most coloured clubs have a Caribbean music and decor. In its golden age, Mr Ambrose Campbell presided over his superb team of drummers, but now the fame of his recordings has beckoned him home on a triumphal tour of Nigeria.[13]

Other musicians had their own patches. Rans Boi, a Ghanaian acoustic guitarist who had come to Britain in 1939, led a high-life band which appeared on television and in West End shows. At the Contemporary Club in Piccadilly, Ginger Johnson played a mixture of high-life, mambos and other West African dance tunes with a line-up that included timbales, string bass and piano. Brewster Hughes, Ambrose Campbell's guitarist, formed the Starlight Tempos Band and took a residency at the Club d'Afrique in Wardour Street which had been opened by Chief Delo Dosunmu.

Apart from high-life, calypso was a firm favourite across Africa in the 1950s. One of the leading exponents, Ali Ganda from Sierra Leone, recorded a series of Melodisc singles including 'Poor Little Monkey', 'Don't Gamble with Girls', 'The Queen Visits Nigeria', and 'Welcome to Our Queen'. Royalty seems to have fascinated Ganda. When the Queen flew to Nigeria, Ganda along with the West African Rhythm Brothers serenaded her from the roof of London Airport's central building. But more important African affairs occupied his attention: in 1957, when the Gold Coast became independent, Ganda recorded an independence song alongside Lord Kitchener's 'Ghana' and 'Good Luck Ghana' by Ambrose Campbell's band.

Other visitors made their mark: high-life star E.T. Mensah, who came to Britain to study dance hall and recording techniques in the late 1950s and appeared at the Festival Hall with Chris Barber. More sensational was the visit from Les Ballets Africains, a Guinean dance troupe put together by a later Guinean government minister, Keita Fodeba. Popular across Europe, Keita's troupe was booked in 1956 to replace a failed comic opera at the Palace Theatre, and offered a breathtaking series of dances to the sound of Guinean percussion, with quieter interludes from two kora players backed by an acoustic guitarist. Les Ballets Africains returned later in the year, and were followed in 1965 by the National Dance Company of Senegal, under the direction of the president's brother, Maurice Senghor.

Nigerian performers in the Royal Tournament in August 1960 treated the audience to horseback displays, Tiv dancing, the Old Calabar march and tableaux featuring Emirs and fishermen, before playing to crowds in Hyde Park.

The following year the South African musical, *King Kong*, which spanned jazz, choral singing and pennywhistle kwela music and jive, came to London and stirred controversy over its apparent lack of political content. Where some might have preferred a stronger political message, Matchet's Diary in *West Africa* commented that *King Kong*

> makes a much greater political impact because it concentrates on being entertaining. Who, after seeing these lively, talented and agreeable people, can stomach the monstrous heresy that they are unfit to exercise the full privileges of citizens?[14]

Such visits doubtless brought Africa to a wider British audience and revived the spirits of the community overseas, but what of the musicians actually based in Britain? For them, music was part of a wider process, something that author and musician Kwesi Owusu describes as 'the struggles for community, dignified labour and autonomy'.[15] Part of the job was to keep the community in touch with its culture and, in so doing, in touch with an identity that was threatened – either by a society that denied black people a role, or insisted that they 'assimilate' into the majority culture.

The African community organized itself into a prodigious variety of clubs and associations. Some were national bodies representing, for example, students from Ghana or Nigeria; others, smaller unions covering different regions and ethnic groupings. African political parties had British branches; schools set up old boys' and girls' clubs in the larger cities. It was these associations that would call artists from overseas – and hire those based in Britain.

Politics remained a guiding force as some countries gained their independence, and others, like South Africa, suffered more of their existing oppression. Musicians joined the cause: in 1962, an 'African Freedom Day' at the Royal Festival Hall featured Ginger Johnson and his Highlife Rhythms Band, Johnny Dankworth, the Ghana Cultural Society, and Fela Kuti with his band Koola Lobitos.

Kuti had enrolled at London's Trinity College of Music in 1958; his band Koola Lobitos became one of the top names on the bustling London scene of the early 1960s, playing for such organizations as the Northern (Nigeria) Peoples Congress and the Ghana Union of Great Britain and Ireland. Although he would later make his individual mark on African music with the creation of Afrobeat – a Nigerian-style based partly on high-life and jazz – Fela Kuti in the early 1960s showed the flexibility necessary to stay popular with most kinds of audiences. One 1962 handbill promised Koola Lobitos with 'the latest highlife, cha-cha-cha, twist etc'.

By now, a well-established network of dance bands had established itself, playing both at West End clubs and at African community social events in town halls and other venues.

African musicians adapted to meet the prevailing tastes. In 1961 Ginger Johnson billed himself as Ginger Mofolounslo Johnson and his Afro-Cuban Latin-American High-Life Cha Cha Cha band; the Abasi band offered the 'best twist and highlife'; in 1963 Ambrose Campbell played a London date with the Fred Quartet ('an all-teenage group to treat you with the twist in any shape or form'); in 1966 the Rhythm Souls offered 'the latest highlife, calypso, pachanga and rhythm and blues'). African and Caribbean bands shared the same bills: in 1968 the Ghana Ashiko's Dance Band was supported by the West Indian sound system expertise of Sir Coxson Down Beat.

As early as 1962, Jimmy Scott popularized his mix of high-life and Latin music with his Ob-La-Di Ob-La-Da band – seven years before the name and his catchphrase 'Life Must Go On' found their way into the Beatles' repertoire. It has been suggested that Scott sold the song to the band for a lump sum.

For most musicians, London offered opportunity – and a struggle made sharper by the fear of returning home with little to show for time spent overseas. One of the top high-life bands of the 1960s was formed by Abraham Onyenobia, a Nigerian musician who had played with Bobby Benson and Victor Olaiya in Lagos. Stung by Fela Kuti's criticisms of Olaiya's band, Onyenobia decided to set up his own outfit, with a fellow Nigerian Akanni Akinde. The band, known as Abraham and Akanni's Highlife Dandies, played regularly for student and community groups. For Onyenobia, London meant hard work. He had arrived as a student, and continued to study economics at a London college. As the band made little money, he also had to take a part-time job; working much of the day, studying and playing music at night.

Professional musicians settled as well. The Manhattan Brothers from South Africa settled in Britain in the 1960s; other South Africans, like Hugh Masekela and Dudu Pukwana, looked for new opportunities away from the restrictions of apartheid; the Rhythm Souls featured members from Roy Chicago's Band and the great Ghanaian Broadway Dance Band. In 1966 their line-up included Sammy Obot, formerly of the Uhuru Dance Band, George Olu and trumpet player Zeal Onyia.

Sierra Leone's the Sound Casters settled in Britain in 1967, later changing their name to the Sand Castles; Eddy Lamptey set up the long-lasting People's Band, while Teddy Osei fronted a string of bands including the Black Star Band, with Eddie Quansah, Teddy Osei's Assembly, in 1968, and Cat's Paw. But it was his work with Osibisa that would bring African music, in the shape of Afro-rock, to its widest public.

Whatever the frustrations, Britain buzzed in the mid-1960s as the rise of the newly independent African states brought an air of celebration to the community in Britain. Michael Osapanin, the Ghanaian musician who would later set up Kabbala, recalls the continuous round of embassy and high commission parties, with bands like Black Star providing the music:

> The Ghanaians in London wanted highlife bands, so I formed two different ones incorporating well-known ex-bandleaders from home. We'd meet up on the day, practise briefly, and I'd say to Sammy Obot 'You take this band, and go and perform, I'll take the other'.[16]

Osapanin's early efforts to break into the mainstream clubs proved disappointing. In the late 1960s Cat Stevens approached him to provide a backing band.

Arguments over money inside the band scuppered the project. A second offer came from Edmundo Ros:

> He was off on a world tour in 1969 and wanted a resident band for his London club. An audition was arranged, but the same arguments broke out over money and who should play. In the end, only two people showed up. Edmundo Ros said to me 'What do you do?' I replied I was a student, 'These people are not serious' he said. 'They're good musicians, but they are irresponsible'. We had our chance and we blew it.[17]

A common feature of the British scene was the large numbers of overseas artists playing the traditional summer and Christmas dances for the student and community associations. Among them, the Nigerian high-life star, Victor Olaiya, in 1963, followed the next year by I.K. Dairo, a pioneer of juju music, the Nigerian urban music based on talking drums and guitars; Roy Chicago, 1965; Dele Ojo from Nigeria, 1966; Ghana's The Ramblers, 1967; Adeolu's Western Toppers, 1967; Tunde Nightingale and his Juju Orchestra; and Sunny Ade and his Green Spots, both 1968; the next year, the Super Eagles, from Gambia; Sir Victor Uwaifo, from Nigeria, juju star Ebenezer Obey and E.T. Mensah, the king of high-life music.

Playing in Britain provided cash, the possibility of overseas exposure, and the chance to buy equipment and record. It also kept Africans abroad in touch with the latest music from home. Many of the musicians came from what had been, or still were, British colonies. But there were exceptions: chief among them Zaireans playing rumba music, which in the 1940s and 1950s had drawn on Latin American music, but by the 1960s had developed its own distinctive pattern of tenor harmonies, interlocking guitars and shuffling, conga-led rhythms. In 1965 the African Students League presented a 'Congo Brazzaville Touring Band' featuring the 'latest hits from Central Africa'. Three years later Los Nickelos, a Belgian-based Zairean band, played in London. In 1969 a Sierra Leonean Students Union dance featured the 21-strong Orchestre Nico Tropicals, led by A. Mputu and offering a line-up of 'rumba Lingala, merengue and boleros' – a prelude to the 1972 London début of Tabu Ley, one of Zaire's great stars, and his Orchestra African Fiesta.

While Africa's underground network hummed with life, African session men started making their presence felt in white rock music. Among them were Ray Allen, a Ghanaian high-life sax player who played with Traffic and other bands; George Lee, a second sax virtuoso from Ghana; Remi Kabaka, a percussionist and multi-instrumentalist who worked with Traffic; Speedy Aquaye, a conga player who worked with Georgie Fame; and Gasper Lawal, whose band, the Sugar Lumps, played juju and roots Nigerian music around the West End African clubs before Lawal established himself with Ginger Baker's Airforce and played sessions for the Rolling Stones, Steven Stills and other artists. Sometimes the artists met on more or less equal terms, as when Fela and Ginger Baker recorded together. At others, they provided a flourish of expertise to lighten an otherwise standard British rock; when for example Ginger Johnson and his drummers played with the Rolling Stones in Hyde Park in 1969.

Session work provided an outlet for African skills but it also showed the difficulties facing musicians who had little hope, at this time, of finding their own way into the musical mainstream. Africa was still 'over there'; and British companies, and the public at large, found it all too easy to ignore the creativity of the scene that bustled around them.

That the situation changed at all had virtually nothing to do with the acumen of British companies, more to do with the strength of African music in Britain – and the work of African businessmen who were prepared to invest their money and energy.

The rise of Afro-rock, swept to the mainstream on a tide of late-1960s optimism and open-mindedness, brought African music for the first time into full public view. The greatest success came from Osibisa, a mix of West African and West Indian musicians who came together in 1969. The membership included Teddy Osei and Remy Salako, who became a leading promoter of Afro-rock bands. As audiences warmed to the sound, leading practitioners such as Osibisa and Assegai signed to large agencies.

Osibisa's success, with singles like 'Music for Gong Gong', and albums like *Woyaya* and *Happy Children*, was immense. It rested on a fusion of West African and western music, tailored for the mass market, and wrapped up with the kind of extravagant rock guitar solos that also endeared Santana, the top Latin fusionists, to wider audiences. A strong African identity helped them push the message: with album sleeves the mixed elements of rural Africa with science fiction; and a stage show that started with a highly effective evocation of dawn in an African village. Juggling and subverting western stereotypes, Osibisa leapt into the mainstream.

But beyond Osibisa's highly effective music and marketing strategy, lay a deeper, cultural message, as leader Teddy Osei explains:

> Our aim was to portray the character of the dress, the colour, the happiness of African music, to portray a traditional cutlure but to play a music that was international. In 1971 we appeared on Top of the Pops wearing African gowns. It made Africans here aware that they could wear their own clothes. Before that it was all suits and ties. This kind of cultural awareness was an important part of our music. Another major thing was that we combined the West African and the West Indian elements. Before that there was a barrier, the West Indians thinking the Africans were bush people; the Africans looking on the West Indians as slaves.[18]

With the 1980s African musicians living in Britain were caught in a difficult position. Public interest grew through the pioneering work of bands like Orchestre Jazira and this led record companies to take a chance. The most notable, Island, signed Nigerian juju star Sunny Ade in 1982, and released two albums of *soukous*, the Zairean guitar-led dance music popular in many African countries.

For locally based musicians, such interest opened few doors. Some companies signed African acts based in Britain – Sterns, for example releasing albums by Hi-Life International and Somo Somo; Beggar's Banquet signing Orchestre Jazira; Oval putting out two singles by African Connexion; Earthworks, a single by Orchestre Jazira; while CBS released singles and an album by OK Jive, a mainly white band which played pop music tinged with high-life and *benga*, Kenya's urban pop music. But such interest could not be relied on and the companies concentrated their efforts largely on artists based overseas.

As a result, African musicians fell on their own resources: setting up their own labels, working with businessmen from inside the community and keeping alive the networks that had sustained them in the past.

Various stylistic approaches came to the fore. Bands like Super Combo, Hi-Life International, African Culture and Taxi Pata Pata worked with well-known urban styles like high-life and *soukous* introducing yet another British generation to 'new' sounds from Africa.

Other bands used Britain as a base for experiment. Mwana Musa, the Sierra Leonean founder member of African Connexion, created a sound whose mix of funk, African music and house, had some of the voguish eclecticism of the mid- and late 1980s. Kofi Busia's *Oh Africa* album, set songs about Africa, its past and future, against a highly individual electronic backdrop; Julian Bahula gave the traditional South African Malombo drums a British jazz setting; while Bushmen Don't Surf mashed South African music into a western funk idiom. Such mixtures were important. 'We want to portray Africa as developing', explains Mwana Musa. 'People here think that the music should be "pure". The media throw doubt on Africa's identity by presenting it as if it was 100 years ago. We're trying to dispel this image'.[19]

For most African musicians, the challenge lay less in representing one particular sound or style, than in creating sounds that reflected their ancestral roots and their new environment. As Kwesi Owusu of African Dawn explains, the labelling and categorization of different 'national' musics remained a largely western pursuit which bore little relation to the work of the musicians, or the 'pan-Africanist trend' which sought shared links rather than arbitrary divisions. In Britain artists from different countries might be two bus stops away. In Africa they would never meet. The opportunities for collaboration and cross-fertilization were enormous as African Dawn demonstrated with a line-up drawn from musicians from Ghana, Zimbabwe, Grenada, Senegal and Uruguay. At the same time, radio and television paid increasing attention to music with disc jockeys like John Peel, Andy Kershaw and Charlie Gillett, who played sounds from Zimbabwe, Zaire and other African countries on their programmes. Television series like the BBC's *Rhythms of the World* and several on Channel 4 brought artists as diverse as Papa Wemba from Zaire and Senegal's Baaba Maal to British audiences who, by now, had been exposed to a range of African music to a degree which would have been unthinkable twenty years before.

The vigour of the African community is one thing. Reaching the mainstream is another. In Paris, Toure Kunda, Mory Kante and Savuka made considerable inroads into public consciousness. In Britain the difficulties remained acute. Most musicians would cite Britain's disregard for other cultures; the conservatism of record companies; real or imagined language problems; the existence of a strong British pop culture which allowed little room for different forms of music. Kwesi Owusu points to an added factor – the selective enthusiasm of those who aim to expose the music and who enjoy a certain amount of power over what is discussed or listened to:

> Musicologists operate with one concept, that of 'discovery'. It is one that goes back to colonial times. Today, different writers and disc jockeys discover different people. But discovery goes with the exotic: you can't be discovered if you are living here, in Britain.[20]

Acknowledgements

Thanks for their help to John Cowley, Jeffrey Green, Gasper Lawal, Mattaya Clifford, Keni St George, and staff at the Royal Commonwealth Society library.

KNIFE DANCERS

Joseph Mogotsi · Rufus Khoza · Ronnie Majola · Jerry Tsagane
Ernest Mohlomi · Boy Ngwenya · Wanda Makhubu

GUMBOOT DANCERS

Victor Ndlazilwane · George Tau · Caiphus Semenya · Wanda Makhubu · Ernest Mohlomi · Josh Makhene · Edgie Mdandana.

(Trained by Ernest Nkosi of City Deep mine Compound)

SPECIALITY DANCERS

Ruth Nkonyeni · Thandi Klaasen   Rose Hlela

CHORUS LEADERS

Men : David Serame
Women : Thandi Klaasen and Ruth Nkonyeni

PEOPLE OF THE TOWNSHIP

MEN : Sidney Motha, Josh Makhene, George Tau, Samuel Kgaswane, Shadrack Tsele, Alpheus Komane, Bernard Zikalala, Josiah Sebete, Caiphus Semenya Johnny Tsagane, Walter Loate, David Serame, Edgie Mdandana, Jerry Chauke, John Lekoane, Boy Ngwenya, Meshak Mosia.

WOMEN : Louisa Emmanuel, Priscilla Booi, Mabel Mafuya, Thandeka Mpambani, Linda Mhlongo, Mary Rabothapi, Letta Mbulo, Petunia Vika, Doris Kumalo, Mimi Edwards, Martha Mdenge, Mamsie Mthombeni.

SYNOPSIS OF SCENES

ACT I

Scene 1	Early morning in the yard of a Johannesburg Township. The present.
Scene 2	Midday in a township street, 1954.
Scene 3	Same as Scene 1.
Scene 4	Back of the Moon, a shebeen on a night when business is good, 1954.
Scene 5	A summer night in the streets of the township, 1954.
Scene 6	The township yard. The present—and the past.
Scene 7	A Sunday in the township, about 1956.

INTERVAL

ACT II

Scene 1	A corner of the township, about four months later.
Scene 2	A road in the township.
Scene 3	Jack's boxing gym, two months later.
Scene 4	Early morning at the bus terminus, a week later.
Scene 5	Jack's boxing gym, 1956.
Scene 6	(a) The township yard. The present.
	(b) In court. February 25, 1957.
	(c) The township yard. The present.

Scenery painted by Alick Johnstone and built by E. Babbage & Co. Ltd. Drapies by John Holliday & Sons Ltd. Lighting by Strand Electric & Engineering Co. Ltd. Costumes made by Gillia Mailer and Yvonne Potter. Stockings by Kayser Bondor. Hoovermatic washing machine used in the wardrobe supplied by Hoover Ltd. (Perivale). Wardrobe care by Lux. Coca-Cola by Coca-Cola Southern Bottlers Ltd. Kangol Berets by Kangol.

IN STAGING THE PRODUCTION OF "KING KONG" IN LONDON JACK HYLTON HAS RECEIVED EVERY COURTESY AND CO-OPERATION FROM THE UNION GOVERNMENT AND WISHES TO RECORD HIS APPRECIATION.

Pages from the programme for the controversial production of *King Kong* promoted by Jack Hylton, at the Princes Theatre, London, February 1961, *Collection: Paul Oliver*

6 Young, Gifted and Black: Afro-American and Afro-Caribbean Music in Britain 1963–88

ANTHONY MARKS

Introduction

The history of Afro-American and Afro-Caribbean music in Britain is inextricably linked with the social groups – both black and white – that adopted new genres as they were imported from their countries of origin. After their initial acceptance, most of these musics were taken up by indigenous practitioners (who often adapted the original styles to meet their own needs); ultimately they became absorbed – in some cases much altered – into the mainstream of popular culture. This chapter surveys the ways in which this process has happened with black popular music from the USA (various kinds of soul music, disco, funk, hip-hop, go-go, and house) and from Jamaica (ska, rock-steady, and reggae).

Some background

The initial acceptance of soul music in Britain must be examined in historical context. During the 1950s there began to emerge an affluent working class of young people with attitudes and aspirations significantly different from those of the previous generation. In part these attitudes were a response to the sudden explosion of teenage culture in the USA, where the images of youth and independence were assiduously marketed to a wealthy, impressionable and ever regenerating sector of the population by a massive, highly adaptable entertainment industry. Such stars as Elvis Presley, James Dean and Marlon Brando represented a teen-oriented culture, and replicas of their supposed attitudes and life-styles were eagerly adopted in Britain in the mid-1950s. Rock-and-roll captured the imagination of young people and was so radical in its message and attitude that it changed their lives.[1] Although this music was rather removed from the Afro-American mainstream, to British youth at the time it represented something exotic and disruptive, something that separated them culturally from their parents.

The teddy boys – white working-class urban youths with a taste for ornate Edwardian clothes and elaborate, often aggressive hair-styles – existed in Britain well before rock-and-roll, but it was music that galvanized them as a youth culture in the mid-1950s. The outrage expressed by the music's many opponents (both moral and musical) became linked with adverse publicity that surrounded its audience. In this case the connection forged between youth faction and music was perhaps somewhat retrospective,[2] but it established a norm. Since that time each successive trend in popular culture has claimed its own music, either by creating it (like the punks) and inventing the culture around it, or by adopting it as part of a general style (like the mods). The entertainment industry, always alert to new opportunities, has capitalized on this tendency. After rock-and-roll several musical trends swept Britain, either spontaneous or commercialized. Some of these had roots in Afro-American music, but the roots became rather obscured. Rock-and-roll, a potent mixture of urban blues and country music, was all too quickly neutralized by the highly conservative establishment of American showbusiness, keen to exploit the new style for its own financial ends. The same was true in Britain. While the first British rock-and-roll singers – for example Tommy Steele, Adam Faith, Cliff Richard and Billy Fury – achieved considerable fame and provoked hysterical reactions among teenagers, none achieved the intensity of their early American counterparts. While these stars formed the basis of the indigenous-style culture that became the backdrop to the success of the Beatles and the Rolling Stones, they bore comparatively little relation to the black musics that had inspired them.

Motown, Stax and the first soul boom

Soul music (the blend of rhythm-and-blues and gospel music first developed by Ray Charles and James Brown in the late 1950s) began to appear on a public scale in Britain around 1962. Its stylistic forerunners had found favour among various types of music lovers; from the mid-1950s one could hear urban blues in folk clubs or even in 'trad' establishments, and rhythm-and-blues and earthy soul-jazz at modern jazz clubs in London like the Flamingo on Wardour Street and the Scene in Ham Yard (off Great Windmill Street). (The Flamingo had a largely black clientele, mainly because it had been a favourite venue among black American soldiers stationed in Britain in the 1950s.) At these clubs the British taste for the jazz-inflected music of Ray Charles and Mose Allison was fostered by such disc jockeys as Guy Stevens. It was fans of this music, not those of the harder Chicago rhythm-and-blues popular at clubs like the Marquee, who adopted soul music when it began to reach this country.[3]

Unlike most other American and Afro-American pop styles, soul became popular in Britain in its original form and retained a stylistic homogeneity for many years. There were several reasons for this. First, it was a minority taste; thus the musical establishment did not at this stage perceive it as ripe for manipulation for commercial ends. Second, its appearance coincided with the growth of the discotheque, which – for the purpose of dancing – established the primacy of the recording over live performance. Soul was largely a recorded music often relying on stylized studio production and large orchestral backings. Thus the identity of the sound, located as much in the backing as the voice, could not easily be copied by British performers, nor readily imitated in British studios. Third, to British audiences soul music was 'exotic'; it was not played on mainstream radio, and knowledge of it was seen as a status symbol and a privilege. It was therefore ideal for adoption by a youth movement obsessed with exclusivity and authenticity – the mods.

The gradual appropriation of soul music into the mod world took place largely in Soho, at the intersections of three distinct but not necessarily mutually exclusive groups: mods, West Indians, and the homosexual community.[4] The first mods were a small group of relatively affluent working-class youths from east and south London, interested in little but clothes – custom-tailored suits and handmade shoes. By the early 1960s they were frequenting clubs like the Scene and the Flamingo, where they came into contact with Motown (from Detroit) and other early soul from such labels as Stax and Volt (Memphis) and Atlantic (New York). In their quest for bright, distinctive clothes they began to patronize John Stephen on Carnaby Street, once the haunt of gay men, and, occasionally, West Indians. As Soho's nightlife became denser, one could hear soul and ska at a West Indian club, the Roaring Twenties on Carnaby Street, or at a gay venue, Le Duce, on Darblay Street. When the mods moved in at the Scene, their life-style had a similar soundtrack.[5]

The original mod movement was over very quickly, almost before the highly publicized fights with the rockers on the beaches at Brighton in 1964. But the media were keen to capitalize on the idea of 'swinging London' and Carnaby Street, right at the centre of the mod world. Thus, in a way that the more marginalized West Indian and gay communities never could have been, the mods were largely responsible for the wider acceptance of soul music. The popularity of the style among such a large and vociferous minority resulted in the music's breaking through to the pop mainstream. Gradually Motown records began to appear in the charts,[6] followed by their Stax or Atlantic counterparts.[7] Black American musicians visited Britain with increasing frequency. In 1965 a 'Motown Revue' toured Britain for twenty four days; on the bill were the Supremes, the Vandellas, the Contours, the Temptations, and Stevie Wonder; later Brian Epstein, the manager of the Beatles, sponsored a British tour by the Four Tops. James Brown and Edwin Starr were also regular visitors. Indigenous soul groups, however, remained few and far between – particularly black ones. The most successful was Geno Washington, a black American former serviceman who settled in Britain and led the Ram Jam Band from 1965 to 1968. Washington had five chart hits between 1966 and 1967, and built up a huge following all over the country; the Ram Jam Club in Brixton was named after the band. Other groups, concentrating more on Caribbean styles, were popular with the West Indian community. Other groups consisted mainly of white musicians imitating Afro-American styles with varying degress of success, such as those influenced by blues (Alexis Korner and Long John

Baldry) or modern jazz (Georgie Fame). Fame, especially, with his band the Blue Flames, helped to popularize a particular fusion of soul, jazz and rhythm-and-blues during a long residency at the Flamingo. Popular among mods were the Action, who sang in the Motown style and signed to Parlophone, but never achieved success. And at the start of their careers, more mainstream rock groups like the Who and the Rolling Stones played cover versions of Motown and rhythm-and-blues. The Who, in particular, gained a large mod following in this way.

By late 1965, the peak of modism's public profile, soul music was gaining an increasingly firm hold on popular taste. This was aided in part by the growing number of discotheques and also, from 1964, the advent of pirate radio stations. The BBC restricted its coverage of pop music to but a few hours a week (and then only to the blander end of the chart material); conversely, until they were banned in 1967, pirates like Radio Caroline and Radio London were able to mirror accurately the tastes of the London clubs, and transmit these to listeners all over the country.[8] Possibly more influential still was the ITV show *Ready Steady Go!*, which gave the rest of the country a visual taste of what was happening in London. Dressed in the trappings of mod, and presented by Cathy McGowan, *Ready Steady Go!* was responsible for showing the earliest televised appearances of soul musicians. Importantly the mods made a taste for soul music a sign of being fashionable and gave it status as something rare, exotic and desirable; partly as a result of this, for many years the concept of black music, particularly among white youth, retained an attractive aura of separateness. This 'badge of exclusivity' was to be worn throughout the 1960s and 1970s by various youth cultures, all eager in some ways to manifest their difference from the cultural mainstream.

Ska

The mods were the first people outside the Caribbean community to adopt Afro-Caribbean music, though it was by no means a new phenomenon in Britain. West Indians had begun to settle in this country in the late 1940s, and by the mid-1950s were encouraged to do so by the British government, which was at that time experiencing a labour shortage. Though they were promised a new life full of opportunity, immigrants often met open racial hostility. Political and economic circumstances forced them into inner-city ghettos where they replicated the Caribbean culture they had left. The first celebration of West Indian music and dance – the Mardi Gras at Paddington Town Hall (later to be the Notting Hill carnival) – took place in 1959, and clubs with a largely West Indian clientele opened in Soho in the late 1950s (including, as well as those mentioned above, the 77, the Sunset, and the Contemporanean). Several West Indians, in imitation of their Caribbean counterparts, set up sound systems – large mobile discotheques – which operated at blues parties (late-night socials in the inner-city areas). Among the most famous sound systems was Duke Vin's, which operated in the Ladbroke Grove area of London. Sound systems were supported by a network of specialist record shops and import labels which were responsible for bringing Caribbean music to Britain in considerable quantities.[9]

During the 1960s ska from Jamaica was one of the most popular forms of Caribbean music, partly because the composition of West Indians in Britain at that time was over 70 per cent Jamaican. Ska – a frenetic dance music with stressed offbeats, played by small groups (electric guitar, bass, drums) often accompanied by a brass section – acquired a large following among black youths all over London and the other large urban centres. It was available on British-based record labels like Bluebeat (so popular that for a time it became the alternative name for the music itself) and Planitone. As early as 1963 some 15,000 records were entering Britain from Jamaica each month, selling almost exclusively to the black community. The BBC never played ska, or any other Caribbean music, and mainstream record shops rarely stocked the records, so it remained an underground taste. But gradually the music found favour among white youths as well, particularly the mods, who in the early 1960s encountered it – along with soul music – at Soho clubs. And while chart success for ska remained minimal (Millie's 'My Boy Lollipop', though it reached no. 1 on the British charts in 1964, was one of the few Jamaican records to do so for many years) it became an essential element of the mod scene, as well as gathering continued popularity in the mid-1960s among West Indians. Among others, records by Prince Buster (particularly 'Madness', 1964) were mod favourites.[10]

After modism: soul culture in the late 1960s and early 1970s

Mainstream soul music – still dominated by the Motown and Atlantic labels – remained a significant presence in the British charts in the late 1960s and early 1970s. Otis Redding toured Britain in 1966 and other soul stars from the USA visited frequently. As its audience grew older, the Motown sound matured: the label's more 'serious' groups, like the Isley Brothers, were just as popular in Britain as the Supremes. Discotheques everywhere appropriated soul as the standard dance music. But the popular imagination got out of step with the clean, sharp Motown style; indeed, the image of the company itself became tarnished as musicians and producers (including the architects of the Motown sound, the Holland–Dozier–Holland team) left the label and corporate wrangling became ever more public. In the USA, and a short time later in Britain, the predominant youth culture changed; the psychedelic movement began in San Francisco in 1965, and altered the tone of the late 1960s. The hippy aesthetic had no room for purely dance-orientated music; longer, intricate records, often highly improvised, became the common form of rock expression. Black American music often imitated this: The Temptations' Ball of Confusion' and 'Psychedelic Shack' are archetypes of 'psychedelic soul', with phased vocals and 'serious' lyrics.

Some took the psychedelic message more seriously than others. In 1968 Sly

Stone was arrested for possession of drugs; the BBC duly cancelled Sly and the Family Stone's appearance on *Top of the Pops*. Stone was a hippy hero, as was the black American rock guitarist Jimi Hendrix, who first performed in Britain in 1966. But for white middle-class youth, who were increasingly dictating the terms of popular culture, this was about the limit of 'acceptable' black music. The wailing guitars, psychedelic imagery, and stretched rhythms of Hendrix and Stone were deemed 'authentic' and 'progressive', but black dance music was dismissed as 'inauthentic' and 'commercial'. Consciously or not, fans of progressive rock relegated the bulk of Afro-American music by insisting that unless it met their criteria it had no validity. It was symptomatic that by 1969, Soho, once Britain's soul centre, was practically devoid of soul clubs as venues turned to the more lucrative psychedelic scene.

Outside London, however, reactions were different. Hippy culture developed more slowly in the working-class areas of the north, where the taste for soul music remained strong. In the early 1960s fans from the northern industrial centres had to visit London to hear soul, but gradually they began to establish clubs in their native cities – the Oodly Boodly in Leicester, the Mojo (and later the Ark and Highway 61) in Sheffield, the Dungeon in Nottingham, and the Twisted Wheel in Manchester. The sounds they favoured were the most energetic, with reverberant backbeats and large arrangements. But by the late 1960s the major American labels were recording this style less and less frequently, turning instead to psychedelic soul, heavy funk, and ballads. Disc jockeys depended for their success on an ever-expanding repertoire; when sources of new material dried up they had to look for old records – often released on small labels in the industrial cities of the American north-east – and bring them to Britain. Disc jockeys (notably Roger Eagle at the Twisted Wheel) became famous for playing records that were ever more rare and obscure. This immediately made a fetish of rarity (some singles changed hands among fans for as much as £50, even in 1970), and the same sense of exclusivity that early mods had enjoyed.

The two cultures share many characteristics – both were white, working-class groups, mostly male, which adopted the music of a distant culture and made it central to their existences. The northern soul scene was a more esoteric form of modism, focused on intense, athletic dancing (the cornerstone of northern soul culture was the 'all-nighter' where dancing was constant from early evening to the following morning). But while the tastes of the mods gradually influenced (and were later invaded by) mainstream popular culture, the northern soul scene became more exclusive. Hardly any of the songs most popular in the northern clubs were chart hits, either in Britain or the USA. The scene was, and remains, one of the more arcane manifestations of the British love of black American music. And importantly, new styles from the USA have continued to make their way into Britain via the northern clubs before heading south. Amid changing styles and trends, there remains in the late 1980s a small but faithful faction of northern soul fans. It has changed, and is not as large as it was, but there are still clubs in northern towns and cities where devotees gather to dance to obscure records made in Chicago and Detroit in the 1960s.[11]

Rock-steady and rude-boys

In the south-east there was a different reaction to psychedelia. While many mods had realigned themselves with the hippy movement, and many had simply grown too old to worry about such matters, there was a core of white working-class youth that was profoundly suspicious of the middle-class appropriation of popular culture. In response, like their mod forebears earlier in the decade, they adopted instead the music and style culture currently popular among West Indians. By the late 1960s they appeared dressed in a menacing reworking of Jamaican 'rude-boy' fashion (cropped hair, Doctor Marten boots, trousers at half-mast, and braces), frequenting the sound systems. The rapid beat of ska had given way by this time to rock-steady – a slower, more intricate incarnation of ska, with shifting rhythms and offbeat stresses. Records by Derrick Morgan, Alton Ellis and Dandy Livingstone (especially 'A Message to You, Rudy') became extremely popular among skinheads.[12] But this new association in turn hardly helped West Indian music to gain mainstream acceptance. The BBC remained wary of rock-steady, less because it was a black music (soul music, it should be remembered, was played often on the BBC by the end of the 1960s), than because of its association with skinheads and violence. Thus the music became marginalized for a second time. (Rare exceptions were the records of Desmond Dekker – most notably 'Israelites', no. 1, 1969 – which appeared frequently on the charts between 1967 and 1975).

West Indian music continued to sell well in Britain, primarily in the community itself; new record labels like Trojan and Island sprang up to meet the demand. At this time, however, they had a captive market that did not depend on hearing records on the radio. The size and buying power of this market was amply demonstrated in 1969, when, despite a ban by the BBC and the resulting lack of airplay, 'Wet Dream' by Max Romeo went to no. 10 in the charts. But the music continually failed to reach large white audiences, and the cause was not helped by the brief association with skinheads. This faction also proved extremely fickle. The aggressive racism that emerged among skinheads in the mid-1970s proved that prejudice ran deep and was not to be eradicated simply because they had adopted black music.

From Philly to disco: soul and funk in the 1970s

If the story of soul music in the 1960s was one of varying degrees of marginalization, then the following decade may be considered as a period of assimilation. Soul emerged from the discotheques to become more popular with pop audiences; moreover, a number of indigenous performers began to establish a British soul tradition. At the start of the 1970s, the interests of fans of popular music were extremely fragmented. Psychedelia and the hippy movement were waning, leaving in their wake a large number of progressive rock groups, whose music was aimed at the same audience. Their work was conceived in terms of albums, and most of them released singles only rarely, if ever. The singles charts, on the other hand, were often filled with uninventive exploitations of the latest teenage fad. In this climate many record-buyers, feeling alienated from the 'white' music on offer, turned to soul and black dance music, and later to reggae. Discotheques, particularly in the north, but also in the suburban south-east, had continued to play soul in spite of other prevailing trends. The singles chart, by this time, seldom responsive to progressive music anyway, gradually indicated an increased interest in soul among record-buyers. Many hits were, as ever, from Motown and Atlantic, but there was also a new wave of activity in the USA, centred around Sigma Studios in Philadelphia, which challenged the supremacy of the major companies. 'Philly soul', a richly orchestrated, propulsive music with compelling vocal harmonies, began to make an impression on the charts in 1971 with 'Didn't I' by the Delfonics. Eventually the soul boom in the clubs – aided by an increasing number of commercial radio stations – gave the music widespread popularity.[13]

While American records formed the mainstay of this boom, there was increasingly significant activity from British musicians. Some of this was based around the club scene – from the mid-1970s northern soul disc jockey Ian Levene was producing recordings for the northern soul market – and had little widespread commercial success. But other musicians managed to make the charts. Combining a Philly shuffle beat with a lyric about martial arts, Carl Douglas's 'Kung Fu Fighting' rose to no. 1 on the chart in 1974 on the strength of a (largely suburban) craze for the kung fu films of Bruce Lee. In the same year Sweet Sensation, a British black vocal group, reached the top of the chart with the balled 'Sad Sweet Dreamer'. Though these musicians fell into obscurity after one or two hits, one black group, Hot Chocolate, had over twenty chart hits between 1970 and 1979, reached the American soul charts on more than one occasion, and remained successful well into the 1980s. These groups tended to appeal mainly to the white chart audience, and were marketed in this way. However, they also achieved a degree of popularity among suburban, middle-class Blacks, who would later become mainstays of the suburban soul scene (see below). Generally, however, this music rarely reached the urban, working-class Afro-Caribbean community, where reggae remained the most popular music.

White musicians began to have hits with soul and funk records. For some – particularly those from the north and Scotland, where the soul tradition had always been strongest – Afro-American styles were a natural medium.[14] For others, the stylistic realignment was a more radical departure. This is particularly true of David Bowie, who, after announcing his retirement from public performance in 1973, moved to the USA and rehearsed with a soul band. He performed with this group at the Tower Theatre, Philadelphia, singing versions of his old hits; this extraordinary concoction is preserved on the album *David Live* (1974), which also contains a lacklustre version of Eddie Floyd's 'Knock on Wood'. But Bowie's biggest soul triumphs, and for many the most successful moments of his entire career, were the albums *Young Americans* (1974) and *Station to Station* (1975), which fuse Afro-American forms with Bowie's own writing style. The title track of the former album, recorded at Sigma Studios, was a considerable hit in both the USA and Britain; later Bowie sang 'Golden Years' (from *Station to Station*) on *Soul Train*, becoming the first white performer to appear on the black soul and dance show.

Bowie, who came from the rock tradition, was criticized initially by some for exploiting another music to meet his own ends. The net effect, however, was much more complex. As a 'glam-rock' star he was famed for frequent changes of style and persona, blurring class and gender. This had won him a staunch following among many different kinds of pop fan, gay and straight, middle and working class, student and 'teenybopper' alike. By shifting his focus to soul music Bowie blurred a further boundary: race. He linked the glam aesthetic, and its many associations, with dance music, making explicit the same cultural exchange – gay/working-class/black – that had happened in Soho in the 1960s. But he was also charting another cultural relationship, already current in the USA: by the time he recorded *Young Americans*, the rise of the disco movement was underway in the USA. Disco culture – the centralization of dance as the *reason* for music – flourished in the mid-1970s among two distinct minority groups: Blacks and homosexuals. Their cultures began to overlap at the venues they shared, and an industry grew up to provide them with music. Bowie's adoption of a soul sound brought the results of that exchange into the heart of suburban Britain.

Disco music was essentially the Philly sound with a peppier beat and more emphatic bassline. Songs were often recorded in versions of up to fifteen minutes long which turned dancing into a marathon. Records were played in an endless stream, continuing for hours without a break. As in the USA, the first people to adopt disco culture in Britain were the Blacks, and most significantly, the gay community. The gay clubs of the 1970s, notably Heaven in London's Charing Cross, promulgated an entire subculture based around dress, music, sex, drugs – much as the mods had done ten years earlier. Interest from the mainstream of pop fans came somewhat later. In the British charts one of the earliest American records readily identifiable as disco was Gloria Gaynor's 'Never Can Say Goodbye' (1974); thereafter a steady stream of disco hits, aided by a marked increase in the number of hi-tech American-style discos, prepared the way for the ultimate boom. This came in 1978, after the release in Britain of the American film *Saturday Night Fever*, with a soundtrack by, among others, the British group, the Bee Gees. When the film broke box office records in the USA it sparked a disco mania across the country. The effect was similar in Britain.[15]

For many people in Britain disco provided a welcome contrast to the rather arid music of punk in the late 1970s. It found its way into the gap between the aggressive music of the Clash and the Sex Pistols, and the bland 'adult-oriented' rock peddled as punk's alternative. A number of British groups began producing excellent soul and disco records. The longest lived of these, the Real Thing, had a no. 1 hit in 1976 with 'You to Me are Everything', and remained successful into the 1980s. Others had similar (if more short-lived) success.[16] At the same time many long-established rock musicians began dabbling with dance music.[17] Amid all this, the now maturing punk movement, aside from its new-found links with reggae artists, sparked a mod revival, initiated by the Jam. Renewed interest in early Motown was so significant that it led the company to re-release much of the material first issued in Britain on Stateside on two new albums called *20 Mod Classics*.

Reggae

Like soul, West Indian music also flourished during the 1970s, but in a very different way. At first it remained most popular within the Caribbean community, played by bands and sound systems at clubs and community centres in major industrial cities throughout the country. The newest development in Jamaican music, reggae, was more esoteric than its predecessors. It was still slower than rock-steady, and heavier and harder, partly because of the influence of Rastafari, which brought about spiritual lyrics in heavy patois, dub mixes and hazy, echoing, ethereal textures (e.g. 'Foggy Road' by Prince Far-I). Because of this it failed to attract large white audiences, and radio play continued to be infrequent. Most reggae reached the radio only as performed by white musicians like Jonathan King, who had little flair for the style. Occasionally lovers' rock records (softer and more lyrical than the hard 'roots' styles) appeared in the charts; these included the later hits of Johnny Nash (among them 'I Can See Clearly Now', 1972) and Ken Boothe's 'Everything I Own' (no. 1, 1974). When slightly harder reggae records were propelled into the charts they were still often ignored; though Rupie Edwards's 'Irie Feelings' reached no. 9 on the chart in 1974, it was hardly played on the radio. This time, however, the cause of neglect was not a ban (like 'Wet Dream'), rather a more general reluctance among disc jockeys to play the record. (Many disc jockeys complained that reggae was 'primitive' and inappropriate for their shows. Only John Peel, given a late-night slot on BBC Radio 1, afforded the music some of the attention it deserved.) Matters began to improve slightly in the mid-1970s; after Eric Clapton covered Bob Marley's 'I Shot the Sheriff' many white fans began to seek out the original. Record companies like Island began to market reggae to rock audiences, with considerable success. From 1975 Marley had regular hits on the UK Chart, and was followed by other groups, both British and Jamaican.

Reggae's real breakthrough into the popular mainstream came with the punk movement that began in 1976.[18] The music's high profile during the punk era had more to do with audience attitude, and a different kind of exposure, than with any increase in reggae activity. In a way that reggae never could have done alone, punk changed the attitudes of radio stations and record companies. Like Rastafaris, punks viewed the musical and political establishment as an enemy; unlike the Rastafaris, punks were prepared to fight the system on a very basic level. The alliance of punk and reggae groups in the late 1970s for Rock Against Racism concerts prompted a surge of interest in reggae, as well as a heady optimism engendered by the sense of working for a common aim. Many British reggae groups, formerly struggling with small record labels, were able to sign to major companies. These included Misty, Matumbi, Aswad, and Steel Pulse; the last-named signed to Island in 1978 for the album *Handsworth Revolution*, which became one of the most successful albums by a British reggae group. New Jamaican groups, like Black Uhuru and Third World, became very popular among punks and new wave fans; as a result there was renewed interest too in the work of longer-established musicians – like Culture, I-Roy, and Prince Far-I – who had hitherto been little known in Britain outside the West Indian community. The reggae record industry, for imports and indigenous music alike, entered a boom period.

Rock Against Racism made admirable political advances, bringing together black and white youths for the purpose of peaceful protest. For a time it seemed that the optimism of Bob Marley's single 'Punky Reggae Party' (1977) was well founded. Marley's album *Exodus* sold over 500,000 copies in Britain. Steel Pulse played support to the punk group Generation X; Aswad toured with Eddie and the Hot Rods. Lee Perry produced tracks for the Clash's second album, though much of the work was never released. Towards the end of the decade, at the tail-end of the punk era, there was a ska revival, instigated by a number of multiracial groups, including the Specials, the Selecter and the Beat. The Two-tone label, which issued much of this music, flourished as the Specials had several chart successes. But while punk fuelled the rise of reggae, it also speeded its subsequent demise. White versions of the style (like Elvis Costello's *Watching the Detectives* and the early work of the Police), though seen at the time by many as gestures of solidarity, distracted chart audiences from real reggae. The decline of the punk ideal was as sudden as it was total, and it left black groups with a diminished audience. Having signed to major labels, some reggae bands (particularly Aswad and Matumbi) found themselves victims of a system that was not prepared to grant them the freedom they needed. In 1981 the death of Bob Marley seemed to mark the start of the decline of reggae's popularity.[19]

After the disco boom

Although the disco craze collapsed rapidly in both the USA and Britain, in neither country did the passion for dancing seem to wane. Having acquired a dance culture, all that dancers wanted to change was the soundtrack. American disco hits, like those of Chic in the late 1970s, began to get slower and sparser, until the backbeat of Tom Browne's *Funkin' for Jamaica* (a hit in Britain in 1980) was so relaxed as to bear more relation to funk of the late 1960s than to classic disco. There was a revival of interest in the music of James Brown and other funk musicians and a huge new body of dance music was created. The hard, percussive funk beat, more pliable and adaptable than the rigid four-square of disco, lent itself to adaptation by musicians formerly unconnected with the Afro-American tradition. Many different kinds of cross-over occurred in the USA: the Talking Heads, a new wave group with art-school pretensions, acquired a brass section and heavy funk bass and percussion for the album *Remain in Light* (1980); former punk group Blondie had a major hit single with

Rapture (1981), full of rumbling basslines and a rap section. This coincided with the growth in New York of a new style of 'street funk', hip-hop (see below).

In Britain the convergence of pop and Afro-American music was if anything more complete than in the USA, as if the mainstream of popular culture suddenly saw fit to confirm what we have already noted – that soul and dance music had been central to huge sectors of the population for many years. Whereas previously most Afro-American music had been marginalized by the white middle class in favour of progressive rock, by 1980 the reverse was the case. Punks had so effectively reviled the idea of 'hippy music' that it became highly unfashionable to confess to liking 'progressive' groups like Yes or Led Zeppelin. Thus when new white groups of the early 1980s (including ABC, Dexy's Midnight Runners, Spandau Ballet, Soft Cell, Haircut 100) marked out their heritage, they adopted another history, that of soul and disco, as their own. By laying claim to black music they gave themselves, in popular terms, a validity which distanced them from the history of progressive rock. In countless interviews in the popular music press, many musicians claimed never to have liked rock, and always to have been more interested in soul. While for some this was undoubtedly the truth – of the thousands of teenagers who filled the discos in the early 1970s, some were bound to become musicians – for others, as in the USA, it was simply an exploitative revision of cultural history to suit prevailing trends.

As if bearing testimony to the rediscovery of all things Afro-American, white British groups began to record in these styles, either covering existing songs or writing their own material. Among the earliest and most successful were Dexy's Midnight Runners, whose first major hit was 'Geno' (no. 1, 1980), a tribute to Geno Washington. Most of the songs on their first album (1980) were accurate pastiches of the Northern Soul sound; included was a cover of the club hit 'Seven Days too Long'. Elvis Costello's album *Get Happy* (1980) consists of new compositions all performed in dance and soul styles redolent of Stax and Motown. The Jam's EP *Beat Surrender* (1982) not only contained the frenetic, Motown-inspired title track, but also versions of, among others, Curtis Mayfield's 'Move On Up' and Norman Whitfield's 'War' (a hit for Edwin Starr in 1970).[20] This recycling of the soul tradition gathered pace during the mid-1980s. The media rapidly noted the popular association of soul with cultural roots and authenticity, and began using old soul songs as the soundtracks to advertisements. Marvin Gaye's 'Heard It Through the Grapevine', used in a commercial for Levis' jeans in 1985, sparked off new interest in old recordings.[21]

Besides this revival of the past, however, there were other more radical adaptations of soul, funk and disco. These ranged from the polite jazz-funk of Level 42's first album (1981) to the flood of new pop groups using such funk hallmarks as thumb-slapped basslines, brass sections, female backing singers, and lengthy remixes.[22] Soul and dance records by white British groups appeared in the American charts so frequently that critics spoke of the 'second British invasion' (the first being the American success of the Beatles and Rolling

Stones in the 1960s). Interestingly many of the most successful groups were from the north, where soul music had always been most popular. New Order, from Manchester, achieved the greatest coup of all when their single 'Blue Monday' went to the top of the 'black music' chart in the American magazine *Billboard* (1983).

At first black British musicians fared less well, though many were making excellent records. Junior Giscombe's hit 'Mama Used to Say' (1981) boasted a pounding backbeat and subtle lyrics which prompted comparison with Stevie Wonder. Linx's hit single and album *Intuition* (1981) and records like Imagination's 'Body Talk' (1981) intimated a new wave of black dance music. Other groups, such as Central Line and Funkapolitan, seemed set to emulate this success. But audiences and the music industry alike had become so accustomed to the sound of American soul music that they were slow at first to foster British talent. Small, independently owned black labels could not afford to promote artists sufficiently to give them broad-based success; many of the major companies would not sign British soul groups unless there was a possibility of their becoming successful in the USA. They thought that British soul had to sound like its American counterpart if it was to reach the American market. Indigenous groups therefore lost out if they allowed their music to reflect their own environments and influences (which were often much more eclectic than those of Americans) rather than slavishly imitating American sounds.

Thus it seemed that by maintaining the duality rock/soul, white musicians, and the record industry at large, tacitly kept their grip on the status quo while exploiting new trends to suit themselves. It took several factors to change this situation. First, there was the meteoric rise in both the USA and Britain of hip-hop – a combination of rapping (speaking in rhyme to a rhythmic backing), electronic funk (played on drum machines and synthesizers), scratching (manipulating the stylus in a record groove to produce rhythmic effects) and associated urban arts (graffiti and break-dancing).[23] Second, the world-wide success of Prince and Michael Jackson, among rock and soul audiences alike, did much to reduce cultural and racial stereotyping. The notions of how a black dance record 'should' sound were effectively destroyed by Prince's '1999' and Jackson's 'Beat It' (both hits in 1983). Third, with the continued exchange of ideas between black and white, British and American musicians created an atmosphere in which the work of black musicians in Britain flourished.

The first hip-hop hit in the UK was 'Rapper's Delight' by the Sugar Hill Gang (no. 3, 1979). It was followed by the substantial club success of Grandmaster Flash, Afrika Bambaata, and other rap artists. Coverage on the radio and increasing exposure in discos (disc jockey Tim Westwood was one of the first to give the music airtime on his show on Capital Radio) contributed to a steady growth of interest in the genre. Streetsounds, a record label owned by Morgan Khan, was one of the first to distribute American hip-hop in Britain. Khan also opened a studio to record local musicians.[24] By 1986 the genre had taken over among urban teenagers as the leading style of black popular music. The widespread success of rap artists from New York's Def Jam label (LL Cool J, Run DMC, Public Enemy, and the Beastie Boys) further confirmed hip-hop's 'cross-over potential' as the hard, electronic rhythms were blended with raucous rock guitar to the adulation of black and white listeners alike. Khan sponsored the first British hip-hop festival, UK Fresh, at Wembley Arena, which starred Grandmaster Flash and Afrika Bambaata.

British rappers learned from hip-hop that they did not need expensive studio productions to make good records, nor expensive equipment to perform live. Gradually hip-hop began to appear in the black communities of south and west London as musicians like the Cookie Crew and Derek B began to perform locally and on radio. The movement was bolstered by the success in the clubs of Black Britain's 'Ain't No Rockin' in a Police State' (1986), and 'Double Def Fresh' by Hard Rock (1987).[25] The albums *Hard as Hell* (1987) and *Bullet from a Gun* (1988) by Derek B were extremely successful in both Britain and the USA, as was the single 'Heat It Up' by the Wee Papa Girl Rappers (1988); by the late 1980s British rap records were in some cases outselling American ones in the USA.

Other styles from the black urban centres of the USA reached Britain in the mid-1980s. From Washington DC came go-go (the more melodic equivalent of hip-hop, with a broader, swinging beat). Go-go records were popular at clubs in Britain as early as 1984, and the success two years later of 'Bang Zoom Let's Go Go' by the Real Roxanne and Hitman Howie T, and 'War On the Bullshit' by Osiris suggested that go-go might supersede hip-hop. However, this was not the case. Though critically acclaimed, concerts by Chuck Brown and the Soul Searchers (London, 1987) and Trouble Funk (British tour, 1987) suggested that go-go was a live phenomenon rather than a recorded style.[26] Go-go's most important legacy is perhaps its influence on New York hip-hop. Many later rap records, particularly many British ones, contain the swung go-go beat rather than a simple four-square hip-hop rhythm.

Possibly the most pervasive American urban style, and certainly the one which has proved most attractive to British musicians, is house, from Chicago. The house beat was derived from the disco staple, but embroidered with fluid basslines and brought up-to-date with the help of advanced technology like digital sampling. It first became popular in Britain with 'Jack Your Body' by Steve Silk Hurley (1986); later that year 'Love Can't Turn Around' by Farley Jackmaster Funk became the first national chart hit in the house style. When clubs began playing the music they were actually ahead of the mainstream in the USA; Chicago record producer Lewis Pitzele claims that 'it took the English media to make the [Chicago] radio [stations] play its own local talent'.[27] This is yet another example of the curious interchange between the USA and Britain, by which new musical trends circumvent many of the more obvious routes to popularity. In the north, house rapidly became the most popular dance music, and by the late 1980s there was a booming industry in Britain making excellent records in variants of the style. Unlike much black American music, which remains regionally fragmented, British dance records often employ elements of hip-hop, go-go and house, as well as rock and other unrelated types of popular music. Bomb the Bass, led by the disc jockey Tim Simenon, blend all kinds of dance music to riotous effect, as may be heard on the album *Into the Dragon*

(1988); interestingly, as well as radical reworkings of contemporary dance styles, it includes a version of Aretha Franklin's 'I Say a Little Prayer'.[28]

As ever, it was not long before the style (particularly the sparse electronically manipulated type known as acid house) made the transition from underground craze to mainstream fashion. White dance groups like the Pet Shop Boys appropriated the idea of the 'acid mix' for some of their recordings, as did the production team Stock, Aitken and Waterman, working with a host of high-profile teenage stars. By summer 1988 even the tabloid newspapers were marketing acid-house t-shirts and BBC disc-jockeys (usually the last to catch on to such fads) were playing acid-style records on their shows. But sudden realization of the (purported) links between the dance cult and the drugs Ecstasy and LSD ('acid') led the *Sun* and other newspapers to campaign for the BBC to ban the music. The BBC capitulated, but the effect of a ban on 'any record that contains the word "acid"' remains to be seen. The fashion itself may anyway have run its course. Nevertheless it is interesting that an entire subculture from Chicago can come to form the basis of a popular club life-style in Britain, and that this in turn can be perceived as so threatening and damaging to the nation's youth that it is banned by the BBC.

Away from the major centres of London, Liverpool and Manchester, however, the suburban soul scene continues to flourish in much the same way that it did in the early 1970s. Though less avant-garde than the clubs in central London, suburban discotheques still flourish by catering to the tastes of local inhabitants. And while metropolitan clubs pursue the radical sounds of hip-hop and house, the suburban clubs of the south-east concentrate on less radical styles. The music favoured is wide-ranging, encompassing everything from jazz-funk by Donald Byrd to the mid-1970s Philly soul of Billy Paul. In general disc-jockeys concentrate on the more melodic, mainstream American music; the suburban scene is largely responsible for the success in Britain (among black and white audiences) of the black American soul singers Luther Vandross, Freddie Jackson, Alexander O'Neal, Cherelle, Anita Baker and Will Downing, all of whom inhabit the smoother, softer end of soul music. However some black British groups who work in this vein have also proved successful: 'Hanging on a String' by Loose Ends (1986) and 'The Way that We Talk' by Hot House (1988) were very popular in the clubs.

After Bob Marley's death, reggae's popularity was hit on two fronts. The decline of punk meant fewer white listeners; the rise of hip-hop among black youth meant fewer black listeners. The latter is underpinned by the fact that contemporary black teenagers are further removed historically from their Caribbean roots than their parents were, and have turned instead to American culture. Nevertheless, the hard core of roots reggae fans remained, as shown by the number of pirate radio stations (incuding the Dread Broadcasting Corporation) that could be found in the mid-1980s playing 'dub' (electronically manipulated and extended re-mixes of pre-existing recordings) and heavy reggae. Records in this style continued to be imported in large quantities from Jamaica (Lee Perry, for example, has remained extremely successful). After a lean period reggae seemed to regain its energy; older bands like Aswad and Steel

Pulse signed new record deals and began to produce new material; Aswad had a no. 1 hit in 1988.[29]

In addition a host of other reggae musicians had hits, mostly in a lover's rock mode: these include Boris Gardner ('I Wanna Wake Up with You', no. 1, 1987), Freddie McGregor, Sophia George, and Maxi Priest. Young British reggae stars like Smiley Culture and Tippa Irie began to make considerable impact, selling large quantities of records. The evidence is that while during the punk era reggae sold to a confined sector of the white population (which stopped buying reggae when punk waned), by the mid-1980s it was crossing over in many different directions, to pop, soul and rock fans alike. Interestingly, by blending hip-hop and reggae toasting the album *Ragamuffin Hip-hop* (1987) by Asher D and Daddy Freddy became very popular among reggae and hip-hop fans alike. As a substyle, hip-hop–reggae crossover is probably unique to Britain, because it is there that these two cultures intersect. The success of such recordings might return to reggae.

Conclusion

The cultural exchange in popular music between Britain and the USA has probably never been as extensive as it is in the late 1980s. The one-way import of the 1960s has been replaced; where once black American dance records sold to white British audiences, now British records, black and white alike, sell to black American audiences. In late 1988 *Billboard's* black music listings revealed, among others, albums by Loose Ends, Jonathan Butler, Sade, and the Pet Shop Boys; and singles by Yazz, S'Express, Bomb the Bass, and the Wee Papa Girl Rappers. Perhaps more interesting is the number of British groups who have worked with veteran American soul musicians. Scritti Politti's 'WOOD BEEZ (Pray Like Aretha Franklin)' (1984) was produced by Arif Mardin, who had earlier produced many of Franklin's classic hits of the 1960s; background vocals were supplied by the black American session singers Fonzi Thornton and Tawatha Agee. 'I Knew You Were Waiting' by George Michael and Aretha Franklin (1986) was produced by American jazz-funk musician Narada Michael Walden. These are but two of many examples of the increased credibility of British soul and dance music in the USA.[30]

Moreover the barriers of race and style seem to be disintegrating rapidly. In 1988 African, Yemenite, Bulgarian, Israeli and Cajun music all reached the charts in some form, often remixed in hip-hop or house style fashion. Technology has made digital sampling available very cheaply, enabling musicians to borrow music from other countries, cultures, or periods of history, and give it a new context. This surge of activity, coupled with the continued buoyancy of the club scene, makes it impossible to define the state of the art; indeed, styles change so rapidly that it is difficult to keep track of them all. Such a mix-and-match approach may offend purists, but British dance music, black and white, Afro-Caribbean and Afro-American alike, seems set to remain vital and vibrant into the 1990s.

7 Trinidad All Stars: The Steel Pan Movement in Britain

TOM CHATBURN

It is not hard to bring to mind the sound of a steelband. Most people in Britain will easily recall seeing or hearing one not only on television or screen but also in some live situation, on stage, in the street, at a party or a dance or even in school. Of the many different corporate musical ensembles, bands and orchestras which perform in Britain, steelband has touched the lives of enormous numbers of people but without necessarily creating an identifiable audience. This, however, is not entirely surprising since it stems from the diversity of its performances and function and, to a lesser extent, its cultural infancy and security in Britain.

Steelband has a popularity, however, which is quite remarkable. No other non-native instrumental ensemble has flourished so strongly in these islands. Few others attract such a wide racial participation and no other ensemble delivers a music with such bright equality of timbre through the seemingly incongruous voice of raw industrial metal. Spectators will regularly gather, giving expressions of admiration as they witness the astounding technique and skill of steelband performers. Others may have a more energizing experience, responding enthusiastically to the highly rhythmicized nature of the musical sound produced. Those expressions of admiration ranging from the technical to the musical are as common today as they were two or three decades ago.

By contrast, a steelband in Trinidad not only touches the lives of most people: those same people are the regular established audience of a large national culture of steelband. A considerable tonnage of raw metal will be involved, refined by expert craftsmen and controlled by vast armies of players from whom highly disciplined, virtuosic levels of performing skill are comprehensively expected. Contrasts of scale need not be over-exaggerated, however. In a large stadium presentation in Trinidad, a band of one hundred performers is appropriate both to the spectacle which it provides and to the sound output necessary. But in smaller gatherings, for example indoors, between five and twenty performers might be perfectly adequate.

What is certain, however, is that in Trinidad, Antigua and elsewhere in the

Caribbean today, some fifty years after legendary discoveries of notes on the end of discarded oil drums, 'pan' as a musical art is thriving on a massive scale. In Britain too, the pan movement appears to be growing with much momentum in circumstances which are both musically and socially very different. Each represents a musical phenomenon which was wholly unpredicted and one which offers not only its own fascinating story but also a remarkable insight into some of the challenges to musical inventiveness and the musicality of the human race in a modern twentieth-century context.

Such challenges in the special context of the history of Trinidad, however, could scarcely be viewed as implying opportunities. On the contrary, it is hard to envisage a situation more culturally restrictive to an African-derived society than that created in Trinidad in 1884 by the banning of African drums in processions and celebrations. Only one white instrument it seems, a political instrument of power in the form of the Peace Preservation Act of that year was needed to effectively silence the drumming traditions and musical expressions of the black majority population. This was therefore a cultural restriction of considerable magnitude and one which was not to be lifted or satisfactorily resolved for over half a century.

It was, none the less, a tool principally designed to strike at the heart of street revelry in its extravagant and often violent forms within which drums were clearly viewed as a particularly sinister and threatening element. Without drums, however, and despite the Act, celebrations such as those of Carnival still continued and they became increasingly more colourful and visually profuse. Although drums were silenced and banished, the musical impulse itself was less easily stifled. Its most obvious outlet was soon to be found in 'tamboo-bamboo' instruments and in 'bottle and spoon' which provided rhythmic and improvisatory opportunities within which pitch differences were also exploited. The tamboo-bamboo instruments were made from bamboo which was cut to different lengths. The names given to them, cutlers, chandlers, fullers and bass described the sizes from small to large, representing pitches from high to low. Hollowed out, but closed at one end, the larger bamboo instruments could be beaten on the ground and the booming rhythmic sound varied by striking at different angles. Others of smaller size were struck with sticks of wood or metal. Tamboo-bamboo bands were soon organized and able to provide a much-needed rhythmic support to Carnival revellers. The bands themselves, each with their layers of differing rhythmic patterns, then began to enrich their instrumentation by other means. Dutch Gin flasks were among the earliest additions to the ensemble and were often beaten with a spoon.

This development marked the beginning of a search for anything else that was portable, loud and bright. Iron and metal devices provided the most obvious and successful additions: biscuit tins, dustbins, car wheel hubs and many other diverse objects were variously pressed into service. Without doubt, the noise produced by this augmentation would have been very considerable and a more-than-adequate replacement for the banished drums.

Bands of the 1930s thus began to develop a distinctively metal sound and among these were the Dead End Kids, Hell Yard Bamboo Band, Newtown

Cavalry Bamboo Band (which later became known as Alexander's Ragtime Band), Gonzales Place Band and others. Like the 'bands' of costumed Carnival groups, most were representative of specific districts and neighbourhoods. These new bands must have looked strange, improvised and impoverished and they may have sounded extremely noisy, but within them were the textural constituents of rhythms differentiated by pitch. In addition, blown instruments such as bugles were also drafted in. The introduction in the late 1930s of larger vessels such as discarded oil drums and gas tanks provided an important new dimension. Further extending the metalizing of a band's hardware, it introduced as a consequence, performing vehicles of depth, shape and sonority which were considerably closer in concept to a drum than anything which had hitherto been substituted. This was to prove a remarkable challenge to cultural instinct, imagination and inventiveness. It marked the very beginnings of steel drumming as it is known today across the world.

In the period before the Second World War, Trinidad was a new country which was politically and economically connected to the Old World. Its links with Europe and the Americas placed it musically on their fringes without giving it a distinctive musical fabric of its own. This made Trinidad receiving territory for musical products of the major continents and older nations. Imported, and reflecting the European and British taste of the ruling classes, its principal language and idioms were further manifest through military bands and film music and through those bands for dancing or festivities which were melodic and harmonic in type. The European-originated tonal/pitch system was much in evidence even if it was not culturally representative of the majority of Trinidadians or their background. That system of twelve equally tempered pitches and associated harmonic procedures could not very easily be ignored, especially by those who, within the life and communities of Trinidad, were attempting to come to terms with the musical void of a severely disabled drumming culture.

Legend tends to obscure the date when that most important development, in which one metallic newcomer, the discarded 45-gallon oil drum began to take on a melodic function of its own. The discovery that surfaces of large steel containers could produce more than one single pitched note was largely simultaneous with the observed cause, that it was imperfect or dented, and the resulting vigorous beating in order to create exactly such variation of the pitch. Winston 'Spree' Simon is most widely claimed to have pioneered this advance. Those experiments upon similar containers with two and, ultimately, more notes were not just a solution to an historical problem; they represented a totally new beginning and a process of Caribbean musical rejuvenation which gained immediate momentum in the enthusiasm which began in Trinidad on the night of 8 May 1945, VE Night. The urge to celebrate was intensified by the fact that Carnival had been suspended during the war years. Reports of the musical turn-out that night testify not only to the vast quantities of steel objects involved but also to the hearing of melody from within the enormous metallic cacophony. Larger biscuit tins and small oil drums were suspended around the neck and played with hands and fists. By 1946, Winston 'Spree' Simon's archetypal Melody Pan reportedly contained as many as fourteen notes. Around this time another legendary figure, Ellie Manette, is widely believed to have personally devised the method of sinking and stretching the head of an oil drum (which also involved heating and tempering the steel) to produce a concave surface which was seamed and then given raised areas capable of being separately tuned to required notes. Famous new all-steel bands arose from former tamboo-bamboo groups: Hell Yard became Trinidad All Stars, Dead End Kids became Desperadoes, Ellie Manette's band, formerly the Oval Boys (and associated with that area known as the Oval) became known as the Invaders.

The steel pan's swiftness of emergence as a wholy self-contained melodic/harmonic instrument is quite remarkable and this occurred without any sacrifice to the original rhythmic function. Consequently, despite its shape, it was like a xylophone; melodio-rhythmic, but possessing all the imaginative characteristics of small gongs implanted upon the surface of a large gong. It was an instrument born of a tradition that included both drums and xylophones but which firmly embraced within its design that European (and latterly western) system of chromatic pitch. By further evolution, a whole family of timbrally unified instruments of different sizes was to emerge exploiting voice division in the manner of strings, brass or human voices, and allowing for the full adoption of Euro-Western harmonic procedures and that organizational system generally known as tonality. An ensemble of steel drums was therefore equipment for providing a musical presentation in terms of two cultures: first of rhythmical drumming, and second, of systemized pitch. This provided opportunity, given appropriate performance skills, to deliver with all the precision and rhythmic sophistication of the former, music originally conceived and expressed within the latter.

Exactly why it should henceforth pursue precisely that direction as a goal is a reflection upon two underlying influences. First, the assimilation of the long-established western diatonic musical language was rapidly becoming complete, comprehensively embracing all cultural varieties of expression from nursery rhymes and commercial or popular music to those of the major classics. Second, a quest for respectability and wider social acceptance of neighbourhood percussive and steel bands became an underlying objective and a matter of pride. For too long violent behaviour had been associated with drumming bands, tamboo-bamboo and steel bands in succession. Rivalry was often intense and a band yard would provide a focus and meeting point for rebellious factions and hooligans. This persisted long after the Second World War and even those boys who admitted to actually playing in a steelband would themselves risk being regarded as of less than good character. The names of the bands themselves indicated the fierce gang loyalties which characterized those early days: Renegades, Invaders, Gay Desperadoes and others. Fights, clashes, band and gang warfare were commonplace, the outcome of oppression and depression in a colonial era. But rivalry proved to be a vital spearhead of musical invention and the object was always to impress. Hence, consistent improvements in craftsmanship and performance meant that developments occurred at a very rapid pace in the space of a few years after 1945.

The 'ping-pong' melody pan was at the forefront, continually increasing in its sophistication and acquiring more and more notes in the process. Not only was it a curious instrument, but also it had arrived with no particular repertoire of its own. A melodic instrument transformed from a rhythmic one, its circumstances were completely new. Hung around the neck, however, this made it eminently suitable for Carnival, for processions and the playing of appropriate festive, popular or marching tunes. The fame of musical innovators from these years, Winston 'Spree' Simon, Neville Jules, Ellie Manette and others is now enshrined in legend. 'Spree' Simon in particular was engaged in extending the range of notes on the melody pan, evidenced by that fourteen-note pan of 1946. To 'Spree' Simon must also be given much of the credit for steelband's eventual achievement of its claim to respectability. While the middle class was fearful and resentful of anti-social behaviour, anti-British attitudes and violence of those warring street bands frequently led by steel pans, 'Spree' Simon was pursuing a more individual and ultimately productive path. He gradually brought the pan as an instrument and himself as a performer into a different social arena by finding engagements as a steel pan demonstrator and recitalist. That absence of any natural repertoire for the pan could now be seen to be a distinct advantage. In more formal contexts the instrument was seen as a great novelty and this was further enhanced as the performer adapted and played such familiar tunes as hymns, the National Anthem, nursery rhymes, calypsos and even classical tunes. Increasingly more well-known and tuneful music of European classical composers from Chopin to Tchaikovsky was attempted and presented. By remarkable memory and timbral transformation it provided an impressive display of both novelty and skill while at the same time pointing itself even more firmly in an 'upward' cultural direction. For with each new 'conquest' of a famous piece of music, the stakes would appear to rise further. Many developments henceforth became strongly influenced by the exacting musical demands and conventions of classical European music.

Evolution, strongly evident in the melody pan with its increasing numbers of available notes, also affected most other versions of the instrument. These were variously larger in size while still derived from the similar discarded oil drums. Musically they functioned in supporting roles, providing the means to offer bass, harmony notes and even subsidiary melody. Although they needed fewer notes than the melody pan, the important means of reproducing the familiar harmonic expressions of western music were established at the outset. The whole ensemble, in practice a band, began to use the term *orchestra*, reflecting both an increasing number of performers and an increasing use of classical repertoire. By comparison with instruments of the 1970s and 1980s, the steel pans of the 1940s and 1950s would seem less than perfect. Where recordings exist, general out-of-tuneness and dullness of tone are in marked contrast to the accuracy of pitch and bright richness of more modern instruments. Whatever inadequacies may or may not have been apparent in those early days, the instruments clearly served their basic aim of accompanying and stimulating physical expression.

Enormous technical problems needed to be solved, however, if the European pitch system was ever to be wholly absorbed in strictly musical terms. This was not a 'hi-tech' craftsmanship and it had to demonstrate competence to over-come the considerable physical-acoustical limitations of the non-scientific basic instrumental design, namely the ability to isolate satisfactorily each single note on a pan and to obtain an acceptable purity of tone. Furthermore, to find the location of any particular note while playing, really meant remembering where you last saw it. The placement of notes in circular fashion was contrary to the established European basis of presenting notes in some form of linear rela-tionship on most musical instruments. Nevertheless, this showed itself not to be a problem to those untrained on western instruments. The layout of pans would vary considerably, each one a particular pan-maker's solution to finding the place where a note sounded best without too much interference from vibrating surfaces of adjacent notes, and to the practical ergonomic considerations of a player executing fast musical manoeuvres among the many different notes. The skill with which such performers apparently did so was one of the observable miracles. It was a new kind of skill not found elsewhere in the world of music and notably involved musicianship in which memory was central. For the whole enterprise of the steelband itself – alert, corporate discipline and acute corpo-rate understanding and interaction – were additional essential features of that musicianship.

Trinidad was not to gain its independence until 1962, and in the 1940s and 1950s National Service with British forces was required of many from Trinidad and Tobago. Consequently it is reasonable to assume that during these years steel pan instruments were both made and played in Britain by those on temporary postings here. Whatever introduction may have been achieved by these servicemen, however, it was the events of the Festival of Britain in 1951 which forged the first important link between the steelband pioneers of Trini-dad and a British audience.

The appearance in London of the Trinidad All Steel Percussion Orchestra (TASPO) was an historic event (see Chapter 4). It was effectively an 'All-Stars' band promoted by the Trinidad Steelband Association, formed in 1950 and organizer of the all-Trinidad steelband competitions. For the first time abroad, Europeans were introduced to this new and timbrally unified orchestra consist-ing of a whole family of chromatically tuned instruments extending across the pitch spectrum and played by some of Trinidad's most accomplished per-formers.[1] TASPO's successful London performances were, therefore, a demon-stration of musical interaction. To Europeans, the melodic/harmonic expres-sion combined with the rhythmic emphasis and bright new timbre of the steel orchestra conveyed itself as a recognizable dialect of the musical language of the listeners themselves. Upon this foundation, the unfamiliar and familiar, road march, calypso, classical opera and concerto were thereby syncretized in one musical gesture, in one single corporate and orchestral presentation. The range of musical repertoire seemed to have few limitations as performers perfected legato as well as percussive playing techniques and the results were as fresh to Europeans as they had been to steelband pioneers of the Caribbean. In the world of steelband, any division between popular and cultivated musics seemed not to exist. Respectability as *musicians*, alongside any other instrumentalists was for the performers, however, a crucial objective and one which seemed more readily to be earned and recognized through the medium of classical music. The success of TASPO's 1951 European tour was therefore of significance not only in the capitals and centres of the Old World but also, just as importantly, back home in Trinidad: here it represented a milestone along that road to musical and social respect. Further significance can also be attached to the initiative of the island's police force in deciding to establish a steelband of its own. While major bands like Desperadoes, Renegades, Casablanca and others retained their earlier prominence, newer bands were beginning to emerge carrying gentler sounding names like Melodians, Valley Harps, Bird Song and Pan Vibes suggesting new musical and social priorities and a sophistication, confidence and maturity across the steelband movement as a whole.

In Britain, audiences had welcomed a music which could not easily be ignored. Its dialectical statements conveyed its intention to entertain across a wide spectrum of public taste without exclusivity to any one. Because of the mixed musical influences within the Caribbean, many different but familiar western idioms were being translated, thereby appealing to more than one generation of listeners. Despite the incidents of violence associated with steelbands in Trinidad (and publicized by the British press), there was no particular identification with the younger generation either in the music played or among the performers taking part. Britain too was already attuned to the calypso and the new rhythmic steel version was absorbed with equal enthusiasm. British audiences thus responded to more than the novel concept of music from oil drums. The instrumental colour itself offered a precision of articulation which was notably attractive and in complete correspondence with the development of most popular music in which the raising of rhythm to higher and higher priority had long been a consistent feature.

Symphonic formations may have inspired instrumental divisions within steelband and also influenced its musical aspirations, but the ensemble was, at this stage, no substitute symphony orchestra. To Europeans it was a popular music band of a vitally new complexion, laying claim to a multitude of tonal musics which interacted according to the mixtures adopted. That very inter-action, however, was ultimately to influence and determine both language, syntax and style of original compositions for steelband right up to the present day. In adapting only by instinctive preference and receptivity to selected musical gestures, the styles, formulae or manoeuvres as 'found objects' in the absence of historical cultural perspective, and creating from them an indi-vidualized mode of musical discourse, steelband pioneers were some of the earliest explorers in a territory later to be shared by many popular musicians and groups.

The possibility of steelband itself taking root and flourishing here began to show in the 1950s and 1960s as immigration from Commonwealth nations gradually transformed the social nature and identity of many larger urban communities. Many former residents of Caribbean countries began to settle here, particularly in the English cities of the south, west and Midlands such as London, Bristol and Birmingham (see Introduction to Part Two). From Glasgow and Newcastle in the north to London in the south, the distinctive sounds of sitars, tabla and harmonium aurally underlined the arrival here of musical cultures which were at first unfamiliar but eventually destined to change and enrich the whole spectrum of musics of British society.

For steelband musicians from Trinidad it was not an easy musical migration. Pan makers (or 'tuners' as they are known) were scarce and those who came found difficulty in obtaining suitable premises for the pursuit of their work. Sinking the surfaces of oil drums with heavy mallets and burning the drums on bonfires of rubber tyres and wood to temper the steel represented less socially acceptable activities which were not much encouraged anywhere. Hence, old disused warehouses or abandoned factories provided depressed, cold and unhappy locations for the English equivalent of the pan yards of Port of Spain. Indeed, to the present day, this operation continues to remain a rather remote and hidden aspect of the British steelband culture. Such conditions were not helpful either to the technical challenge which steel pan instruments faced more acutely in this their new 'Old World' environment. It was one of pitch precision, vital for the accurate performance of European musical expression. Control of the single note and mastery of its harmonics has consequently been a matter of constant refinement by tuners and designers during the last thirty years. Colour or timbre of a band derives exclusively from a tuner's decision upon depth of sinking, the location of individual notes, the amount of harmonic vibration which he allows to affect related notes or adjacent notes. Hence it is often possible to differentiate aurally between the sounds of different bands and that tone quality is often referred to by the degree of 'sweetness' involved. Indeed, the oft-quoted references to 'sweet Pan' are not only expressions of pleasure and admiration but also an indication of a positive shift in taste which has tended to move away from hard metal origins to a smoother and more lyrical quality overall.

Unlike the more ancient or sophisticated instruments of the Indian continent however, the cultural framework in Britian for steel pans, especially of the new standard chromatic types was receptive and always potentially wider than that brought by the participants themselves. Not unnaturally, the kind of music first played by the new British bands was that which most reminded the players of the Caribbean life they had left behind them, music of Carnival and of festivity. In the calypso, above all, they possessed a music which was identifiably their own and now a universal trademark of the steelband itself. Bands were smaller, less polished both musically and technically, but their social function was assured. Reaching out from city communities of diverse race, colour and cultural backgrounds, they became a familiar voice and their instruments equally capable of adoption by those whose origins were not Caribbean. The steelband in Britain became an ensemble of popular appeal associated especially with live music-making and in this respect soon occupied a position which no other musical band, orchestra, pop or rock group could emulate. Steelband offered something quite new: the opportunity to participate in a musical enterprise from, and within, a local community. Its corporate ethos, which also embraced the learning and rehearsal processes as well as performances, was thus wholly comprehensive. No other European ensemble prepared itself in quite this way: most depended upon earlier intensive individual effort and practice in recognized stages of progression.

The first serious interest from another quarter was that of schools and educators. Similar processes were already established, for example, in recorder groups and in singing classes. Steel pans therefore were seen, in method, to be natural partners to these kinds of activities. But here the similarity ends because school music-making was largely conducted through, or directed towards reference to the western system of written music and notated pitch. In steelbands a new concept of performance musicianship existed in which written music was avoided. Notes on a steel pan were rarely found in any linear European-based scalic progression. The frequency of use of a note, e.g. C or G, might be one factor determining its focus or advantageous placement on a pan by comparison to a lesser-used note, e.g. E flat. The chalked alphabetic characters on a pan surface were also the only visual reference. Hence steelbandsmen had adopted from the western tradition familiar names for all their notes (and tuned them in some accord with recognized pitch) without adopting the practical systems within which those names functioned, for example, that of instrumental design incorporating ascending-descending note fingering or its visual written equivalent, the five-lined stave with note symbols. So long as music was being effectively produced without such refinements, the need to accept their influence was clearly completely unnecessary. Western music-making, it could be argued, co-ordinated and exploited the relationship of pitch and scalic images visually presented on paper with the related design of linear note progression on many musical instruments. With the accent wholly directed towards memory, musically realized through an unconventional instrumental design, steelband found traditional European notation virtually useless and obsolete.

Music educationists had, however, another important stimulus to their interest in steelband and this derived from the fact that some schools had already become a youthful microcosm of the new multiracial communities which they served. Clear cultural problems were therefore posed if society and school represented differing concepts, values and directions. The steel pan now offered new opportunities. It was a drum with wide appeal to children of all backgrounds and importantly it offered an access to music-making without reference to or dependence upon theoretical systems. Consequently this meant the removal of a significant barrier to participation and progress.

During the 1960s and 1970s decades of traditional musical thought and practice were effectively set aside by the introduction of steel pan instruments to many schools in the public sector, most notably those in London. This development provided probably the easiest means of access to instrumental music for young children ever devised in this country. At the same time it meant that relevance to popular music and the use of musical styles of the day would become ever more important in our schools. It seemed consequently less probable too, that steelband would ever resume the focus for delinquent behaviour in the new English context.

That association of steel pan playing with child culture and the younger generation was a significant cultivation however. It effectively established the steelband as a domestic musical ensemble and provided a nursery for a whole generation of enthusiasts and performers. The framework of British youth festivals and competitions which have long encouraged high standards and a competitive approach to musical performance also provided a stimulus to competition in steelband playing. But despite this, steelbands have not really found easy acceptance within the existing network. One inevitable consequence, therefore, has been the need for steelband to devise and develop its own festivals and competitive outlets in Britain, thus setting it apart as a specialised musical art.

In many ways this departure symbolized an important act of self-confidence by the steelband movement and by those Caribbean-born practitioners who had, as leaders, been associated with most of the British initiatives, instrumental and educational. It established a separate identity for the steelband culture and invited a much more positive relationship with the maturity of its parental counterpart in Trinidad.

By now the steelband movement in Trinidad had become a national industry. Steelband competitions from the early 1960s developed into an immense public spectacle and became officially part of the Carnival celebrations. In 1963 the now-famous pre-Carnival steelband competition called Panorama was launched for the first time. A national steelband body, Pan Trinbago, was also established in 1973. The size of individual bands themselves had expanded enormously involving up to one hundred players with perhaps two hundred instruments often stage-mounted upon large movable floats. A huge and dramatic spectacle with its equally huge output of sound in front of crowds of many thousands quickly generated industrial and commercial sponsorship on a grand scale. Oil companies and others were quick to realize the benefits of projecting their image on the armoury of these vast musical regiments. This was evident in the new names adopted by the bands: Amoco Renegades, Witco Desperadoes, Iscott Casablanca, Heineken Pan Vibes, Guinness Cavaliers and many others. The sheer professionalism of those taking part required nothing less than total commitment. It extended also to the technology of pan manufacture which not only achieved very high standards of musical perfection but also developed extravagant futuristic concepts of raised and side-mounted pans much resembling batteries of rocket launchers in appearance. Key personnel in these new big bands were the musical arranger, the Band Captain and, not least, in the driving calypsos, the much expanded metal rhythm section including its array of dynamic car wheel-hub players. Not forgotten, however, amid the intense excitement of this new age of floor-mounted steelbands were the older traditional walking bands which were separately cultivated and generally known as 'pan-around-the neck' bands.

It was unlikely, given such thriving developments in Trinidad, that steelbands in Britain would be totally unaffected. Young bandsmen who had emigrated to this country bringing with them the seeds of the British movement have tended to retain links with their former Caribbean life, homes and families. These same people, now in middle age, remain active as today's respected leaders of bands, organizers, teachers and tuners in Britain. The British scene has, in a number of different ways, come to reflect that of Trinidad, for example in the establishment of the Steel Band Association of Great Britain, specialized music festivals and, not least, Britain's own 'Panorama', a premier competition focus for British bands today. The City of London 'Carnival' itself is the best known of the major events for steelbands. This takes place in August and large numbers of different bands take to the streets and participate.

Instrumentally, British-made pans are also improving in quality and appearance. New-style pans like 'Quads' and 'Tripletones' are being introduced as well as 'bored' pans in which the surface seams separating adjacent notes are perforated (see Figure 1.) However, there are perhaps only a handful of really skilled tuners who are responsible for actually making pans and their services are consequently much in demand. Today, new instruments made in Britain are quite expensive and this is one factor which is restricting the emergence and establishment of new bands. Today's tuners are facing a particular problem

Quadrophonic Pans by Victor Philip, Coventry. *Photograph: Tom Chatburn*

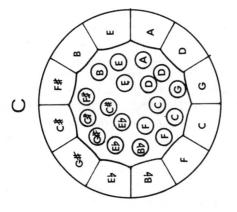

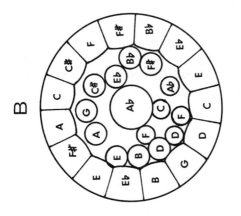

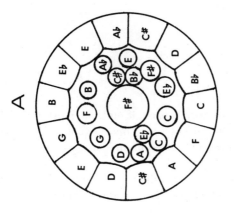

Figure 1

which is perhaps unique to the decade and results from the increasing use of recycled steel products of varied origins by manufacturers of oil drums. The steel pan of today, like any other sophisticated musical instrument, requires the same perfection and consistency of its basic originating materials.

It is interesting to consider that steel pans in frequent use may ultimately become worn out since the stretching, grooving, tuning and performance activities are all centred upon the head of the drum. Similarly the many small areas selected for the notes themselves, being subjected to consistent pressure and vibration in use are likely to go out of tune from time to time. The regular re-tuning by a specialist tuner of all instruments in a band is therefore an important musical consideration.

Nevertheless, the instruments to be found in bands in Britain vary from the very old to the very new. In timbre they may range from those which are very bright to those which are soft and mellow. The lack of standardization in note layout will seem surprising and the following typical examples which one may find of the highest pitched melodic pan will bear this out. In Figure 1, A and B are older designs but still in use, and C is a more modern type based upon an anti-clockwise presentation of fifths.

Even the names given to the instruments are different. These melody pans, for example, are known by the modern name of 'soprano' or by the older, more traditional 'tenor'. A band using modern names for its instruments might have the following range of types.

Soprano
Alto
Tenor
Guitar
Cello
Bass

A band using more traditional terminology might have:

Tenor (formerly ping-pong)
Double tenor
Double second
Guitar
Cello
Bass

Lower-pitched instruments usually consist of multiple pans, two or more, but played by one performer. Here the notes are almost equally distributed between the pans allowing the performer corresponding use of left and right hand beaters (see Figure 2).

Particularly dynamic, versatile and athletic performances are to be seen in the territory of the basses in which players may have to control six or more pans with extreme agility. Whatever the instrument, however, a player will certainly learn the exact placement of all available notes and this obviates the need to

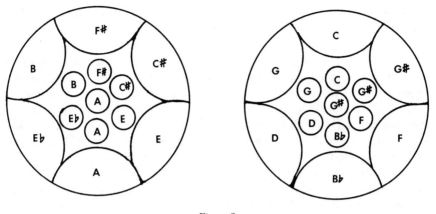

Figure 2

inscribe note names on the playing surface unless the person involved is a beginner.

The nomenclature adopted for instruments derives from conventional musical terminology in much the same way as the alphabetical names for the notes themselves. Both features may in fact show early influence from military bands. Some Trinidadians in the process of serving in British forces acquired both musical experience and training, later becoming steelband directors and arrangers.

The transmission of music itself to steelband players is rarely if ever conducted through the language of musical notation, the translation of which remains a special and sophisticated skill of the arranger. In Britain steelbands have continued to function in this way with reference only to twelve convenient note *names* and in isolation from the traditional notated system of a written music. (Consequently the five 'black' notes found on a keyboard, musically expressed as either a sharp or a flat, e.g. C# = D♭, will have only *one* of these two possible identities in a steelband.) Without the symbolic system, it can be assumed that there are therefore difficulties to be overcome in the transmission of musical data, e.g. note patterns and chords, to players. With children, on the other hand, it will be recognized that almost any solution or alternative method is nearly always an advantage, enabling practical music-making at an early stage without any theoretical barrier or encumbrance. The enormous extent of that musical data is most apparent when considering the range and size of repertoire which a typical band will perform during the course of a single programme – perhaps up to two hours in length. Characteristically this may include popular hit tunes, sophisticated calypsos, transcriptions of big band jazz plus complex classical overture, symphonic or concerto exhibition items, all delivered with a seemingly relaxed spontaneity which derives from being wholly memorized and well rehearsed.

It follows then that steelband players practise assiduously and as a team. This may be done under the direction and care of a musical mentor who might be an arranger, or, through the band's leader, often referred to as the captain.

In rehearsal the notes are commonly conveyed in one of two ways: either by ear, in which the arranger/captain demonstrates a fragment at a time, and to each separate section of the band, the notes and rhythms involved, or by means of a special notational scheme which a band itself has adopted. In the case of the latter, there are many interesting versions which rely upon horizontal successions of note names carefully arranged in sections or boxes representing the group of beats or bars and layered rather like a musical score to show in vertical formation the parts for all participating sections of the band. The whole fabric of a section of music may thus be chalked out in this form on blackboards displayed around the walls of a band room (see Plate below).

It is of course vital that a particular passage of the 'score' is satisfactorily learned before it is replaced on the blackboard by a succeeding passage and players may spend several rehearsal sessions dealing only with a comparatively minute section of complicated music. In the case of classical music, a blackboard layout could never rival the precision of normal musical notation and instead presents a space-time version of note names for which actual rhythms have to be learned by ear. Although these rhythms may be very sophisticated, nothing is more astounding than to witness the virtuoso rhythmic grasp of very complex classical musical materials by young players with no conventional musical training whatsoever. From this fact alone may be recognized the different nature of the musicianship involved: one which requires prodigious feats of musical memory, a store with seemingly endless capacity, constantly accommodating more and more materials coupled with an ability to draw upon that memory at a moment's notice.

'Score' for steel pans being chalked on a band room blackboard. *Photograph: Tom Chatburn*

Steelbands in Britain today involve thousands of participants. They may be all-black, all-white or have members drawn from a variety of ethnic groups. In the opinion of Terry Noel of the Steelband Advisory Service, however, white musicians are now in the majority. Principal leaders within the movement include Mr Noel himself, a highly respected figure and former Trinidadian, living and working in Britain, who retains active links with steelbands and music education in Trinidad while leading a number of successful bands in Britain including the Groovers and, more recently, BWIA Melodians. The importance of Trinidad and Tobago as the centre of steelband culture remains very strong and many British players seek their inspiration by visiting the islands, especially to witness the colourful and musically extravagant celebrations of Carnival time. Steelband musicians usually earn their living by other means and are therefore, in status, amateur, but their commitment to playing will be very considerable. Some, perhaps no more than fifty in the country as a whole, will earn a living professionally from steelband.

From the activity generated in schools, a large reservoire of enthusiastic young steelband musicians exists and, as a consequence, a number of very proficient youth bands has emerged with an age range from approximately thirteen to twenty-seven. These bands are competitive as well as performance bands and are certainly pace-setters, noted for their high levels of energetic technique, showmanship and virtuosity as well as state-of-the-art instruments and sometimes orchestral dimensions. Among these could be mentioned the Phase One Steel Orchestra (Coventry), City of London All-Stars, Maestros Steel Orchestra (Birmingham) and Paradise Steel Orchestra (Leeds).

Steelband music is essentially a live music and a band might be found playing virtually anywhere in Britain, from a dignified international reception to an outdoor carnival, from a cathedral setting to that of a north country working men's club. The variety of venues at which a band will perform may require some emphasis in repertoire, either calypso, rock, religious or symphonic. A successful band must adapt itself to such demands and respond equally well to each musical challenge. Television and radio appearances are quite common-place but few British bands make commercial recordings, unlike their counterparts in Trinidad. In one respect this accords with that broadly amateur status of British bands, but at the same time it also reflects upon the very real technical difficulties in faithfully recording such a dense array of percussive metallic sound, especially indoors or in studio conditions.

A steelband must also meet high financial overheads if it is to respond to the many performance opportunities which come along. Many bands function only because a rehearsal base has been established perhaps at a local community centre or a school tolerant of high levels of noise and musical exuberance. Beyond this, financial support is often needed for instruments and to cover the margin between the actual cost of the orchestra attending an engagement and that which a promoter is willing to pay. (It is widely assumed by many promoters that a steelband will provide inexpensive entertainment.) Consequently, commercial sponsorship, long associated with the movement in Trinidad is increasingly becoming a life-line in Britain too. One particular result of this in recent years has been to enable bands to develop their participation in festivals and competitions and to allow them that important opportunity of concentration upon musical skills and musical development through demonstration and exhibition pieces. It is these which have supported the tendency of bands to maintain their two original musical directions: popular and classical. Certainly British bands in pursuit of the classical direction need very little in terms of inspiration or initiative from Trinidad if only because our culture supports such a wealth of classical music performance, both professional and amateur, at local, regional and national levels. Within the steelband movement are also many music teachers who are trained only in the European tradition and who, quite naturally, exploit their knowledge of musical repertoire through their school steelbands. Hence in a youth band, perhaps led by a Trinidadian who is likely to be particularly experienced in calypso and popular music, the complementary expertise of the native British musician may sometimes be sought.

Whatever its source, popular or highbrow, the musical repertoire of British steelbands is very largely second-hand and consequently what one hears most often today are musical arrangements of familiar materials perhaps, but delivered in the now-familiar timbres of the steelband. The exploitation of a distinctive idiom may be a principal objective of the arranger, i.e. drawing upon musical gestures and devices which have been well-used before and therefore known to be effective in steelband terms. Nowhere are such sound types more vividly explored, however, than in Trinidad herself, where original works for bands are composed, full of effects and vital musical ingredients to provide the brilliant-sounding showpieces of modern steelband competitions. Discovery of that idiom has been a long and gradual process, drawing extensively upon devices exploited in earlier popular and classical arrangements. The results can be fascinating, while at the same time predictable: a completely hybrid music of complex and driving melodic-rhythmic intensity but built upon the textural sophistication and tonal adventure of symphonic expression and particularly embodying all the familiar dramatic gestures and devices of the nineteenth-century symphonic or operatic composer. Nowhere else can one experience the famous extended 'Rossini ending', a formula of emphatic final chords rhythmically spaced out in time to achieve maximum climactic effect, each one separated not by the essential dramatic silence but by the filled-in concerted non-stop clatter of a driving ten-piece rhythm section of car wheel-hub players and other percussion!

Effects such as this are intensified by the whole scale of the replica: some sixty or so orchestral symphony players may be replaced by perhaps one hundred pan players. This lends a new challenge and dimension to the drama as each musical gesture is considerably magnified, e.g. the simple crescendo is likely to acquire a thunderous quality never before heard in that style. Even the more delicate nuances of the concert hall will become much more highly charged when translated into components of mighty stadium or outdoor dramas. The original classical product, however, has not been completely abandoned in Trinidad and one suspects that certain key works, e.g. Offenbach's overture

'Orpheus in the Underworld', will long remain in use as exhibition pieces. In Trinidad pan *is* the national culture and by comparison the British movement may be seen to represent a branch of that principal Trinidadian activity. It is, however, by far the largest, being more extensive than those in other countries, e.g. Switzerland, the USA or Canada. In Britain today it is a thriving popular art. Although it involves thousands of practitioners and is also competitive, the movement remains, nevertheless, slightly underground and somewhat secretive, possessing its own non-amplified instruments which are exclusive to its culture and instrument makers ('tuners') who are not involved with other musical instruments. The sense of enclosure is completed by those unique methods of learning and playing which together represent a very special kind of musicianship. It provides corporate, energetic, stand-up-and-play, stand-up-and-dance music and its public face is frequently festive, popular and versatile. Unlike a brass or military band, a steelband cannot help but promote its youthfulness and modern informality. And, unlike an amplified pop group, a steelband does not *demand* attention, it *attracts* it. Consequently, it may function equally successfully as foreground or background music.

The adoption and absorption of steel pan instruments into schools remains a valuable strength and an important means of access for young people. A recent handbook, *Play Pan* by Terry Noel and Jill Scarfe, although designed for use in schools, will provide many interested readers with a useful and very practical guide to the steel pan.[2] Interestingly it also explores a newer and quite fascinating educational concept of steel pan playing as an avenue to conventional musical literacy. In this it points to a remarkable departure from the decades of aural tradition. The influence of GCSE might reinforce and help to maintain the future existence of steel pan in education, but its effects upon the movement as a whole will not be felt until recognized routes towards defined and higher performance levels are also established. More critical for the future of pan in this country is the continued dedication of that group of former Trinidadians who are the active leaders of youth bands in various regional centres.

Herein, however, lies one particular dilemma of the British steelband. It is smaller than the exhibition bands of Trinidad and belongs as much to the old world of Europe as it does to the Caribbean. Consequently some of its leaders would wish to build a particular distinction upon the classical and conventional musical tastes of Britain and Europe, a kind of strength which would give a special identity and also fit in with general objectives of a basic British music education. Hence, in theory, a British band might play calypso less well than a band in Trinidad but it *ought* to play Handel considerably better! As a direction for the future, however, this would not seem to be particularly promising, for when steelbands play classics to a British audience, the result may often be viewed as a mere novelty and in the case of an orchestral work, the scale of the steelband performance is likely to be much reduced from the original. Only when the steelband actually magnifies the original musical work, e.g. a keyboard fugue, is the impact likely to be a strong one.

Consequently in terms of repertoire, there may possibly be a slight difference

of view between what the British public today likes to hear from a steelband and
what some pan practitioners themselves would prefer to play as a demonstration of their skills and musicianship. One is tempted to speculate that if
steelbands in Britain continue in the future to build upon their Caribbean
nourishment and to concentrate upon distinctive and popular music-making,
the movement possesses the vital means to secure its future and preserve its
identity here. If it does not, there must be a real risk that despite laudable
artistic and educational objectives, it may become an easily forgotten novelty,
divorced from its roots and devoid of its characteristically youthful musical
momentum.

Young steel band performers playing at an open-air festival, 1989. *Photograph: Tom
Chatburn*

8 Bhangra 1984–8: Fusion and Professionalization in a Genre of South Asian Dance Music

SABITA BANERJI AND GERD BAUMANN

From the mid-1980s the dance and song genre Bhangra rose to be the most widely known music of South Asian communities overseas. Bhangra music, in all of its widely divergent styles, represents the fusion of a rural Punjabi dance and its songs with sounds, social forms, and production strategies associated with disco music and pop. In its more adventurous styles, it has further come to take up influences from hip-hop and house, as well as dance techniques such as spinning, body-popping, and breaking. To the British media of the late 1980s the Bhangra Beat appeared both an exciting example of musical fusion and the unexpected cultural expression of an 'Asian' identity in Britain. Not surprisingly the media hype did little to make Bhangra more audible in the concert of musics in Britain, and much to update mainstream stereotypes.

Leaving aside the pros and cons of classifying highly diverse communities of immigrants and people born in Britain as 'Asian' or, for that matter, 'black', Bhangra is at once more and less than 'black music in Britain'. It is performed and enjoyed by Punjabis of Sikh, Hindu, Muslim, Jain and Christian religious orientations throughout the India–Pakistan borderlands, and has been taken abroad by Punjabi communities to the USA, east Africa and Australasia. In these countries and in Britain it continues to be the music and dance for parties, functions, and the lavish wedding celebrations of the Punjabi communities, while in the Punjab it is still performed, together with its counterpart, the unaccompanied women's songs *Giddha*, at the harvest festival of *Vaisakhi*. Such simultaneity of performances, contexts and styles is of the essence of Bhangra, for the British Bhangra scene remains part of a network of musicians, listeners and tapes travelling across the continents of Punjabi settlement.

The position of Bhangra music in the west shows a number of contradictions for which it is difficult to find parallels in other genres of black music in Britain. Its aesthetic tenets, as well as virtually all of its texts, are Punjabi, and not easily accessible to non-Asian listeners; in circles devoted to world music, on the other hand, we have heard it called 'too British', 'too westernized' or 'too much like disco pop' to be acceptable as 'authentic world music', such as, for instance, *qawwāli* (see Chapter 9). What many commentators recognize as its most exciting potential, that of a fusion of hitherto disparate styles, moreover, can be seen as the oldest virtue of Punjabi culture, rooted in a region characterized by immense cultural diversity and intense cross-fertilization for most of its history. In this chapter we aim at an appraisal of Bhangra by combining our two distinct but complementary perspectives. The first part, written from the vantage point of a music journalist and commentator within the South Asian music scene, provides a social and musical history of Bhangra in Britain, and isolates the key issues arising from the relationship between Bhangra and the music industry. The second part, written from an ethnomusicologist's perspective, addresses these issues as forming part of a process of professionalization.

The social and musical history of Bhangra in Britain

Sabita Banerji[1]

South Asian communities in Britain have remained invisible, and their music inaudible, for a surprisingly long time. The reasons for this relative obscurity, as for the misconceptions that have arisen and for their struggle to make themselves heard, are closely connected with their cultural and political history. As early as 1873, there are records of Indian pedlars selling cotton cloth and spices in British cities and towns; wandering Indian street entertainers are an exotic, but none the less familiar phenomenon in Wilkie Collins's novel *The Moonstone*, and Indian tea shops, precursors of that most British institution, the Indian restaurant, were well established along the waterfronts of Britain's harbour towns. The first generation of Indian immigrants, however, were not settlers, but more often sailors, ship's cooks and galley hands who plied whatever trade they could on land before enlisting on another homebound ship. It was not until the economic boom after the Second World War that a steady influx of immigrants and settlers began. Often, they were recruited directly by factories to compensate for the loss of unskilled labour suffered in the war, and traditionally 'loyal' areas like the Punjab became a source of much cheap labour for British industry. The immigrant workers tended to be farmers and craftsmen from rural areas; rather than escaping from extreme poverty, they were likely to be replenishing the fortunes of their families for a transitional period. As from their employers' point of view they were a temporary stop-gap in the labour force; they, too, saw working in Britain as a short-term emergency measure to rescue the honour and wealth of their families. Britain remained a cultural vacuum for most: an alien, immoral, hostile world which they were neither encouraged, nor inclined, to participate in. Early immigrants tended to keep in close touch with community affairs at home, with village and local news, and with the folk and film music to which they were accustomed.

Among the first to commit themselves to settle more permanently were those who established businesses as market stallholders, middle-men in the cloth trade, car mechanics or restaurateurs. Some of the qualities of these early settlers seem to have engrained themselves into the British imagination as characteristic of 'the Asian immigrant'. Wholly erroneous images were all the easier to form and succumb to, as Indian settlers tended to make little of their cultural activities at this stage. Seeing their time in Britain as temporary, and fearing the censure of white neighbours, immigrants neglected their celebrations of religious festivals, birthdays, traditional harvest days, and other visible and audible occasions; they usually contented themselves with an occasional party in a friend's room, accompanied by folk records imported from India. It was not until their families came to join them, and more settlers began to move into individual homes, that celebrations became possible. Many of the unskilled workers had also found that it was no longer possible for them to return home to villages where their place had been filled by others, their share of the family land had been commandeered by a brother or cousin, or their children might feel disorientated for a time. With the sending for wives and children left in India and with the birth of children in Britain, the cycle of birth, marriage and death was now set to resume and religious ceremonies once again made full sense. Yet as Indian families moved into more spacious homes, spent time and money on celebrations, resumed their ceremonies and reasserted their culture, their isolation from British life was increased. British neighbours, politicians and media professed to feel threatened by the increase in immigration, and long-term settlers felt their womenfolk and children to be under threat from the comparatively loose moral life of the west. Mistrust and mutual ignorance sealed the closed door between the two cultures, and it has taken many years for that door to be prised open.

This opening has, to a remarkable extent, relied on music as its means of communication, and developed furthest in the genre of Bhangra. Neither is a coincidence. The isolation of the immigrant South Asian community, combined with its efforts to maintain its cultural identity, created a kind of cultural greenhouse for its music to grow in. Bhangra music, in turn, is the heritage of the largest group of South Asian immigrants, those from the region of the Punjab, straddling the post-Partition border of Pakistan and India. Punjabis of both nationalities appear to dominate the cultural scene among South Asians in Britain, a community that includes, among others, Sylhettis from Bangla Desh, Gujaratis, Bengalis, Tamils, and the descendants of South Asians who had previously emigrated to east Africa. Much of what is said in this essay does not apply equally to all of these groups, and it is well to keep in mind the cultural, regional, religious and linguistic diversity of South Asians in Britain. What is special about Bhangra, however, is its uniqueness as the first large-scale and successful musical fusion to grow from the very heart of a South Asian community in Britain. To appreciate this fusion, its appeal to other South Asian settlers, and its promises and chances of success, it is useful to survey the musical heritage of Punjabis.

This heritage consisted, in the main, of four categories of music. Beside religious music and hymns performed in Sikh and Hindu temples, and the narrative songs accompanying peripatetic puppet or theatre shows, virtually all Punjabi villagers were and remain familiar with celebratory folk music and with Indian film music. Celebratory folk music accompanies all important points in the agricultural calendar, as well as births and weddings. Of these, Bhangra has for long been the most prominent genre in the Punjab, and is identified most closely with the celebration of harvest and the New Year, known as *Vaisakhi*. In its traditional form, Bhangra is characterized by the distinctive rhythm of the *dholak*, a wooden barrel drum beaten with sticks, and the smaller *dholki* beaten by hand. The *dholak* drummer, with his instrument slung around his shoulders and therefore able to move around, is considered the 'leader' of the dance, with the principal singer as 'deputy leader'. The often humorous or romantic lyrics in couplet form may be improvised, and end in a burst of the drums, to which dancers perform a vigorous, acrobatic display of their agility and strength. In the rural Punjab, Bhangra remains a most vital expression of a community's social bonds and functions, and it has re-established this function also in Britain. That it was able to do so effectively, it owes in part to the Indian music industry that grew up alongside Indian film music.

Indian film music is the subcontinent's equivalent of western 'pop' music in that it is the most prolifically produced, widely marketed, and commercialized form. Since the beginnings of an Indian film industry in 1912, and throughout its growth to being the world's largest producer, Indian films have given a prominent place to music and songs. Their musical style represents a mixture of traditional Indian folk and light European classical formats, scored for both Indian and western instruments, and including, more recently, synthesizers and electronic gadgets. In South Asia as also in many parts of south-east Asia and north and east Africa, it is heard not only in cinemas, but also on radio stations, records, and cassettes. Despite the vast number of films produced in India, the film song scene is dominated by remarkably few singers who, as 'playback artists', provide the sound tracks to which actors and actresses mime. Singers like Lata Mangeshkar, Asha Bhosle and Kishore Kumar have enjoyed success-ful careers that span decades and top world-wide recording figures. Their popularity remains unchallenged also in British South Asian communities, where performances of celebrated stars continue to fill halls and sports sta-diums, and tapes and cassettes find a seemingly insatiable market. To the growth of Bhangra, Indian film music has been indispensable in at least two ways: aesthetically it has fostered an openness to fused musical styles, while industrially it has provided experience and resources for the mass production and marketing of popular music.

The recording industry in India was first established in Calcutta, the centre also of Indian film-making, at the beginning of the century. The British-based Gramophone Company, exercising a virtual monopoly over the following fifty years, banked on booming film sales, low production costs, and all too often on outdated equipment, cheaply imported from Britain. The latter is perhaps one of the reasons why the South Asian market seems less discerning about the sound quality of recordings and more amenable to second-rate pirate fare. Pirated records and cassettes, often available a few days after the original recording and at half price, remain a problem in India, even though competi-tion by the Polydor Company succeeded in breaking the Gramophone Com-pany monopoly and in raising standards. Pirating remains a problem also for

Indian musicians in Britain, and one that dates back to the very beginnings of imports from India.

With the growth of a permanent South Asian community in Britain, Indian records, and later cassettes, began to find a further market for export. The structures of the market however, remained peculiar. It was not until 1980 that the largest British importer saw any need to recruit Indian staff into its Indian music department, and distribution continues to rely on a few specialist shops in areas of dense South Asian settlement, such as Southall in west London. The economics of retailing are similarly peculiar, as on the one hand, cheaper production costs in India allow for low prices, but even the lowest prices are easily undercut by pirated versions. Pirating has indeed remained so vast, secure and lucrative a business that one of the largest bootlegging companies could afford the jump to legitimacy and now exhorts its customers to buy nothing but the genuine original. A further economic idiosyncrasy of South Asian, music in Britain may be seen in the fact that its biggest selling category, film music, requires no advertising other than that paid for by the film producers themselves. Given such peculiarities, the South Asian music market proceeded to evolve in its own way, largely independent of the mainstream music economy, reflecting, perhaps, the isolation of the community at large, and increasing that of its musicians.

Economic and cultural isolation, however, began to decrease with the growth of a generation of British South Asians raised in Britain. Toward the end of the 1960s Hindi film music and mainstream rock and pop appear to have been equally popular among the youngest generation. South Asian bands who mimicked film songs, word for word and note for note, now started producing Hindi and Punjabi versions of light western pop such as Boney M and Abba. Their appeal was short-lived in a generation whose integration with British society was hampered by the fears and prejudices of both South Asian and British communities. Many of them had no memory of an Indian 'home' to return to on some mythical day, no illusion of transitory passage to cling to in the face of hostility or indifference, and less fear of western life-styles than their elders. Young British-born South Asians are often more hurt and perplexed by their separateness than their parents, a separateness which is imposed by a generation with different paradigms of experience and by the insidious racism encountered in education, at work, and in the minds of many British people. Faced with this dilemma, children and young adults seem to have tried more stridently to assert their own, as opposed to their parents' or their white contemporaries' culture, and to search for a musical voice to state unequivocally who and what they are.

In music, the first blow on the closed door between the two cultures was the Indi-pop of the early 1980s. For the majority of young Britons, it was perhaps just another of the short-lived novelties of which the pop world is constituted; yet its effect may have been greater than is usually credited. Indi-pop, a blend of western pop and Indian elements, showed that there were many more facets to Indian music than were known from the Beatles' interest in Ravi Shankar, or Shankar's duets with Yehudi Menuhin. Headed by Steve Coe and Martin

Smith, the Indipop label produced line-ups including young Whites and South Asians. The best-known of these bands was Monsoon, fronted by Sheila Chandra who subsequently, in a solo career lasting some five years, introduced listeners of her album *Quiet* to the classical Ragas. Most Indi-pop was well produced, smooth disco with Indian resonances appearing in percussion or in lyrics. Instrumentation could include Indian instruments together with electric guitars, synthesizers, and electronic drum machines. It was distributed mainly through the independent channels and tended to reach those already interested in Indian or receptive to experimental music. Through its short life-span, it was more popular among westerners, and in particular in Scandinavia, than among South Asians. It might be said that it represented but one of a number of 'national flavours', alongside Japanese gongs and south American guitars, that were used, at times self-consciously, to stem the vicissitudes of the pop music industry. It could equally be argued, however, that it opened a way toward an east–west fusion in popular music which the success of Bhangra has been able to build on.

In addition to the imitators, or perhaps translators, of Boney M and Abba, there were bands who played traditional folk music, particularly Bhangra, at weddings and birthday parties within the South Asian community. There were also musicians who sang hymns in Hindu and Sikh temples. These two were, in a sense, the true musicians of the South Asian community, and it was from them that the latest and most successful fusion has grown.

In 1984 one of these groups, Alaap, approached Kashmiri-born arranger and session musician Deepak Khazanchi with the idea of producing a Bhangra album. Khazanchi, who had played in Uganda and Britain with a large variety of bands covering most of the mainstream western and Caribbean styles of music, introduced to Alaap's traditional Bhangra some elements from these musics, most notably the more electronic elements of disco. The resulting album, *Teri chunni de sitare*, was a success that shook all concerned. Accompanying live daytime concerts attracted thousands of young Asians into concert halls to see, hear and most importantly dance to the 'Southall Beat'. The new style was exactly what the new generation wanted. Young, fresh, lively and modern, it was as genuinely Indian as it was recognizably disco. Some of its appeal may be based on the rhythm of the *dholak*, the drum which, much more than the sitar, represents Indian music over a wide area of the subcontinent and at every level of musical activity, folk, classical and film music (*filmi*). It might also be more likely to appeal to a wide British audience than the elite and tonally complex sitar.

From the mid-1980s Bhangra groups mushroomed in all British centres of Punjabi settlement, and London and the Midlands cities such as Birmingham, Wolverhampton and Coventry soon maintained upwards of fifty groups. These tended to consist of a large (ten to fifteen) all-male, all-Punjabi line-up, and their style of self-presentation, moulded as it was on the gaudy tinsel-glamour of Hindi movies, was often reminiscent of the 1970s: flared white trousers and sequined shirts were the characteristic uniform of musicians, most of whom tended to be somewhat over thirty-five and slightly overweight.

None of the Bhangra groups were, or are, fully professional. All musicians kept down their full-time jobs even when, as in the case of the most successful groups like Alaap, Holle Holle and Heera, they were booked out for three to four evenings a week over the next two years. The pressures for and against professionalization will be addressed more fully in the second part of this chapter. They have taken several years to emerge as the first Bhangra productions were distributed through South Asian grocery shop chains whose owners bought outright, and often for a pittance, the distribution and other rights to recordings. Fortunes were made out of musicians who themselves saw little or nothing of the profits. Changes occurred only as Bhangra grew into a more firmly established, widely known, and commercially promising music form. Production and distribution began to take on professional forms with the consolidation of recording companies such as Savera Multitone, Gramophone Company/EMI, and the Arishma label owned by Deepak Khazanchi. Independent British producers founded the Cartel, a nation-wide distribution network that contributed to make Bhangra available in mainstream record shops, as well as Asian outlets. This spread of Bhangra music into the mainstream market became the chief topic of concern around the late 1980s.

The British media 'discovered' the vibrant Bhangra scene from late 1986, at a time when Holle Holle and Heera attracted audiences of up to 3,000 to London venues such as the Hammersmith Palais. Images of girls in glittering dresses and energetic boys flocking to the largest discos of Central London captivated the white press who had always assumed Asian youth to be shy and introverted, suppressed by authoritarian, ultra-conservative parents. The music media, too, pricked up its ears: music papers ran articles on Bhangra, and Andy Kershaw and John Peel gave it some air time, BBC Radio 2 did a feature, and Alaap appeared twice at the Bristol-based World of Music Art and Dance Festival. Bhangra had become news, and the possibility of emancipating Bhangra into the mainstream of the British music industry was a preoccupation of producers and at least some groups.

The term most widely invoked in this connection is 'cross-over'. For production and distribution, cross-over holds out the promise of recognition of Bhangra as part of British youth culture, as much a chord in Britain's multicultural medley as Reggae has become. Musically cross-over is sought in experimentations at fusion between the Bhangra-disco style well established since the mid-1980s, and other influences ranging from pop to house. The problems of this cross-over, however, remain immense, as might be shown by detailing one particular case, exemplary for the position of Bhangra in 1988. It concerns the move, by Morgan Khan, to adopt Bhangra music into the commercial repertoire of the Street Sounds label, reform its marketing, and perhaps win it greater audibility in the British mainstream.

Morgan Khan, part Scottish and part Pathan, born in Hong Kong and based in Britain, had worked his way up from being post boy to head of the R and B section in Pye Records (now PRT) in the space of a year. Having worked with artists like Donna Summer, Gladys Knight and Barry White, and having launched the career of Imagination, he eventually left to form his own label

(Street Sounds) and struck gold with affordable compilations of otherwise unavailable import tracks. While his musical upbringing on R and B, American soul, funk, hip-hop and house would initially have alienated him from the Bhangra sound, he decided, in 1987, to add Bhangra to his repertoire of introductions to the British music market. Hurdles, however, were not long in coming up. Khan was surprised to be faced with a reluctance from most quarters of the Bhangra industry to cooperate, which he put down to incestuous business ethics, envy, and a desire to remain 'confined to a small corner of the market-place'. The truth might be that, having run the industry entirely on their own terms and within their own cultural paradigms, most South Asians were unlikely to be willing quickly to hand over the reins to a fast-talking, Americanized, breezy outsider. Yet much of what to an outsider might appear as underhand or duplicitous business strategies is merely politeness and self-protection so far as the South Asian businessman is concerned.

Khan's interest in Bhangra, and his overtures to the industry, are but the latest, if perhaps a crucial, stage in the processes of professionalization that industry and musicians have undergone over recent years. These processes will be discussed more fully in the second part of this article. It is possible, with regard to Morgan Khan's plans, to delineate some of the difficulties that would have to be overcome.

The most serious of these is perhaps the 'price trap'. Bhangra records are sold in South Asian shops for the same price as records imported from the sub-continent, about half the price of an average British LP. Ironically the new generation of South Asians are no strangers to record shops such as HMV and Virgin, and are not discouraged from buying western pop and rock records at high street prices. Observing this, Khan is determined to break through the 'price trap' in Asian shops themselves. Success with this plan would have wide repercussions, but might enable musicians at last to see some concrete reward for their work. At present, even the most successful Bhangra musicians rely on daytime jobs for material security, and take most of their musical earnings from live concerts. It is these, in the South Asian music scene, that promote records and cassettes, when in the mainstream the link goes the other way. Material security for musicians is important also in view of the fact that, unlike reggae and hip-hop, which began as low-budget street music, Bhangra has already evolved into a highly studio-orientated genre which calls for high levels of investment.

A further problem Khan, or anyone else, would have to overcome, is that of the Bhangra image. In the video-intensive music scene of the 1980s, enamoured of lean and sullen young men, it will be a challenge to market the glitteringly bright, cheerful, jolly-uncle image of even the most musically competent Bhangra bands. Indeed, Khan signed up a group of two Asian boys, Culture Shock, whose outward style appeals more to mainstream expectations, and whose music aims at a 'cross-over' into the western field, working in some South Asian themes to carry their present audience with them. Similarly Deepak Khazanchi of Arishma Records signed up a chic, westernized female duo, Romi and Jazz, as his offering to the mainstream market. One could see these as the commercial safety valves – westernized South Asian kids doing Indianized covers of western pop and waving the banner of their community until the Bhangra bands are ready. When and how this will happen is a matter for the future. What the case of Morgan Khan has succeeded in demonstrating with a new clarity, however, is the range of issues in production and marketing, pricing and styling, that will bear on the further development of Bhangra in Britain.

Bhangra between professionalization and community ethos

Gerd Baumann

The issues outlined above have remained crucial, and indeed grown in urgency during the period 1988–9. They can fairly be conceptualized as between the demands and promises of further professionalization, and the maintenance of an ethos hitherto characteristic both of Bhangra as a genre and of Punjabi popular musicians. The push and pull between these poles is not unusual, of course, in the musics of communities that have migrated. Expected though this creative tension is, however, there is nothing predictable about the aesthetic, social and entrepreneurial choices that are taken up to resolve it. Bhangra music in Britain stands out from many comparable cases in that the tensions between professionalization and the retention of cultural roots has arisen over an extremely short span of time. Within the past five years, the genre has taken on board new instrumental line-ups, new performance contexts, new sound and production technologies; has found favour with other South Asian communities both in Britain and overseas; has entered a wide range of new musical fusions; and has come to negotiate the threshold of entry into popular commercial music culture.

While the situation is still fluid in many regards, it is possible, perhaps, to glean from a detailed observation of events over the season of 1987–8 some of the bearings at a critical phase of development. The events and views cited originate from a variety of sources, including interviews with musicians and audiences in Southall (west London), discussions with school students, and the first eight issues of *Ghazal and Beat*, the first professionally produced and well-informed Asian music paper in Britain.[2] The data gathered from these and some incidental sources call for an approach to professionalization from three contrasting angles: first, the promotion of public live events or 'gigs', and second, the production and distribution of albums and tapes that cover the entry of Bhangra into the 'music industry'. By contrast to these, a third perspective should consider the performance of Bhangra at private, rather than public, live events, such as weddings and other celebrations: combined with musicians' own programmatic statements, this allows for some views of the roots and ethos of Bhangra. These need to be taken as seriously as the news of commercial break-through or crisis, for they form part of the creative tension which Bhangra has thrived on so far. My plan, therefore, is to trace the public and commercial facets of Bhangra where they indicate processes of professionalization, and to leave the reader to assess these against the data and views taken from private or community contexts.

In discussing the dynamics of professionalization, public live performances such as discos and gigs are of particular interest: it is from this sphere that Bhangra emerged into the media limelight, and here that entrepreneurial change and initiative are most directly effective and promises and claims of groups and producers most openly assessed. The classic public event for Bhangra music is the 'daytimer' disco, news of which was discovered by the British media in 1987 and helped to give Bhangra the publicity which album releases had been denied. Not all this publicity was welcome, for apart from its often patronizing tone, its pictures of a new generation of Asian youth regularly bunking off school to attend live shows created images that did justice neither to parents' attitudes nor to youngsters' aspirations. Daytimers organized by and for young Asians date back to at least the early 1980s, when sound systems and DJ crews attracted, usually male, audiences to community centres and hired halls, playing dub reggae and some soul, and, from 1983–4, jazzfunk and hip-hop. The considerable Afro-Caribbean influence, audible in musical tastes as well as in the names of the first Asian scratchers and mixers (Xzecutive, Senator Sabzz Zulu Warrior and Mixmaster PJA) yielded to more distinctive preferences around 1984–5. Sound systems such as 'Gidian de Shingar' and 'Pa Giddha Pa' began to specialize in Bhangra, and daytimers to include as much Bhangra as hip-hop. The first professional promoters, 'Onyx' and 'Moni', began to hire more prestigious London venues such as the Hammersmith Palais (1986) and the Empire Ballroom, Leicester Square (1987), which could draw audiences of up to 3,000, made up of young people from west London as well as the Midlands, and of young women as well as men.

In this emancipation of Bhangra as the self-expression of young people in particular, two constellations seem to be worth noting both with regard to musical influences and with regard to the dynamics of professionalization. Musically, Bhangra in Britain developed hand-in-hand with the technology of disco music, as is evidenced in the unprecedented successes of Holle Holle ('Holle Holle', 1986) and Heera ('Diamonds from Heera', 1986) built upon the imaginative use of sampling techniques and high-tech synthesizers; a similarly courageous appropriation of new musical influences appears to be in progress at the time of writing when Bhangra groups particularly from the English Midlands envisage a fusion of Bhangra with house. With regard to social constellations, it is worth noting that Asian daytimers were invented not by professionals, but by young people who, beside school, job, or college, sought for active musical expression on their own initiative, paralleling the example of other post-immigration youth cultures. The publicity of Bhangra music, on the other hand, relied on a small number of highly professional promoters and the colonization of prestigious and visible venues.

Ironically, the height of British media attention coincided with, and perhaps contributed to, the first professional crisis in the history of Bhangra. The Christmas season of 1987 saw sixteen separate Bhangra shows, at times four on the same day and two or three in walking distance of each other; on Valentine's Day of February 1988, four simultaneous Bhangra shows in Central London condemned one another to failure when venues planned for 3,000 struggled to attract a few hundred people on to empty dance floors. An acute sense of crisis was shared by the most astute observers of the Bhangra scene: Sanjay, a one-time pioneer of Onyx promotions, is quoted as saying: 'This year could be the end for the Asian Bhangra gig shows, and for many promoters chasing too few venues'.[3] What the media hype had indeed done was to call forth a deluge of new would-be promoters, ranging from the tone-deaf businessman to the breezy college student, all going for the same undifferentiated market. Professionalization had succeeded so well, with Onyx, Moni and their few competitors, that it produced more professional promoters, instead of more patronage for good Bhangra.

At the time of writing it appears that Bhangra promotions have responded to the crisis by two familiar entrepreneurial strategies: concentration and specialization. Established promoters, such as can command bookings and even block bookings at the most prestigious of the London venues, formed a cartel named United Promotions; smaller, independent promoters, including the first one directed by a woman, aim for crowds of 300, rather than 3,000, with uncompromisingly 'hardcore' or 'underground' dance music, rather than Bhangra. The public live scene in the cities of the Midlands suffered far less from the crisis of over-promotion. Venues such as the Dome in Birmingham, Rotters in Manchester, or the Coventry or Wolverhampton clubs continued to attract local followers, and coachloads from elsewhere of fans enthusiastic about the Midlands groups that had emerged into stardom over the previous year or two. Musical tastes and social composition were similarly far more heterogeneous than those catered for in London, given the greater popularity of house. One promoter from the Midlands even dared to try to break the London hegemony by 'poaching' some of the most sought-after venues of the capital.

The professionalization of the public live scene has thus gone through a remarkable cycle in the space of less than five years. Promotions having been started from the rank-and-file of Bhangra fans, had grown into a lucrative, more capital-intensive, entrepreneurial venture. The very success of the music, helped perhaps by the publicity, however one-sided, bestowed on it by British mainstream media, had brought the entrepreneurial bubble to burst. An increasing diversity of tastes within and around the Bhangra scene appears now to allow for the emergence, alongside the established cartels, of independent promoters with new programmatic ideas. Whether professionalization in the promotions field might spell the fragmentation of Bhangra into substyles and subsets, or might encourage musical experimentation and creative development of the genre, musicians are, as might be expected, loath to predict. 'If some good Bhangra comes out of it, it's good' is a phrase I heard in a number of interviews. That, however, will depend to a high degree on the production and distribution of albums and cassettes, for it is these that promote concerts, gigs and other live events.

To follow the dynamics of professionalization in the production and distribution of Bhangra, the British-based music industry must be set in a larger context. As a genre of music with deep roots in Punjabi culture, dispersed across all continents, and excluded, in Britain, from the mainstream music industry, its economic infrastructure is full of contradictions. The first part of this chapter has already mentioned Deepak Khazanchi, whose 1984 production of 'Teri chunni de sitare' by Alaap gave Bhangra its first great success and its longest-lasting best-seller. Khazanchi remains the single most influential producer of Bhangra from the best-liked established groups, such as Heera and Holle Holle, as well as branching out into exploring the cross-over market. In a descriptive history of Bhangra production, the name of his Arishma label and Waikiki Studios would figure prominently, as would the names of Savera Multitone Company and, at certain junctures, of GramCo. In tracing the dynamics of professionalization, however, concentrating on such fully professional producers would be misleading. Even one of the most competent producers, Kuljit Bhamra, whose twenty or so releases include at least four successes qualifying for platinum and as many for gold, continues to work full-time as a civil engineer.

The production of Bhangra albums was doubtless pioneered and made commercially viable by a very few names indeed. The complexity of Bhangra economics, on the other hand, remains its most distinctive feature. The Bhangra market in Britain still comprises productions made by musicians themselves and recorded in a converted front room at home. The cost of such home productions could, in some circumstances, be as low as £3,000. Such amateur production remains a tempting, if in the end often self-defeating, strategy especially for the proliferation of new groups formed since the 'Bhangra boom' of 1986–7.

It remains a further possibility to produce in India. The most famous case of this option is probably that of Golden Star, a highly influential group based in Handsworth, Birmingham. Its lead singer, Malkit, widely praised for his lyrics and honoured with a Gold Medal from Khalsa College, Amritsar, succeeded in capturing enthusiastic audiences with the Indian productions 'I Love Golden Star' (1987) and 'Puth sardara de' (1988). Even where production is undertaken in Britain, as is the case with the Arishma label of Deepak Khazanchi, cutting is often done in India. Thus Khazanchi is quoted as explaining the delay in 1988 of long-awaited releases by Holle Holle and Heera: 'We cannot release either of the albums in this country first, because otherwise they will be pirated in India'.[4]

The strategies of piracy indeed remained crucial to the particularities of the Bhangra music economy, although they received some attention both in India and in Britain. The Indian Government's Copyright Amendment Act of 1984 was followed by the establishment of anti-piracy units by legitimate recording companies, which culminated in a number of police raids in 1987. There appears to have been some progress compared to 1985, when Dubashi estimated that some 95 per cent of all cassettes sold in the Lajpatrai market of Delhi were *nagli* (pirated) copies.[5] The problems that piracy posed to established or newly set-up legitimate companies, however, proved tenacious, as pirating remained profitable by avoiding not only the payment of royalties, but also the payment of a staggering 26.5 per cent sales tax.[6] 'In such an atmosphere,' writes Peter Manuel, 'most of the legitimate companies either have folded or have taken to piracy themselves'.[7] In Britain commercial pirating of Bhangra tapes is a wide-spread complaint of musicians as well as producers.

Thus Multitone/Savera, responsible for probably three-quarters of the commercially produced Bhangra groups in Britain, decided to counter piracy by insisting on both civil and criminal proceedings, successful by May 1988 in at least one hundred cases. According to an estimate of Pran Gohil of Multitone, commercial piracy may have accounted in 1988 for some 25 per cent only of cassettes played at home.[8] Bhangra musicians in Britain shared, of course, their colleagues' losses of royalties from home pirating. Their economic prospects were lessened further by the fact that very few indeed had joined the Performing Rights Society or the Mechanical Copyright Protection Society before 1988, when the former began to campaign among Asian musicians in Britain. Piracy, both commercial and private, remains a key factor in the reluctance of Bhangra musicians to go professional.

For producers, the problems of piracy can sometimes be devolved by colluding with pirates and taking a cut. This option, not only less honest but also less profitable than any producer could possibly wish, is a direct outcome of producers' lack of control over distribution. Most readers of this article are unlikely to have seen Bhangra albums or cassettes on the shelves of their local music shops. With sales figures of upwards of 45,000 for a successful production, of which there were some three to five per year from 1986,[9] this is a clear indication of the marginalization of Bhangra in the British music market, and of the cultural presumptions surviving in it. The weekly sales figures of best-selling Bhangra records are not achieved in the 660–700 record shops monitored by GALLUP to determine the British charts, nor indeed does the 'check panel' of a further 700 or so outlets include one of the major Asian retailers. The benevolent interest of mainstream DJs did as little, up to the time of writing, as the shy advances of World Music promoters to help the distribution even of professionally produced Bhangra. Established Bhangra producers, too, continue to be criticized by musicians for their lack of commitment to, and investment in, wider publicity and distribution networks.

In 1988, when Bhangra had, for the first time, succeeded in giving visibility to South Asian music in Britain, producers and distributors turned increasingly to new designs. These seem to be based on the assumption that a South Asian 'cross-over' into the mainstream market might more easily be achieved by music that follows the established images, tastes and styles of mainstream pop and the charts. The business proposition of a South Asian cross-over has begun to attract a wider range of producers. The first part of this chapter has already mentioned the duo Romi and Jazz who, on the Arishma label, were to produce the first successful Asian–pop cross-over, as well as plans by Morgan Khan of Street Sounds to sign on Bhangra groups and to market the group Culture

Shock with their intended fusion of Bhangra and house. It was a telling comment on the distribution of Asian musics when Annil of Culture Shock explained, in an interview with Veeno Dewan:

> We are not supplying house Bhangra to any Asian record shops because we don't want to be put into a category as another Punjabi group, although we are proud of our Punjabi roots and will draw upon it for the future prospects we have planned.[10]

Difficulties of distribution, publicity and image might further be overcome by the involvement, in South Asian music productions, of professionals from other backgrounds. Thus Ian Scott and Bunt Stafford Clarke produced Najma Akhtar's 1987 release of 'Ghareeb', a collection of Ghazals aimed at the cross-over market, and John Mostyn and Andy Cox put their experience with 'Fine Young Cannibals' behind the promotion of Sarbani Mukerjee's 'Ishka deh marmaleh' (1988). How far such ventures with different styles will be of benefit to the promotion of Bhangra, is a question wide open at present. The gradual professionalization of Bhangra in promotion, production, and perhaps distribution appears set to continue. Yet even the most professionally minded musicians I interviewed appeared unlikely to embrace strategies of a merely market-orientated hybridization. Bhangra musicians often showed pride in the authenticity and 'deep roots' of their genre, and even those with exceptional experience of blending and fusion professed their deep 'respect', as it was sometimes called, for the mixture of robustness and subtlety that the genre combines in its vigorous beat, spontaneous improvisations, and artful lyrics.

What must be asked, therefore, is how far Bhangra musicians themselves have engaged in professionalization, and what forms this process has taken. In this context, it is essential to clarify that professionalization cannot be regarded as an unquestionable or even obvious value in itself. While the promotion of public live events and the production and distribution of recorded music must be founded on a measure of professionalism to be effective, the creative development of any genre feeds on such values as courage to experiment, time-consuming devotion to detail, and a host of other virtues that musicians often call simply a 'love' of their music, and that characterize the 'amateur' in the best sense. Professionalism, after all, is to serve the dual aim of producing the best music for the greatest number.

With this in mind, the following examples should be read not as a comparison of 'successes' to professionalize as against 'failures', but as an indication of the actual range of the push and pull between professionalization and the mainte-nance of the ethos of Bhangra. Not surprisingly, professionalization developed most conspicuously among the Bhangra groups that had been well established by 1986–7. Some examples may suffice to illustrate the range of professionaliz-ing strategies. Alaap, founded in 1977 and highly popular ever since, had been well known for their exceptional care about professional stage management and lighting, a competent road crew, and a prominent part in their own productions and arrangements. In early 1988 they were the first Bhangra group to employ a professional manager, Nigerian-born Freddie Anne, and to consider giving up their daytime jobs. Manjit Kondal, star of Holle Holle, took leave of his job as an engineer for the professional recording of his 'Wicked and Wild' in the same year. Among more newly established groups, Chirag Pehchan of Birmingham sent their lead singer Mangal to gain professional experience by recording for a number of films in Bombay, including the highly successful 'Yaari jat dee' (1988). Of the latest generation of Midlands groups, DCS founded their wildfire success particularly among the youngest Bhangra fans on a fully professional road crew taking their 70,000 watt PA, lighting rigs and special effects machinery to every major venue, and on recording their albums in their own studio. Without adding further examples, the three groups mentioned, however, make it clear that professionalization is by no means an unambiguous process.

The social structures associated with music in the Punjabi community are recognized even by the most professional performers. All members of DCS are related by kinship, and there always was, and continues to be, a network of alignments and realignments in the membership of established groups, with musicians from different groups forming new ones. Groups such as Alaap are not above playing for expenses when asked by good friends to perform at a wedding, and Heera could be seen, in the summer of 1988, to play for expenses for a school-girl's fourteenth birthday party in Southall (west London). Manjit Kondal of Holle Holle explained to me very clearly the pitfalls of professionalization when taken as a sole value in itself:

> In the end, it must be about good music. You mustn't try too hard. It's like Karate in a way: when you first learn it, you can't wait for a fight, just to win. But when you have learnt it, and it has matured in you, you will enjoy it for doing it well.[11]

Other musicians interviewed often echoed this sentiment, and not a few insisted that 'music should be a hobby'. This reluctance toward professionalization is connected to the international appeal and market of Bhangra which allows the best amateur groups to tour Canadian, Kenyan and some Australasian cities to full houses and tumultuous audiences. It is also connected to the vagaries of the musical profession in Britain, as to the losses of potential earnings through piracy. Even a group with two medium-sales albums to its credit, and a schedule of performing weekly at weddings and parties is likely to need several years' savings to afford a van for transport. Such privately booked live performances remain the mainstay of Bhangra musicians' efforts and reputation for all but a handful of groups. They also remain an indispensable source of feed-back among musicians and between musicians and their audiences. Punjabi weddings excel in generous hospitality, joyful celebrations and, no less importantly, long and enthusiastic dancing of Bhangra, be it in a more traditional or in the 1980s disco style. It is remarkable how, on such occasions, two and three generations can mix on the dance floor and share a very extroverted enthusiasm in a music and dance that evoke much of what is best in Punjabi culture. Such privately booked performances contribute much to the continued vibrancy of Bhangra, as also to parents' openness to their children's musical tastes and venues: even a Bhangra style that relies on sampling and drum machines more than on the beat of the *dholak* or the improvisatory finesse of a singer commands respect also from the oldest generation of Punjabis in

Britain as a genre in the language and tradition of the region. Not all people of the parental generation, or indeed all musicians,[12] are happy with school students absconding to daytimers; but Bhangra, even where it takes its inspiration from disco or house and the promises of cross-over, has retained its legitimacy and credibility as the music of a distinctive cultural community. As such, it continues to contribute both to its best traditions and to its internal debates. Thus Nirmal of the group Shava Shava is one of several musicians dedicated to furthering in Bhangra lyrics the heritage of Punjabi poetry in the succession of its modern classic Shiv Kumar Batalvi.[13] An innovative group such as Golden Star, conversely, can direct its Punjabi texts to social criticism and even protest, and be given a fair hearing where it matters most.[14] Where Nirmal insists that he is 'not here to produce Punjabi music in an English way' but does not fight shy of scoring for mandoline, flute and violin, exponents of house Bhangra such as Culture Shock still profess to serve a genre of 'our parents' music, which we are proud to inherit'.[15]

Such rootedness in a cultural community and loyalty to the genre's communal ethos are not immediately recognizable to the outside listener struck by deceptively western rhythmic and instrumental patterns. An English academic colleague indeed posed the question whether 'western influences' might not 'conflict with the function of the music as supportive of cultural identity'.[16] Yet Bhangra performers and their South Asian and British Asian audiences are apt, in response, to point to the Punjabi language and its distinctive conceptualizations, to the recognizable Bhangra metre and phrasing, and to the place that the genre fills in the communal life of Punjabi, and indeed other South Asian settlers in Britain. Musicians also point out that Punjabi culture, originating from the crossroads of Muslim, Sikh and Hindu traditions, has for long been known as a culture of mutual adaptation, cross-over, fusion and amalgamation in many other domains. The communal embeddedness of the genre, however, does not go easily with the pressures of all-out professionalization. The tensions thus raised might well be vital if Bhangra is to achieve many musicians' dual aim: of continuing to cultivate a genre of and for the community, and at the same time gain this music, and the community whose it is, the audience and the respect they deserve. The future of Bhangra in the British music industry is as yet undecided. It would be a loss in many ways if Bhangra musicians sold out their genre to the latest British fad; a greater loss, however, and one that is more likely, if the music industry in Britain were to fight shy of the authentic, deeply rooted yet highly adaptable, styles of Bhangra in favour of one of its own purpose-built, synthetic, rootless and toothless hybrids.

9   *Qawwāli in Bradford: Traditional Music in the Muslim Communities*

JOHN BAILY

In this chapter I examine some of the constraints on music-making that tend to operate in more traditionally orientated Muslim societies and outline some of the characteristics of *qawwāli*, a type of Muslim religious music associated with Sufism in the Indian subcontinent. I then discuss two Muslim Asian communities in the city of Bradford, the Mirpuris and the Khalifas, which have very different ideas about music. I look at one particular *qawwāli* singer in Bradford and advance some reasons why this traditional Muslim music has relevance in modern Britain.

First, a short explanation of the term 'Asian music' is required. When people in Bradford talk about 'Asian music', which they contrast to 'English music', they refer to those genres of music which are identified with the Indian subcontinent. There are certain political nuances to this usage. People from Pakistan often wish to avoid the term 'Indian music', while it does not make much sense to speak of 'Pakistani music', a term which would be equally unacceptable to people from India. Partition of the subcontinent in 1947 drew an artifical boundary across what was in some respects a homogeneous music culture area. Indians and Pakistanis can agree on the term 'Asian music', and disregard the fact that the subcontinent is but one small part of Asia.

The Muslim communities in Britain have been established mainly, though not exclusively, by peoples who migrated from the Indian subcontinent, notably Pakistan, Bangladesh and India. Immigrant communities bring not only their own distinct genres of traditional music and indigenous musical instruments to their countries of adoption, but also carry wider aspects of their music culture with them. These include ways of identifying and discriminating categories such as 'speech/song' and 'music/non-music', ideological reasons for affixing different values to such categories, and sets of beliefs about the place of music in human experience.

Music occupies an ambiguous place within the Muslim value system and has been the subject of theological debate within the Islamic world for many centuries. A large literature exists on the subject.[1] Although the Holy Koran does not make any explicit statement about music, a number of Koranic verses have been variously interpreted as sanctioning or condemning it. The Traditions of The Prophet, and the Traditions of the Companions of The Prophet are also equivocal. The idea that music is unlawful and contrary to Islam arose soon after the death of The Prophet in AD 632 and in many Muslim countries persists to this day. There is general consensus that music plays an appropriate role in certain Muslim rituals and celebrations, but for other purposes such as entertainment it is judged by orthodox religious authority as a worthless and even sinful activity.

This puritanical view is ameliorated and counterbalanced by popular and Sufi traditions which emphasize the positive spiritual values of music, describing it, for example, as 'food for the soul'.[2] This idea of the positive value of music in human experience finds its most complete expression in the use of music for religious (devotional and ecstatic) purposes by various Sufi Orders. Sufism may be defined as the mystical tendency within Islam which seeks to promote direct communion with the Divinity, and in the Indian subcontinent *qawwāli* music is used extensively by Sufis for this purpose. Despite opposition to music, Muslim societies have a great diversity and wealth of music-making. Highly cultivated art musics and theoretical writings about music have existed for many centuries, and Islamic music has had important consequences for the history of music in Europe.[3] The dialectic between the supporters and condemners of music within Islam, evident in the debate about the lawfulness of music, has to be understood as a central part of Islamic music culture.

The Muslim concept of what constitutes 'music' differs in some ways from the European. Broadly speaking music is classified as the product of playing musical instruments, especially melodic instruments, while unaccompanied singing is not defined as 'music'. This excludes from the category of 'music' various kinds of religious singing, such as Koranic recitation, the call to prayer, the unaccompanied singing of mystical poetry, and Sufi *zikr* (a ritual which involves the co-ordination of chanting, musical rhythm, breath-control, and physical exercises to excite ecstasy). By connecting the concept of 'music' strictly with the sound of musical instruments Islam is able both to condemn music and to condone religious singing.

A religious music such as *qawwāli* challenges this taxonomy, for it combines religious texts whose poetry expresses the most profound religious and spiritual sentiments with musical accompaniment played on instruments such as the harmonium and *tabla*. There is little doubt that the development of this musical genre over many centuries owes much to the example of the revered place of music within Hinduism, and its use in a spiritual context. *Qawwāli* is problematic from the point of view of Islam, but because its texts are religious, and because of its very wide occurrence in the subcontinent, it is not usually condemned outright as unlawful.

The condemnation of music has important implications for the status of musicians in Muslim societies. The performance of music at public or semi-public gatherings, such as wedding parties and concerts, is very often in the hands of hereditary professional musicians. They usually occupy a low position in society, often stereotyped as social deviants. Popular imagination connects musicians with drinking alcohol and prostitution. The work of the professional musician may be regarded as *harām* (prohibited), and often it seems that music is condemned because of the social behaviour of musicians. In the Middle Eastern Muslim world professional musicians are frequently recruited from ethnic minorities, such as Jews, Armenians or Gypsies.[4] In the Indian subcontinent the music profession is associated with a number of low-ranking Muslim castes, often called Mirasi (from *miras*, inheritance). In the cities of India and Pakistan, especially former royal courts, there are also higher ranking hereditary musicians, practitioners of the various schools of vocal and instrumental high art music. Neuman has examined in detail the process by which low-ranking Mirasi families have become elevated to the status of higher-ranking instrumentalists and vocalists.[5]

Of course, not all musicians in Muslim societies are from hereditary musician families, and there is usually, though not always, an important amateur component. The distinction between amateur and professional status is often of great importance to the people themselves. Amateurs strive to dissociate themselves in the public eye from hereditary professional musicians, emphasizing that they play and sing because of their compulsive love of music, not merely to make a living.[6] The occurrence of amateurism in music, and the degree to which amateurs allow themselves to gain public prominence, is an indicator of the strength of secular trends in a Muslim society.

As a musical form *qawwālī* employs the same structural principles of *rāg* (melodic mode) and *tāl* (metric cycle) as other types of subcontinent music, and is considered to be a 'light' form of Hindustani ('Indian classical') music. It is distinguished by its mystical and devotional poetry, group singing, hand clapping, and the way it alternates between poetic couplets sung in a slow unmetred manner and fast, highly rhythmic singing. Great importance is attached to the song texts, which are usually *ghazals*, composed by the great mystical poets of Persian, Urdu, Hindi and other regional languages such as Punjabi and Gujarati. It is exhilarating and uplifting music, full of joyous affirmations of belief in Islam, The Prophet Muhammad, the saints, and the possibility of ecstatic communion with God.

In the subcontinent the proper setting for a performance of *qawwālī* is the Sufi shrine, the burial place of a saint. Such places have been an important part of Indo-Muslim culture for many centuries. Large shrines like the tomb of Mu'inuddin Chishti at Ajmer-e Sharif in Rajasthan and that of Nizamuddin Auliya in Delhi are the sites of huge annual gatherings to commemorate the death of the Saint and his union with God. *Qawwālī* music is performed during the *samāʿ*, the 'gathering for listening', regularly held at a shrine in the presence of senior figures of the Sufi hierarchy, who exert a direct control over the performance. In the *samāʿ*, members of the gathering may enter into varying degrees of ecstasy. The role of the musicians is to elicit a strong response from those present, and financial remuneration depends directly upon success in this respect. Listeners usually enter an ecstatic state upon hearing a particular line of poetry. When this happens the musicians repeat the 'triggering' line a number of times in order to consolidate the ecstatic state, and to give time for offerings of money to be made. The rhythmical nature of the music is likened to *zikr*, the chanting of the Sufis, which is also characterized by repetition, as though a formula such as *Allāh Hu* ('He is One') were being constantly recited. Increases in tempo are also used to heighten ecstasy. A *qawwāli* performance is very fluid, with constant interaction between musicians and listeners: listeners' reactions directly shape the course of the musical performance. An excellent account of *qawwāli* performance at the Nizamuddin Auliya shrine in Delhi is given in Qureshi, while Currie provides an indispensable general account of the shrine at Ajmer.[7]

Qawwāli, which is widespread in India and Pakistan, also exists outside the context of the shrine, and has become an important genre of concert-platform music. *Qawwāli* 'stars' like the Sabri Brothers, Nusrat Fateh Ali Khan, Yusuf Azad and Jani Babu Qawwal sell vast quantities of records and draw huge crowds to their concerts. In Pakistan *qawwāli* has assumed great importance as a national music. It is regarded as a specifically Muslim music distinct from the more classical forms of vocal and instrumental music, which are seen as tainted as Indian music, despite the fact that for many centuries, and still today, this court music was in the hands of Muslim hereditary musician families. *Qawwāli* has also achieved some prominence as a form of film music, though in this context song texts are usually on the theme of profane rather than spiritual love.[8] Film *qawwāli* is often performed by groups of women musicians, unknown in the shrine context.

Cities in modern Britain vary widely with respect to the relative size of the various minority communities living in them. In the mid-1980s the population of the Bradford Metropolitan Area was about 350,000, of which perhaps 60,000 were Asian, principally from Pakistan, Bangladesh and India. In Bradford Muslim Asians predominate; the Hindu and Sikh communities are comparatively small. Perhaps 85 per cent of the Asian community are Muslim; the majority have come from Pakistan, especially from the Mirpur District of Azad Kashmir.[9] Other sections of Bradford's Muslim Pakistani population are Pakhtuns and Punjabis.

We are fortunate in having access to a good deal of information about Mirpuris from research carried out by two anthropologists, Verity Saifullah Khan and Roger Ballard, who both worked in Bradford and Pakistan.[10] According to their researches, Mirpur District, an area approximately 30 miles by 20 miles (technically in Kashmir State but administered by Pakistan), has a long tradition of sending excess manpower out as migrant labour. Mirpuris were prominent in the British merchant navy, which is how the first emigrants found their way to Britain in the 1930s, usually working as itinerant pedlars. Mirpuris started coming to Bradford in significant numbers from the early 1950s, and were actively recruited in Pakistan as cheap labour by agents for the various textile mills. Mirpuris also settled in other parts of Britain, such as High Wycombe and Bristol. The pattern of migration was normally for young men to come first, and for their wives or brides to join them after some years.

Thirty years later the community is well established in Bradford, though the textile industry is now in a state of decline. Large areas of the city of Bradford are predominantly Asian. There are many mosques, Asian shops and restaurants, and many Asians work as doctors, dentists, estate agents, accountants, lawyers, architects, school teachers, civil servants and community workers. In 1985–6 Bradford had its first Asian Mayor, Mohammad Ajeeb Khan, a Mirpuri, once a Bradford bus driver. Mirpuris maintain close links with their communities in Pakistan, many visit their home villages every few years, and some retire there. The repercussions for the local Mirpuri economy of the input of foreign exchange from Britain and from the Gulf (which also has a large Mirpuri work-force) have been discussed in detail by Ballard.[11]

The Mirpuris are regarded by other Asian communities in Bradford, and apparently elsewhere, as rather unsophisticated people. They come from a rural area of Pakistan and the original immigrants were unfamiliar with urban culture. Many of them are committed to an orthodox Islam with – in recent years – fundamentalist overtones. Although they want to be attuned to modern British life, they actively resist compromising with certain of its values. They seek to establish a strong Islamic society in which institutions such as purdah (the veiling of women) are continued, and often argue that there should be separate education for boys and girls. There can be no doubt that there is strong pressure within the Mirpuri community to maintain a way of life which is in harmony with the values of Mirpur, especially with respect to maintaining the honour of women.

The Mirpuris are not great patrons of music. In Mirpur itself the place of musician is extremely low in the social order, being the domain of a Mirasi caste, whose speciality appears to be drumming. They perform in the context of wedding festivities, country fairs and political events.[12] Ballard observed little in the way of music-making during his fieldwork in Mirpur. Mirpuri weddings in Bradford do not usually employ groups of musicians. As one young man explained to me, 'That would lead to a mixed party' (i.e. men and women together). There seem to be no Mirasi musicians amongst the Mirpuri community of Bradford, and if any Mirasis from Mirpur have migrated to Britain they seem to have kept their origins hidden, for very understandable reasons. As a British community the Mirpuris evince little interest in music. They may enjoy it in the Hindi and Urdu movies they watch on their home videos, or in the daily broadcasts of Pennine Radio's Urdu programme *Meeting Place* (which plays records of Asian disco, film songs, *ghazals* and *qawwālis*), but music is not something they want to perform themselves, nor wish their children to learn about, in or out of school.

Muslim reservations about the value of music are well known to school teachers in Bradford. The dissertation of Patricia Jones, herself a Bradford teacher, gives much valuable information.[13] In general, she found amongst Pakistani children at middle school level (95 per cent of whom spoke a language other than English to their parents) that although some listened to a good deal of music at home (English as well as Asian), very few had any involvement in practical music-making.

> The children appear to be protected from 'live' music situations. Very few of them play an instrument or have an instrumentalist in their family; very few of them ever learned any songs as small children, had any songs sung to them, or experienced any singing at home; very few of them are allowed to attend school discos. On the other hand, all the children listen to a considerable amount of music at home of various descriptions and watch films, as well as television programmes, which include dance.[14]

Many Bradford school-teachers noted that Asian children experienced problems with singing in music classes at school. Out of a total of 1,010 children receiving peripatetic instrumental lessons in western music that year only 25 were from 'non-European families'.[15] Up to 1986 there was very little provision for Asian music in Bradford schools. Many teachers believed they should meet the needs of Asian children by introducing Asian music in the classroom but felt that they lacked adequate knowledge or resources.

Jones's experience in Bradford is not surprising in view of the fact that the majority of the children she calls Pakistani are probably Mirpuris, amongst whose parents prejudice against music-making and music-makers is strong. Jones conducted interviews with a number of Pakistani parents:

> Mr A appeared to have a fairly liberal view about music-making in school itself but talked, at length, about the Islamic cultural view of music which still sees 'musicians' as having rejected Islamic teaching, and being 'outside' the faith. This is their choice [he said], and they are regarded by the religious community as having the lowest 'status' in the community.[16]

In 1986 when I was working in Bradford, the city's Directorate of Educational Services decided to adopt a more direct role in promoting Asian music in school, and advertised for a co-ordinator to organize a teaching programme. The directorate also sponsored a series of school visits by a group of local musicians to give demonstration concerts. The directorate wanted to move cautiously, worried that there could be a negative reaction from Asian parents who did not want their children to be taught Asian music in school. There had been difficulties in accommodating Muslim expectations before, over such issues as the provision of *halāl* meat for school meals, and separate physical education for boys and girls, and another controversy was to be avoided if possible. Some of my time in Bradford was spent going out to visit schools with the small group of musicians who gave the demonstration concerts. It was in this way that I was introduced to musicians from the Khalifa Muslim community.

Besides the Pakistani community in Bradford (numbering perhaps 30,000–35,000 people), another much smaller Muslim community originates from Gujarat, in India, numbering several hundred. They call themselves Khalifa.

Most of the Khalifas are 'secondary immigrants' who came to Britain from various east African countries in the late 1960s. In many cases they left Africa under duress, feeling threatened by the policies of Africanization adopted by countries like Kenya, Tanzania and Uganda after they became independent from Britain. They differ from their Mirpuri co-religionists in several important respects. First, the Khalifa pattern of migration to Britain was rather different from that of the Mirpuris. They were more like refugees in that entire families, spanning three or even more generations, arrived together. Second, they came originally from a different part of the subcontinent and in some ways have more in common with the Gujarati Hindus of Bradford, with whom they share a language and regional culture. Third, they have a more sophisticated urban experience, having lived for many years in cities such as Nairobi, Dar-es-Salaam and Kampala, where Asians formed the middle tier in the socio-economic system between Europeans and Africans.

The Khalifa community presents a completely different profile from that of the Mirpuris. Whereas the Mirpuris left their Mirasis behind when they came to Britain, the Khalifas derive from, or have connections with, just such a Mirasi community. They constitute a small subcaste in the Valsad region of Gujarat, whose traditional caste occupations include those of barber and musician. In the early twentieth century large numbers migrated from British India to east Africa, then also under British rule. There was a demand for the services traditionally supplied by barbers, and members of this subcaste in Gujarat, geographically close to east Africa, took advantage of the situation. Once in east Africa they encouraged their children to turn to higher-ranking and economically more rewarding occupations, but the connection with barbering and music remained strong. The Arabic term *khalifa* has a variety of meanings, including 'caliph'. In Gujarat it means 'barber'. The connection between the professions of barber and musician is also evident in Afghanistan where the term *khalifa* is often used to address a barber.[17]

In 1986 the size of the Khalifa community in Britain was about 1,800 persons, scattered over a number of towns and cities, mostly in the north of England. Each local community has its own Khalifa society, affiliated to the Federation of the Gujarati Muslim Khalifa Societies of the UK. There are two Khalifa societies in Bradford, and they are also found in Coventry, Leicester, Wolverhampton, Dewsbury, Blackburn, Nuneaton, Luton and Southall (west London). The Khalifas have a keen sense of their own identity, and through their membership lists know of everybody in their community. Each local Khalifa society has its cricket and football teams and competes in Inter-Khalifa Tournaments, which are important occasions for bringing the members of the scattered community together. Wedding celebrations are also important in this respect, when several hundred guests gather in a building such as a community centre. Burials serve a similar role in bringing large numbers of the community together.

Unlike the Mirpuris, the Khalifas have a high level of involvement in music-making. Several of the most prominent Asian musicians living in London are Khalifas, often seen as accompanists on BBC Asian music television programmes, and some are members of Indi-pop groups such as Alaap, playing a form of modern dance music which combines elements of Asian and western pop music (see Chapter 8).[18] In Bradford there is little scope for full-time professional Asian musicians, but there is a high incidence of amateur musicianship amongst the Khalifas. They think of themselves as inherently musical, saying that 'music is in our blood'. As musicians they are mainly interested in Asian rather than in English music. The Khalifas are remarkable as an example of a hereditary musician social group which is becoming 'de-professionalized', but still holding on to the activity which defined its identity in the past.

The participation of Khalifas in music-making in Bradford is clearly manifest in the make-up of Bradford's two principal Asian music bands, Naya Saz and Saz aur Awaz. Naya Saz ('New Music') represents the sound of modern Asian music. Naya Saz play mostly modern film songs and dance music of the Bhangra type. Their music is strongly amplified and they have a large rhythm section. The songs they sing are mainly in Hindi, Punjabi and Gujarati. In 1986 the band consisted of Kadar Esmail, keyboards; Karvar Javad, electric guitar; Hamid Khalifa, *dholak* and vocal; Champak Kumar, bongo drums; Ali Hussein, conga drums; Hamid Abbassi, vocal; Rozina, vocal; Rahim Khalifa, tambourine; Nazir Musa, *dholak*. Two new members were Hema Patel, keyboards, and Richie Patel, Boehm flute. What is of interest about this line-up is that half the band members are from the Khalifa community (Kader Esmail, Hamid Khalifa, Ali Hussein, Rahim Khalifa and Nazir Musa). Champak Kumar, Hema Patel and Richie Patel are Gujarati Hindus; Karvar Javad and Hamid Abbassi are from Pakistan; while the girl singer, Rozina, is from a Gujarati Muslim background but is not a Khalifa. (A brief description of the Asian musical instruments mentioned in this chapter is given in the Appendix, p. 166.)

In contrast to Naya Saz, Saz aur Awaz ('Music and Song') is a group that performs the more traditional genres of Asian music: *qawwāli*, *ghazal*, and older film songs. In 1986 the group consisted of Gulam Musa, vocal and harmonium; Fakir Khalifa, electric 'banjo'; Yusuf Esmail, *dholak*; Shaukat Ishaq, vocal and harmonium/electric keyboard; Farook Musa, *tabla*; Imran Ishaq, *tabla*; Anvar Musa, tambourine; Daud Karim, *kāj*. Gulam Musa, the leader and organizer of Saz aur Awaz, is a Khalifa from a hereditary musician family. He formed his band, Saz aur Awaz, in the 1970s, with his father playing *tabla*. The personnel of the band had changed periodically, but was recruited mainly from his Khalifa relatives. Thus, of the line-up mentioned aboved, Fakir was his brother-in-law, Yusuf and Daud were cousins, Farook and Anvar sons. The only non-Khalifa members of Saz aur Awaz in 1986 were Shaukat, and Shaukat's eleven-year-old son Imran, who was learning *tabla* from a well-known Hindu guru in Manchester, Pandit Manikrao Popatkar. Shaukat is a Mirpuri; he is a motor mechanic with his own business, who developed a passionate interest in music several years earlier and joined Gulam's band in 1984. This is the group with whom I worked in making the film *Lessons from Gulam: Asian Music in Bradford*.

Gulam Musa, *qawwāl* (*qawwāli* singer) and leader of Saz aur Awaz, emerges as a figure of some importance in the Bradford Asian music scene. His family comes from the village of Amalsad, in Valsad district of Gujarat. He has only fragmentary information about his forebears in Gujarat (he learnt a certain amount on a visit to his ancestral village some years ago), and what he knows of his musical genealogy looks like this:

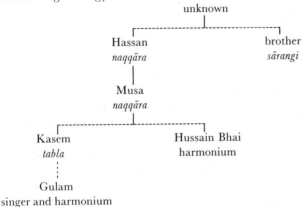

Gulam's father, Kasem, was the student of Chota Usman Khan, of Kathiawad in Gujarat. Musa, Gulam's grandfather, was a virtuoso on *naqqāra*, throwing his sticks into the air on the *sam* beat (the first beat of the metrical cycle), and folding his turban into wonderful shapes. It appears that the musicians amongst the Khalifa forebears in Gujarat played mainly *shahnāi* and *naqqāra*, a combination of instruments commonly used for wedding and other festivities. Their status is unclear but they appear to have been rural Mirasis of the kind described by Neuman.[19]

Gulam's father, Kasem Musa, was a professional *tabla* player who went to Kenya as a musician with a touring theatrical troupe, and found that east Africa presented possibilities for a professional musician. His family later joined him in Nairobi. Kasem Musa did not want his son to become a musician and did not set out to teach him anything about music when he was young. Gulam learned from another relative and later regretted not having learned more from his father about *tabla*. In Kenya Gulam worked as a storeman and semi-professional musician. *Qawwāli* was very popular in Kenya at that time, and Gulam became a well known singer of this genre. His group Aaghaz Party won the annual *qawwāli* competition in Nairobi in 1964 and was awarded a silver cup. In the late 1960s, faced with the choice of leaving Kenya or renouncing their British citizenship, Gulam and his family moved to Bradford. The Asian population in Bradford at that time was comparatively small and there was no possibility of earning a living from music. Gulam worked for British Rail for many years and was made redundant in the 1980s. He is an elder of his Khalifa community, a former secretary of the local Khalifa Cultural Society, and a member of the Bradford Council of Mosques.

Saz aur Awaz is essentially an amateur group; its members play together for their own enjoyment, mainly at Sunday afternoon 'rehearsals' at Gulam's house. The rehearsal is structured somewhat along the lines of a *qawwāli* performance in a concert hall. It starts with an instrumental *naghma* intended to warm up the musicians, Gulam and his accompanists perform several *qawwālis*, and the session often ends with 'Mast Qalandar', a song associated with the shrine of Lal Shahbaz Qalandar in Sind Province, Pakistan, and which is commonly used to end *qawwāli* concerts. The rehearsal is not confined to *qawwālis*, though. Gulam may sing some *ghazals* and older film songs, and Shaukat also takes his turn with *ghazals* and film songs.

The rehearsal is not the context in which individual lessons take place: it is an opportunity for the whole band to play together, and it is more of a session than a rehearsal. If Shaukat needs help in learning a particular *ghazal* or film song, or if Yusuf needs detailed instruction with a *dholak* pattern, they get together with Gulam for that purpose at another time. Sometimes friends drop in to listen to the music but Gulam does not keep open house. On one occasion when we were filming a Sunday rehearsal an older relative was present, soon to embark on the pilgrimage to Mecca, and Gulam sang for him a *qawwāli* about the pilgrimage.[20] Gulam's front room is clearly very different from a Sufi shrine for *qawwāli* performances: a picture of the shrine at Ajmer hangs on the wall. The audience, if any, is small, and nobody is transported into a state of overt ecstasy. The musicians are competent, and their rendition of *qawwāli* conforms to the various criteria set out above, but they are not virtuosi. Nevertheless, at its best the band creates a moving emotional experience and the passion of *qawwāli* comes across.

Gulam has in his possession a number of song books, hand-written volumes of song texts in several languages, including Urdu and Gujarati, and he usually sings reading from a book propped up on the harmonium. In part the song book is an *aide mémoire*, but it is also a prop, something for Gulam, a rather shy and retiring man, to hide behind when performing, and he uses a song book even when singing songs he knows well. The song book has, I think, a further purpose. In *qawwāli* great importance attaches to the text, usually a *ghazal* by a famous poet whose own burial place may well be regarded as a holy shrine and place of pilgrimage. Such poems are in themselves quasi-sacred texts and importance is attached to their accurate rendition. The song book affirms the accuracy of Gulam's performance. It suggests that he is literate, that he has learned the poetry from the written word, and that if in doubt he will refer back to the text.

Sometimes the band performs in public, most commonly at Khalifa wedding parties, when they share the stage with other Khalifa musicians. Since they are fulfilling obligations to their community, they do not expect to be paid, though they may receive tips from the audience. They occasionally play at private parties, or for functions such as the opening of a doctor's new clinic. On rare occasions Saz aur Awaz play in a concert situation. The fee paid for such performances is invariably low, and since the band is large, individual payments are small. Saz aur Awaz is not a money-making concern: its members are amateurs who share a passionate interest in this kind of music-making.

In 1986 Gulam was attempting to modernize the sound and repertory of Saz aur Awaz. Inspired by the success of Indi-pop groups such as Alaap and Heera in London, he hoped to broaden his appeal to the younger generation of Asians in Bradford so that the band would get more professional engagements. The band had obtained an electric keyboard (usually played by Shaukat) and some amplification, and was awaiting the delivery of a set of conga drums (these new instruments and equipment were bought with a grant from Bradford Council). They had plans to write their own songs, which would be more firmly rooted in *rāg* and *tāl* than most modern film songs. Gulam was grooming Shaukat to be the band's lead singer for this new sound, a role that would have required Shaukat to dance about on stage as he sang, like the singers in *Naya Saz*.

According to Shaukat, Gulam was not keen on this more modern music:

> He hates doing it. He doesn't like to be like that, he's all classical, well, he sings *ghazals* and *qawwālis*, *qawwālis* is the main thing. That's the only reason he's doing it, then people will want him more.

And Shaukat himself was no keener than Gulam:

> I like *ghazals* and *qawwālis*, I like the more classical [music]. If we can write and compose our own songs which are in proper *rāgas*, we can make them together in modern type, then I'll probably like them. Some [film] songs that I do like are in *rāgas*.

Gulam confirmed these comments:

> I don't see any good poetry in the new songs nowadays, I'm talking about the modern days. We have so many film songs, very very old songs, which are in *rāga* and good *tāl* like *Dādrā, Tintāl, Rupak, Jhaptāl*. And we still can't forget those tunes, and we love singing them. But not nowadays, the way they sing, I think I can't do it.

I suspected that Gulam and his friends were too committed to older and more traditional genres of Asian music to succeed in these ambitions.

Gulam's role in the Asian community, manifested through Saz aur Awaz, is that of music teacher. His special gift lies in organizing and leading a music group, mainly to perform *qawwāli*. He instructs his accompanists in both how to play their instruments and in holding their individual roles in the ensemble. His group is a workshop, and people, mainly Khalifas, join it for varying lengths of time in order to learn more traditional forms of Asian music. Gulam does not claim the status of *ustād*, 'master musician' – he feels his own limitations in musical knowledge too keenly – and certainly does not act like an *ustād*, but the data indicate that in the Bradford context that is in fact his status. There he is the doyen of Asian music, the local expert. He sometimes teaches in Hindu Temples and Sikh Gurdwaras in Bradford, and also plays religious music for their festivities. He has a repertory of Gujarati *bhajans* (Hindu religious songs) and no doubt back in Gujarat his ancestors had performed for Hindu patrons for generations. In 1986 he was appointed as one of four peripatetic Asian music instructors in Bradford, to teach the harmonium. The other instructors were from outside Bradford: a Sikh from Leeds (harmonium and keyboards) and two Muslims from Manchester and Blackburn (*tabla*).

Many plan to go, but the plans go awry.
Only those pleasing to Khwaja may reach Ajmer.
My friend! From town to town, on various paths I walk,
Kindling the fire of love.
I have lost my home, and even my being.
I am consumed by the fire of love.
Ashes on my face declare my faith,
And repentance as my instrument accompanies
    my songs to Khwaja.
Enchanted, I am enchanted by Khwaja!   Sahrai Sanbhari[21]

This text, often performed by Pakistan's celebrated *qawwāls* the Sabri Brothers, decribes the goal of any *qawwāli* singer, to visit the shrine of Khwaja Mu'inuddin Chishti in Ajmer, India. There are no Sufi shrines in Bradford, nor indeed anywhere in Britain, but Gulam made a visit to Ajmer a few years ago and played at the shrine like any other visiting *qawwāl*. Is it this possibility, of maintaining contact with the holy places of the subcontinent, that explains why *qawwāli* exists in Britain when there is no real context for its performance? I think not.

If music-making in the Muslim communities of Britain were left to the Mirpuris there would be little in the way of musical performance. The Khalifa community is a different matter: they are 'born in music', music is 'in their blood'. It seems clear that their musicality is an important part of their self-identity as a community. In the Indian caste system which they have to a large extent left behind them the Khalifas had a low rank as hereditary musicians. In Britian they live in a society where higher value is placed on music and where some degree of musical performance is seen as an integral part of a child's education. In the British context the Khalifas are an upwardly mobile community whose members may realize that the profession of musician is unlikely to match other available professions in terms of income and security, but still they feel an attachment to music-making. Gulam's role in the Khalifa community is to provide informal musical training for those who desire to put that predisposition into practice.

Gulam, himself a devout Muslim and a prominent member of his community, is in no doubt that music is condemned by orthodox Islam.

According to our religion music is not allowed. I know, because I am a Muslim, and music is not allowed in Islam, no matter whether it is dance music or classical music or light-classical music. But from my point of view if you do it respectfully it's okay. We take our Holy Prophets' names, we keep remembering them, that they worked a very good job for our Muslims. And they are very very near to God and if you pray to them [through singing *qawwāli*] God can listen to them very easily. You can go all over the world, to any corner of the world, and you will find music, either in Muslim countries or anywhere else. I don't do anything wrong with music. I always sing respectfully *ghazals* and *na'ts* [songs specifically about The Prophet Muhammad] and *qawwālis*. I have no reply if religious people tell me it is wrong. But I will do it and I am going to do it.[22]

Though not strictly speaking a Sufi – he does not belong to a Sufi Order such as the *Chishtiyya* – Gulam is able to reconcile the apparently irreconcilable, music and Islam. *Qawwāli* combines highly revered religious and mystical poetry with an overtly emotionally powerful music, and follows the precedent of hundreds of years in the subcontinent, traced back to the 'founder' of *qawwāli*, the thirteenth-century courtier, poet and Sufi, Amir Khusro Balkhi, who is buried in Delhi.

This ideological framework, which gives music a revered place within Islam, allows British Muslim Asians, especially those like the Khalifas who come from a hereditary musician background, to reconcile the conflicting worlds of music and religion. This justification is required for their relationships with other Muslim communities such as the Mirpuris, who condemn music-makers (but enjoy music), and for the Khalifas' own image of themselves as worthy of Islam. As long as this need is felt – and the settled nature of the Muslim communities in Britain suggests that this will be the case for the foreseeable future – then *qawwāli* singers like Gulam Musa will continue to play an important role in British Muslim society.

Appendix – Asian instruments mentioned

Electric 'banjo' – a long zither of the *bulbul tarang* type, with a single melody string and several drone strings. The strings are strummed with a plectrum and the melody string is stopped by pressing down on a row of keys. Fitted with pickups for amplification.

dholak – twin-headed barrel or cylinder drum played with the hands.

harmonium – small portable 'Indian' harmonium with bellows pumped by one hand, the digitals fingered with the other.

kāj – glass clappers, made from two pieces of thick glass, a pair held in each hand.

naqqāra – pair of small kettle drums played with sticks.

sārangi – bowed lute with a skin belly and many sympathetic strings, fretless, usually used to accompany vocal music in Pakistan and India.

shahnāi – double reed aerophone of the oboe family.

tabla – pair of kettle drums played with the hands, extensively used to accompany all types of Asian music.

Acknowledgements

My information about music in Bradford derives from a three-month stay in the city for the purposes of making the documentary film *Lessons from Gulam: Asian Music in Bradford*. The project was funded by the Leverhulme Foundation with a Film Training Fellowship administered by the Royal Anthropological Institute and tenable at the National Film and Television School. My profound gratitude is due to all those who helped me with the project in Bradford, and particularly to Mr Gulam Musa Qawwāl. My thanks also to anthropologists Roger Ballard and David Pocock for help and advice; they are not to blame for my errors. I assume that my findings have some applicability outside Bradford, but further research will be needed to substantiate this claim.

10 Conclusion

PAUL OLIVER

A conclusion? More of a pause for reflection on the questions that these essays have raised, and on some which will have to be considered in the future. Though the theme is 'Black Music in Britain', it is one that no single book can claim to cover comprehensively. In part this is due to the uncertainties in the concept 'black music', which have already been discussed. But it is also a field that has been insufficiently researched hitherto, and on which there are inadequate historical data. In consequence, any initial study which endeavours to draft the outlines and, at least partially, to fill in the shapes defined, must sketch the history of the genres as well as attempt to solve some of the problems that they raise.

Aside from a few references to the slender evidence of early black musicians and entertainers in Britain, the period reviewed in this book has been from the beginning of the nineteenth century to the present. This is a period on which there is more available, if uneven, documentation. Methodologically there are considerable differences in the research that can be undertaken with reference to much of this time-span when it is compared with the last thirty years. For instance, first-hand interviews with a group of musicians are impossible when one is speaking of the nineteenth century, or even of much of the twentieth century. Information and deductions must come from close scrutiny of a variety of documentary sources – performance reviews, contemporary accounts, published memoirs, printed ephemera and early recordings, where they exist. Even as recent a musical phenomenon as calypso in Britain has not received prior examination, and recordings of the music, whether made in the West Indies or in Britain had never been comprehensively listed and analysed. Documentary history may play a secondary part when the genre is of recent date, for its roots may be traced and its functions examined by direct association with the musicians and their audiences within their cultural milieu. Nevertheless, memories are faulty, many musicians have died or are no longer traceable, and not infrequently they have returned to their homelands. The raw material of black history in Britain as a whole, let alone of black music, awaits systematic collecting, housing, referencing and, one need hardly add, financing.

As we have seen, throughout the nineteenth century and until after the Second World War there was a very small black presence in Britain. In the late 1950s the black population grew more rapidly and its base was broader, with the coming of West Indian, African and later south-west Asian immigrants, and with the maturation of first- and second-generation young Blacks born in Britain. Consequent upon this is inevitable uncertainty about the nature of the kinds of audiences which were drawn to black music. At one stage there was only a minority black community which could be addressed by black musicians, and their performances were essentially for the entertainment of Whites. Later, there were changes in the kinds of audience that listened to the bands and singers: wholly black audiences drawn from localized communities bound either by their countries of origin, or by their newly adopted cities; and later still mixed white and black audiences of young people.

Similarly the nature of 'black music' itself underwent substantial changes. New genres followed in quick succession: slave songs and minstrelsy, ragtime and early jazz, calypsos and steel band, Indi-pop and Afro-pop among them. Though there have been valuable studies of specific genres, musicians or groups – the Jubilee Singers and their songs, Paul Robeson, the Southern Syncopated Orchestra, Bob Marley and reggae, contemporary African music, and so on – an overview which located them in time, culture and place did not exist. Not that location is in itself a simple task, for the performance venues of black music have also undergone many changes, from the street show to the minstrel show, the concert stage to the theatre stage, the society club to the jazz club, the disco to the rock concert, the dance hall to the school hall. Back room and garage, provincial park and city carnival have all been host to black music. Again, there have been developments in the media which have paralleled the growth of black music and sometimes influenced it: broadsides were replaced by music sheets, gramophone records augmented radio, television and video eventually dominated all other vehicles of transmission.

Even from these brief observations it is evident that while black music in Britain is in no way homogeneous stylistically or ethnically, its context has not been consistent either. In the English tradition of music hall, whose history largely paralleled that of black music here, the venues were substantially similar and the performances were dependable within the conventions of the idioms of music hall. Hence the audiences were able to rely on both the kinds of artists they were to see and the context in which they would enjoy them. In so volatile a field as black music this was by no means always the case; audiences that were continually exposed to new sounds and new genres from the Americas, the West Indies, Asia or Africa had continually to readjust. Small wonder that many found the syncopated rhythms of ragtime hard to accept after the sweet laments of the Jubilee Singers, or that many wished to cling to the styles and types of music that they had learned to enjoy and even love. In retrospect, it should not be a source of surprise that audiences were sometimes unappreciative of new musical imports.

Audience attitudes and responses to black music, more than hinted at already in several chapters in this book, could well be the subject of future detailed research. For it is also evident that there was a considerable degree of positive interaction between the kinds of new music that were introduced, the places where they were heard and the constitution of the audiences that were able or inclined to attend them. More remarkable perhaps, than the resistance of white audiences to black music before the 1960s was the dedication, even fanaticism, of enthusiasts for jazz, when they shared neither colour, nor culture nor even country with those Blacks who brought it to Britain.

When black popular music in Britain is compared with black music in the USA many differences become apparent. The spirituals, work songs, ragtime, gospel music, New Orleans, Kansas City and Chicago jazz, modern jazz in its many forms, the varieties of blues, zydeco, soul, rap and other types and sub-genres have had profound influences on music styles throughout the world. Popular music as we have known it in the twentieth century is inconceivable without the massive injections of these black idioms which have sustained it. The diversity and vitality of North American black music is indisputable, which is not to argue that white musicians did not play a considerable part in many of these idioms – in the formative stages of the spirituals, the composing of ragtime, the development of jazz. But there are others to which Whites had little to contribute in their early years though they may have assimilated them in the course of time: hollers, blues, soul among them. What is particularly noticeable is that these were idioms that took shape on American soil. Retentions of African practice have been detailed and disputed over two centuries but however strong they may have been in rhythm, scale, timbre or expression, however much they may have given a distinctive colouration to black musics in their emergence, those that have been mentioned above were distinctively American in their maturity.

In Britain the circumstances are different. None of the black music forms that have thrived here appears to have had its origins in this country; though they represent black music in Britain they are not, at source, British black music. Some have been brought over by or developed under the influence of black American musicians, like the jubilee songs, jazz or soul. Or they have been introduced by immigrants, like calypsos, steel band or *ghazals*. And, in a few more recent instances, introduced by visiting Africans, as is the case with *kpanlogo* or *soukous*. If there has been a particular function of the British musicians in this respect, it has been subtly to transform these imported musics, giving them a different flavour as they became adapted to the particular needs and tastes of black culture here.

One does not have to look far to account for this. For well over a century Blacks have constituted at least a tenth of the total population in the USA; in certain states, such as Mississippi, Georgia, Alabama and Texas the proportion has been far higher, with some counties having a predominance of Blacks in the formative years of many musical genres, and even today in a large number of southern counties, over a third of their population are black. These concentrations have created cultural milieux in which new musical forms were able to flourish and be expressive of the emotions and collective identities of the people.

Compared with the USA the black population in Britain until the 1960s was minute, and even now is proportionately a fifth of that in the USA – perhaps 2–3 per cent. Not enough to encourage a new musical form to emerge and permit it to develop on a comparable scale. With the growth of black communities in Britain this may well change – indeed, it may already be changing. In the first decades of the next century we may witness the evolution of new, British, black musical forms. To date the function of black musicians in Britain has been to incline the genres of their overseas heritage to the liking of Whites, to that of black residents already here, and to the youthful tastes of black, British-born teenagers. With another generation of British-born Blacks, local styles may soon emerge.

Among the many points that arise from the comparative smallness of the black population for most of the past two centuries is the question of audience expectation. As Michael Pickering has shown (Chapter 1), audiences in the nineteenth century gave a mixed but by no means wholly unsympathetic reception to the black music brought by travelling troupes and individuals. That their responses were coloured variously by imperialist jingoism, by reports from missionaries of 'native savagery', or by revulsion of slavery, is scarcely surprising: the mores of the times were very different, the media were fewer (if not more controlled) and accessible to a much smaller sector. In the endeavour to please their audiences performers may have substantially altered their styles of playing and delivery, consciously or subconsciously compromising in the process. Audiences on the other hand would have developed expectations of the musicians and singers which further conditioned their performances.

Jeffery Green (Chapter 2) has suggested that preconceptions of black music permeated the concert-hall, so that musicians playing in the popular classics vein were obliged to 'Africanize' their repertoires. The quesiton whether such expectations always apply, and to every kind of black musician, generates many further questions: Are black musicians *always* conforming in some measure to stereotypes – even when playing to Blacks? If they do *not* play 'black' music, are they regarded as being suspect by their own communities? Is there a black equivalent for 'playing for Whitey'? Are the expectations that, say, Jamaicans play reggae, as much within the culture as outside it? Are black musicians sometimes trapped *by* black music?

Such questions – and there are many – though uncomfortable, may be more answerable now than in the past, if only because black musicians can express an opinion on them. As Howard Rye makes clear (Chapter 3), the audiences for early jazz were often little better informed than those of the previous century to the music they encountered. Newspaper critics ranged from the cautious to the hostile, but there is no question that jazz was welcomed in a number of clubs and on the theatre stage. In part this was a response to vigorous promotion and the advocacy of British white musicians who were excited by the new developments. Many of the British band-leaders employed black Americans. Jazz and swing became commercial business and were it not for the blinkered view of a stubborn Musicians Union, which imposed the notorious ban already discussed, might well have generated work. Not only could this have been advantageous for those who instrumentally backed up the American jazzmen who visited these shores, but also it could have stimulated a lively home musical market that would have given further employment to musicians, both black and white.

Indications of the potential market, and also the initiative of the enthusiast in providing the driving force behind new enterprises in both entertainment and media, are to be found in the activities of a number of British entrepreneurs over the years: band leaders like Jack Payne and Ambrose, record company owners like Carlo Cramer or Guy Stevens, record shops like Doug Dobell's or Stern's, radio presenters like Charles Fox or Charlie Gillett, club and concert promoters like Ronnie Scott or Harold Pendleton, and innumerable magazine writers and critics like Spike Hughes or Denis Preston.

Preston's enthusiasm for the black music, which extended well beyond jazz, is evidenced in his single-handed promotion and recording of calypsonians in the 1950s, as John Cowley has recounted (Chapter 4). When his enterprise collapsed in litigation, calypso declined, but whether coincidentally or as a partial outcome of his misfortune is a matter of debate. Clearly however, the motivations and attitudes behind entrepreneurship in black music require more detailed examination. Possibly the most important aspect is the role of Blacks in the music industry. With a few exceptions such as Hazel Miller, of Ogun records or Remy Salako, the lack of black Artist and Repertoire recording executives, concert promoters, radio producers, disc jockeys, even critics and writers is conspicuous (as is the lack of women). Black musicians and writers have complained of racism in these areas, and though the sincere support for black music of such persons as those listed above is beyond doubt, the issue demands close scrutiny. While it could reflect adversely on the music industry as a whole, many other factors, including the aptitudes, motivations and commercial experience of Blacks, in the past as in the present, would also have to be considered.

So far reference has been principally made to the history of black music in Britain as performance and entertainment, with their related genres, locales, audiences and promoters within the music industry. Though there are circumstances that are special to each, they have in common the broad principles of marketing and entertainment which bear upon all forms of popular music. With the growth of the black communities in Britain there were new forms of music that were introduced which did not exist for, or depend on, the audiences of the dominant white society. Increasingly black music came to serve other audiences. As Chris Stapleton has demonstrated in the case of African musicians in Britain (Chapter 5), their presence had been sustained over a long period but their numbers were too small for them to establish a significant identity: in the 1940s African musicians worked in jazz and Caribbean groups.

With the 1960s and independence from Britain and other colonial powers, African musicians found increasing work, overcoming the presumed exoticism of African music, which was at first a hindrance to their entry into the mainstream of popular music. This was still the objective of many African musicians, as Stapleton's interviews reveal. They were torn by the pulling power of opposing trends: the growing demand for their music, particularly high-life and juju, from within the resident African community, and their own aspirations for professional success. This conflict between minority group identity through music and the musicians' aspirations to professional success was to be shared by many black musical forms in the ensuing years. Success, it was widely assumed, was commercial, measured by record sales, exclusive contracts, media appearances, concert tours, air-time and the entire apparatus of the popular music industry which was directed at the larger, and therefore predominately white, society.

Professionalism and identity

There is of course no special reason for believing or expecting that the Anglo-Saxon and Celtic strains of the British people should want to hear the music of Africa. It could be argued that the public welcomed African music to an extent which indicates a surprising liberality of taste. To the African performer working in Britain the perception has generally been different: the slow recognition of his music was often seen as prejudice, the lack of recording contracts and bookings as evidence of racial bias. There is little doubt that racist attitudes have existed, and continue to do so, in both public responses to music and the operation of the industry. It may have been the reason for the almost total disregard of West Indian ska by the BBC, though the BBC's characteristically conservative rejection of the music may have stemmed from a genuine belief at the time (1960s) that it had little but a minority appeal. To ascribe failure to achieve commercial success solely to the deliberate suppression of talent on the grounds of race is inadequate. It is the essence of commercial enterprise that it responds to market forces which it can only do effectively when there is a demand. By the mid-1980s, and progressively since in fact, African-derived music has achieved a wide measure of exposure and popular appeal – as the summary for 1988 in the Introduction indicates.

Part of the process of gaining a wider public has been one of musical acculturation. Traditional African styles of music from Burkino Faso, Kenya, Nigeria, Senegal, Zaire or Zimbabwe may have certain elements broadly in common, but they are also differentiated markedly from each other in instrumentation and performance techniques. While this particularly applies to the older forms it is also apparent in the variations of 1960s high-life, or later, in the diverse types of music which have combined, say, traditional drum rhythms with electric guitars and other modern and western instruments. In making it more accessible, compromises have been made, consciously or subconsciously, as presentation techniques have been polished, musicians show-cased, fashions adopted, mannerisms affected. The gains and losses, musically and professionally, have still to be evaluated, but this process of musical assimilation and synthesis continues today, enlarging the potential of African-derived music while at the same time increasing its audience.

Nevertheless, the black musician, whether from Africa, the Caribbean, Asia or from an urban ghetto in Britain, has frequently felt marginalized, a member of a minority within a minority group. Anthony Marks (Chapter 6) observes that in the early years, British soul was popular in clubs which served both the black and the gay communities, sometimes overlapping and both marginalized; it took the advent of the (white) mods for the music to move into wider venues. Black musicians have felt that they had good reason to be suspicious of the industry, regarding it as an instrument of the same powers that repressed black initiative and kept large numbers of young Blacks unemployed. For Rastafaris the 'dread tunes' of 'real reggae' was the authentic music; they contrasted 'raw reggae' with 'sweet reggae', the commercialized and compromised version which was directed towards a white British audience.

British Rastafaris protected the authenticity of the Jamaican music of the rude-boys and the West Indian rastas, and expressed their identity and their defiance of establishment mores through it. There was always a fair measure of security in minority taste, and a resentment of popularization which has run counter to the demand for recognition. The subculture protagonists of many kinds of specialized popular music genres have insisted on wider acknowledgement for 'their' music when it has been the province of a minority interest – and subliminally regretted the loss of its exclusive nature when it had achieved greater popularity. Yet alliances *were* made, unlikely in the case of the soul–skinhead union, somewhat more believeable between punk and reggae. Challenging and anarchic as all these musical forms may have been, they succumbed to the blandishments of the record industry and the material rewards of popular success.

For such success to be achieved there had to be a white audience – the size of the black audience could hardly sustain it commercially in the view of the major record companies. It was inevitable that many young white musicians should also adopt the music they supported, until the boundaries dissolved and white British groups were even scoring hits among black Americans. Part of the process was assimilation: the rhythms, expressive intonations, instrumental and vocal techniques, and repertoires appropriate to the specific genres, interpreted by the white imitators. In the case of the steelband it was more complicated: there was an alternative musical organization to be learned, a different kind of instrument to be mastered, and a repertoire which drew from light classics and martial music as much as from popular songs. Thomas Chatburn's analysis (Chapter 7) of the means by which the Trinidadian music was transferred to Britain, highlights the technical challenges in learning to play an unorthodox instrument within a large ensemble.

Pan music has retained its integrity largely through the diversity of the pan layouts, and the competitiveness of the steelbands. These factors have ensured a high measure of solidarity within the ensembles, while the complexity of the pieces learned by ear exerts a strict discipline upon their members. Loyalty to the band and identification with the music may now be shared between young Blacks and Whites alike, but its in-group, subcultural nature is still its strength. While the Caribbean source of steelband music is not in question, its authenticity may be in doubt as the bands consciously seek to refine their instruments and to play ever more ambitious, even symphonic compositions. To what extent it remains a 'black music', now that the proportion of young white performers may exceed that of Blacks, is indicative of the problems that are generated by the processes of popularization.

The social implications of professionalism in the music of an ethnic minority, and the issues arising from the meeting of genres are emphasized by the rapid rise of South Asian music in Britain in recent years. In part, as Sabita Banerji has reminded us (Chapter 8), the synthesis of Punjabi Bhangra with western genres had already begun in Indian film music, and when it became popular in Britain in the mid-1980s, it largely assumed the glamour of *filmi* in the eyes of young Asians; perhaps this prepared the way for the surprising capacity of the Bhangra groups to assimilate West Indian idioms, Afro-American hip-hop and electronic media. Yet, Gerd Baumann indicates (Chapter 8), the Bhangra musicians teetering on the verge of going professional have been inhibited by the realities of the recording industry, and particularly of pirated releases. And there is another factor which emphasizes the duality of black music in Britain: the recognition by many young Bhangra musicians of their musical roots and their pride in playing for traditional Punjabi weddings held in Britain. Bhangra has achieved a measure of compromise between its celebratory roles and the aspirations of its performers.

How important music is to some ethnic subgroups within the Asian minority, and how serious the problems that they face are when transposed to a new environment are underlined by the instance of *qawwāli* musicians of the Khalifa Muslim sect (Chapter 9). A complex web of loyalties links them to others of their faith. Of Gujarati descent, by way of east Africa, they are hereditary musicians who have been able to bring professional skills to a variety of musical contexts, when required to do so. Even though they have lost some of their professional status they have retained a devotion to their music which acts as a bond between the small and dispersed Khalifa groups. It is simplistic to assume that there is invariably a direct relationship between musical performance and the maintenance of ethnic identity; John Baily compares the Khalifas with another sect, the Mirpuris, orthodox Muslims who deprecate the playing of music and associate it with the low-rated Mirasi caste. But this close focus on the values of Muslim sects in a single British city nevertheless emphasizes the central place accorded to music in the lives of many within the multi-stranded Asian community.

Black music, Britain and the future

It is clear that there is no entity that is 'Black Music', no single definition that will satisfactorily encompass all that the convenient, but ultimately misleading term seems to imply. Even the unity that is implicit in the assumption that 'black music is that which is played by black musicians' is threatened when the performance of popular concert music by Blacks, or the participation of Whites in the playing of musical styles initially developed by Blacks, are considered.

Contradictory though they may be in certain respects, some features of black musicians in Britain can be identified. Perhaps the sharpest distinction can be made between the musicians of Caribbean, African and Asian descent, but as we have seen, these are further divisible between Nigerians and Ugandans, Jamaicans and Trinidadians, Muslims and Hindus, and many other subsets drawn along national, religious and class lines. But a distinction may be made that cuts across such cultural definitions to identify those black musicians who came as visitors to Britain, intending to return to their home countries, and those who came as immigrants to settle in this country (or are their descendants), bringing music with them as part of their heritage. Another distinction, no less important, is to be made between the non-professional musicians and the professionals, and between those that perform for, and within, their subculture and those who play for a larger musical audience.

Such distinctions between musicians may similarly be made between the genres which these musicians, singularly or in groups and ensembles, represent. While by no means all are shared by every genre, some are common to a number of them. In particular the latter: the distinction between the genres which serve ethnic communities in Britain, and those which have been moulded to the demands of popular music media and professionalization. As we have seen, 'authenticity' in black music in Britain since the 1950s, however popular the idiom, requires that it is rooted in, and is nurtured by such community functions.

Just as evident as the fact that there is no single, all-embracing definition of black music in Britain is the diversity of positions from which its various musical forms may be perceived. Musician, ethnomusicologist, historian, sociologist, anthropologist, educator – members of all these disciplines may contribute to an understanding of this complex phenomenon, and have done so in this collection. There are numerous areas which have hardly been touched upon, many aspects which will need scrutiny. Among the most important of these is musical analysis. Not only should specific genres be closely examined for their essential musical structures, but also comparative studies should be undertaken in order to ascertain the extent to which common elements may be traced between them. Song forms and themes require transcription and analysis, the significance of lyrics identified and the relevance of the idioms to black community life-ways explained. In all such areas the study of British music of Afro-Asian derivation is decades behind that of the musical forms in the USA of African-American origin – ragtime, jazz, the blues among them.

If any clarification is to be achieved in the definition of black music in Britain it will be necessary to enlarge upon, and extend beyond much of the material in this book. For example, the importance of the media in any form of popular music is fundamental, but though our knowledge may be growing, a great deal remains to be done in the documentation of stage appearances, club venues, repertoires, radio broadcasts, discographies and much else. Serious and detailed research is essential if sound theoretical arguments are to be advanced and valid interpretations reached; for this reason, a number of empirical papers have been included in the present collection.

It is perhaps appropriate in an initial survey which endeavours to chart the waters and identify the obstructions and difficulties on which theories may founder, that the contributors are observers of black music first and, in the case of one or two musician-authors, participants second. It is the earnest desire of all the present contributors and the series editors that black writers will be motivated to research into their music traditions, and the creative processes now taking place. Future studies will benefit greatly by the personal experience of black musicians from within the genres, and the diverse cultural contexts from which they spring.

Meanwhile, this present collection of essays on the Afro-Asian contribution to popular music in Britain is offered with great respect for their achievement and with gratitude for the pleasure they have given us.

The popular Punjabi Bhangra band 'Heera' in action, 1988. *Photograph: Paul Slattery*

Notes

Introduction to Part One

1 Tagg, P. 1987, 'Open letter about "Black Music"', 'Afro-American Music' and 'European· Music' (mimeo) Göteborgs Universitet, Musikvetenskapliga Institutionen.

2 Oliver, P. 1985, 'Review of Eileen Southern, *The Music of Black Americans: A History*', *Popular Music*, 5, p. 297.

3 Nettl, B. nd (*c*.1964), *Folk and Traditional Music of the Western Continents*, Englewood Cliffs, NJ: Prentice-Hall, pp. 69–187. Oliver, Paul 1970, *Savannah Syncopators: African Retentions in the Blues*, London: Studio Vista.

4 Forbes, J.D. 1988, *Black Americans and Native Americans*, Oxford: Basil Blackwell, pp. 83–92, 123–4, 193–5.

5 UNESCO 1952, *The Race Concept: Results from an Enquiry*, Paris: UNESCO, para. 9, p. 15.

6 Blacking, J. 1973, *How Musical is Man?*, Seattle, Wash: University of Washington Press, p. 62.

7 Herskovits, M. 1934, 'Freudian mechanisms in primitive Negro psychology', in E.E. Evans-Pritchard, R. Firth, B. Malinowski and I. Schapera (eds) *Essays Presented to C.G. Seligman*, London: Kegan Paul Trench, p. 76.

8 Merriam, A.P. 1964, *The Anthropology of Music*, Evanston, Ill: Northwestern University Press, pp. 223–7.

9 Blacking, op.cit., p. 54.

10 Fryer, P. 1984, *Staying Power: The History of Black People in Britain*, London: Pluto Press, pp. 80–81.

11 Hugill, S. 1966, *Shanties from the Seven Seas*, London: Routledge & Kegan Paul, pp. 9–18.

12 Salter, J. 1895, *The East in the West: Work among the Asiatics and Africans in London*, London: S.W. Partridge & Co., pp. 20–21, 62–5, 131–3.

13 Nathan, H. 1962, *Dan Emmett and the Rise of Negro Minstrelsy*, Norman, Oklahoma: University of Oklahoma Press, pp. 159–209.

14 Playbills and song sheets from the collection of the Center for Popular Music, Middle Tennessee State University, Murfreesboro.

15 Anon. nd (*c*.1926), *Williams' Colored Singers*, Chicago, Ill: Rosenow Co., booklet from the collection of the Center for Popular Music, director Paul Wells, to whom I'm

indebted for his help and interest.

16 Charters, A. 1970, *Nobody: The Story of Bert Williams*, New York: Macmillan, pp. 69–77.

17 Lotz, R. 1986, 'Will Garland and his Negro Operetta Company', in R. Lotz and I. Pegg (eds) *Under the Imperial Carpet: Essays in Black History 1780–1950*, Crawley, Sussex: Rabbit Press, pp. 130–44.

18 Goddard, C. 1979, *Jazz Away from Home*, London: Paddington Press, pp. 81–6.

19 Quoted in Lovell Jr, J. 1972, *Black Song: The Forge and the Flame*, New York: Macmillan, p. 410.

20 Field, F. and Haikin, P. 1971, *Black Britons*, Oxford: Oxford University Press, p. 4.

21 Summerfield, P. 1986, 'Patriotism and Empire: music-hall entertainment 1870–1914', and Shephard, B. 1986, 'Showbiz imperialism: the case of Peter Lobengula', in J. McKenzie (ed.) *Imperialism and Popular Culture*, Manchester: Manchester University Press, pp. 37 and 97.

Chapter 1

1 On minstrelsy, see the references in Pickering, M. 1986, 'White skin, black masks: "Nigger" minstrelsy in Victorian Britain', in J.S. Bratton (ed.) *Music Hall Performance and Style*, Milton Keynes and Philadelphia: Open University Press, pp. 70–91.

2 *The Athenaeum*, 640, 1 February 1840, p. 94.

3 *London Chronicle*, 18 February 1764, cited in Hecht, J.J. 1954, 'Continental and colonial servants in eighteenth-century England', *The Smith College in History*, 40, p. 49; Fryer, P. 1984, *Staying Power: The History of Black People in Britain*, London: Pluto Press, pp. 69, 81, 449 fn 15; Buchan, J. 1926, *The Three Hostages*, London, p. 110, and see p. 109 for his jaundiced sketch of a London night club with dance music provided by a 'nigger band'.

4 Walvin, J. 1973, *Black and White: The Negro and English Society 1555–1945*, London, p. 199; Fryer, op.cit., p. 230.

5 Grant, J. 1838, *Sketches in London*, London, pp. 20–7, 42–4; Smeeton, G. 1828, *Doings in London*, London, pp. 120–4; Smith, J.L. 1817, *Vagabondiana*, London, pp. 33–4; Shyllon, F. 1977, *Black People in Britain, 1555–1833*, London and New York, p. 162.

6 Edwards, P. and Walvin, J. 1983, *Black Personalities in the Era of the Slave Trade*, London, p. 164; Hindley, C. 1878, *The Life and Times of James Catnach*, London, p. 135; George, M.D. 1967, *Hogarth to Cruickshank: Social Change in Graphic Satire*, London, pp. 169–70; Billy Water's death-bed reference is to Tom and Jerry, the rakish men-about-town who feature as the main protagnists in Egan's *Life in London*.

7 Edwards and Walvin, op.cit., p. 163; Hindley, op.cit., p. 138; Shyllon, op.cit., p. 161.

8 Chernoff, J.M. 1979, *African Rhythm and African Sensibility*, Chicago, Ill., p. 28.

9 Farmer, H.G. 1954, *History of the Royal Artillery Band 1762–1953*, London; Farmer 1950, *Handel's Kettledrums*, London; Farmer 1912, *The Rise and Development of Military Music*, London; Farmer, 1980, 'Janissary music', *New Grove Dictionary of Music and Musicians*, London, IX, p. 497 (with J. Blades), etc.; Fryer, op.cit., pp. 79–88; Wright, J. 1986, 'Early African musicians in Britain', in R. Lotz and I. Pegg (eds) *Under the Imperial Carpet: Essays in Black History 1780–1950*, Crawley, Sussex: Rabbit Press, pp. 14–24. See Southern, E. 1973, 'Early African musicians in Europe', *Black Perspective in Music*, 1, fall, p. 166 for the earlier quotation.

10 Lorimer D., 1978, *Colour, Class and the Victorians*, Leicester, ch. 3.

11 *Bath Morning Post*, 8 December 1789, cit. Wright, J. 1980, 'George Polgreen Bridge-

tower: an African prodigy in England 1789–99', *Musical Quarterly*, January, pp. 65–82.

12 Angelo, H. 1830, *Reminiscences*, 2 vols, London, 1, 448–51; Wright, 1986, op.cit., pp. 23–4; Fryer, op.cit., pp. 97–8; Parke, W.T. 1830, *Musical Memoirs*, 2 vols, London, 1, p. 264; Buckingham, Sir James Silk, 1855, *Autobiography*, 2 vols, London, 1, pp. 166–71.

13 Mayhew, H. 1967, *London Labour and the London Poor*, 4 vols, London, III, p. 191; II, pp. 490–3; IV, pp. 425-6; and Trotter, J.M. 1969, *Music and Some Highly Musical People*, Chicago, Ill., orig. pub. 1880, pp. 306–8.

14 Southern, E. 1982, *Biographical Dictionary of Afro-American and African Musicians*, Westport, Conn. and London, p. 207; and see her 1983, *The Music of Black Americans*, New York and London, pp. 107–10, 112–16. On Johnson, see also Sanjek, R. 1988, *American Popular Music and its Business: The First 400 Years*, 3 vols, Oxford, II, pp. 215–17.

15 Reynolds, H. 1928, *Minstrel Memories*, London, p. 78 (for a possibly apochrypal story of Sweeney's construction of the non-gourd, modern-type banjo around 1839); Marshall H. and Stock, M. 1958, *Ira Aldridge: The Negro Tragedian*, London, pp. 28–47, 71–81.

16 LeRoy Rice, E. 1911, *Monarchs of Minstrelsy*, New York, p. 48; Winter, M.H. 1947, 'Juba and American minstrelsy', *Dance Index*, 6, pp. 28–48; Stearns, M. and Stearns, J. 1968, *Jazz Dance*, London, pp. 44–8; Dickens, C. 1966, *American Notes and Pictures from Italy*, London, p. 91.

17 Reynolds, op.cit., p.163.

18 Reynolds, op.cit., pp. 163–6.

19 Toll, R. 1974, *Blacking Up*, London and New York, pp. 199–200, 212–13 (on Hicks's business competitiveness), 215, 259–61; Reynolds, op.cit., pp. 165, 206–7; Winter, op.cit., p. 42; Daly, J.J. 1951, *A Song in His Heart*, Philadelphia, pp. 64–5; *The Era*, 11 December 1897, p. 21; *The Merthyr Express*, 11 December 1897, p. 5; MacQueen Pope, W. 1951, *Ghosts and Greasepaint*, London, p. 111; Green, J. 1984, 'The case of James Douglass Bohee (1844–1897)', *Black Music Research Newsletter*, 7, 1, Fall, pp. 4–5; Stearns, op.cit., p. 51.

20 Trotter, op.cit., pp. 67–87.

21 Blind Tom's London concerts in 1866, for instance, realized $100,000, according to Scobie, E. 1972, *Black Britannia*, Chicago, Ill., p. 125.

22 See for example the testimonies of Moschelles and Halle in Southall, G. 1979, *Blind Tom: The Post Civil War Enslavement of a Black Musical Genius*, 2 vols, Minneapolis, II, pp. 54, 56. See also her 1975, 'Blind Tom: a misrepresented and neglected composer-pianist', *Black Perspective in Music*, 3, 2, May, pp. 141–59.

23 *Dwight's Journal of Music*, 26, 665, 29 September 1866, pp. 316–17; Trotter, op.cit., p. 144.

24 Rutling, T. *c.*1910, *Tom: An Autobiography*, Torrington, N. Devon, and for general histories of the Fisk Jubilee Singers, see Pike, G.D. 1874, *The Jubilee Singers and their Campaign for Twenty Thousand Dollars*, London, and Marsh, J.B.I. 1877, *The Story of the Jubilee Singers*, London. For a recent summary, see D. Seroff in Lotz and Pegg, op.cit., pp. 42–54.

25 *The Standard*, 7 May 1873; *Hawick Advertiser*, 10 January 1874; and *Sheffield and Rotherham Independent*, 7 February 1874.

26 Oliver P., Harrison, M. and Bolcom, W. 1986, *The New Grove Gospel, Blues and Jazz*, London: Macmillan, pp. 1, 7–8.

27 Marsh, op.cit., p. 70; *Scarborough Express*, 9 August 1973; *Hawick Advertiser*, 10 January

1874; *Daily Telegraph*, 8 May 1873; *Musical Times*, XX, 1 August 1880, p. 396; *Whitby Times*, 22 September 1876.

28 *The Standard*, 7 May 1873; *Hull News*, 9 August 1873; *Sheffield and Rotherham Independent*, 7 February 1874; *Leicester Chronicle and Leicestershire Mercury*, 18 April 1874; *Derby Mercury*, 18 February 1874; *Hawick Advertiser*, 10 January 1874; *Derby and Derbyshire Gazette*, 13 February 1874; *Birmingham Morning News*, 8 April 1874.

29 *The Standard*, 7 May 1873; *Scarborough Express*, 9 August 1873; *Daily Telegraph*, 8 May 1873; *Hull News*, 9 August 1873; *Sheffield and Rotherham Independent*, 7 February 1874.

30 *The Orchestra*, 2 April 1984; *Birmingham Daily Mail*, 10 April 1874; Seroff, op.cit., p. 46; *Birmingham Morning News*, 9 April 1874. See also the more informed articles, which had appeared a few years earlier, by Higginson, T.W. 1867, 'Negro spirituals', *Atlantic Monthly*, XIX, pp. 685–94, and Barrett, W.A. 1982, 'Negro hymnology', *Musical Times*, 1 August, pp. 559–61.

31 *The Review of Reviews*, VI, July–December 1892, p. 264. (The tradition of their harmonized group singing continues today, as for example with the Ladysmith Black Mambazo choir.)

32 Stearns, M. 1956, *The Story of Jazz*, New York: Oxford University Press, p. 139.

Chapter 2

1 Sayers, W.C.B. 1915, *Samuel Coleridge-Taylor, Musician: His Life and Letters*, London: Cassell, was reprinted in 1927 and in facsimile in the USA in the 1960s. His mother's identity is noted in Green, J. 1985, 'A note on Coleridge-Taylor's origins', *Musical Times*, August, p. 461 and in McGilchrist, P. and Green, J. 1985, 'Some recent findings on Samuel Coleridge-Taylor', *Black Perspective in Music*, 13, 2, pp. 151–78. His half-sister's recollections are in Evans, M. 1986, 'I remember Coleridge', in R. Lotz and I. Pegg (eds) *Under the Imperial Carpet: Essays in Black History 1780–1950*, Crawley, Sussex: Rabbit Press, pp. 32–41. See also Coleridge-Taylor, J. 1943, *Genius and Musician*, Bognor Regis: John Crowther; Coleridge-Taylor, A. 1979, *Samuel Coleridge-Taylor*, London: Dennis Dobson; and Richards, P. 1987, 'Africa in the music of Samuel Coleridge-Taylor', *Africa*, 57, 4, pp. 566–71.

2 Geiss, I. 1974, *The Pan-African Movement*, London: Methuen; Fryer, P. 1984, *Staying Power: The History of Black People in Britain*, London: Pluto Press; Green J. 1985, 'Perceptions of Samuel Coleridge-Taylor on his death (September 1912)', *New Community* 12, 2, pp. 321–5.

3 Marshall, H. and Stock, M. 1958, *Ira Aldridge: The Negro Tragedian*, London: Rockcliff; Southern, E. 1982, *Biographical Dictionary of Afro-American and African Musicians*, Westport, Conn: Greenwood Press; Scobie, E. 1972, *Black Britannia*, Chicago, Ill: Johnson Publishing. Amanda Aldridge's papers are in the Special Collections Library at Northwestern University, Evanston, Illinois.

4 Sadie, S. 1980 (ed.), *New Grove Dictionary of Music*, 15, pp. 534–5; obituary in *The Times*, 17 October 1988.

5 Green, J. 1982, *Edmund Thornton Jenkins: The Life and Times of a Black American Composer 1894–1926*, Westport, Conn: Greenwood Press; Hilmon, B. 1986, 'In retrospect: Edmund Thornton Jenkins', *Black Perspective in Music*, 14, 2, pp. 143–80.

6 Southern, op.cit., p. 25.

7 Green J. 1982, 'Roland Hayes in London, 1921', *Black Perspective in Music*, 10, 1, pp. 29–42; Southern, op.cit., p. 173; Sadie, op.cit., 8, p. 414.

8 The Jamaican Choir details are under publication in the *South African Theatre Journal*,

scheduled for September 1988. For Drysdale see Green, J. 1986, 'A black community? London, 1919', *Immigrants and Minorities* 5, 1, pp. 105–16.

9 Robeson has several biographies and that based on family papers is under publication in New York. See also Green, J. 1987, 'High society and black entertainers in the 1920s and 1930s', *New Community*, 13, 3, pp. 432–4; Crowder, H. 1987, *As Wonderful As All That?*; Chisholm, A. 1981, *Nancy Cunard*, Harmondsworth: Penguin.

10 Vaughan, D. 1950, *Negro Victory: The Life Story of Dr Harold Moody*, London: Independent Press; Fryer, op.cit.

11 Dunbar's autobiography is under publication in England.

12 Southern, op.cit., pp. 354–5.

13 Thompson, L. 1985, *Leslie Thompson: An Autobiography*, Crawley, Sussex: Rabbit Press; obituaries appeared in *The Times*, *Observer* and *Independent*.

14 Murray-Brown, J. 1974, *Kenyatta*, London: Fontana.

15 Green, J. 1986, 'John Alexander Barbour-James (1867–1954)', *New Community*, 13, 2, pp. 250–6; interviews with Amy Barbour-James, London.

16 Interviews with Shirley Thompson.

17 Ofori, A. T.-A. 1976, 'Conversation with Ian Hall', *Black Perspective in Music*, 4, 3, pp. 313–19.

18 Ehrlich, C. 1985, *The Music Profession in Britain since the 18th Century: A Social History*, Oxford: Clarendon Press.

Chapter 3

1 Blesh, R. and Janis, H. 1971, *They All Played Ragtime*, rev. edn, New York: Oak Publications, p. 155; 'The variety stage', *The Referee*, 7 January 1906, p. 4.

2 'Our Belgian Fund: Ciro's Restaurant Club', *Daily Telegraph*, 19 April 1915, p. 11; 'Ciro's in London', *The Era*, 21 April 1915, p. 17.

3 'Three shot dead: terrible act of jazz band leader', *News of the World*, 27 June 1920, p. 5.

4 Rye, H. 1988, 'Visiting firemen 14: Joe Jordan 1915', *Storyville*, 134, pp. 55–8.

5 'Variety Gossip', *The Stage*, 6 May 1915, p. 7.

6 'Jottings', *BMG*, XIV, 1917, p. 93.

7 'Minstrelsy as in the old days', *Newcastle Evening Mail*, 22 June 1915, p. 4.

8 Concord, 'The Savoy Ragtime Band', *BMG*, XV, 1918, p. 146.

9 'London variety stage: London Opera House', *The Stage*, 12 October 1916, p. 15.

10 Brunn, H.O. 1963, *The Story of the Original Dixieland Jazz Band*, London: Jazz Book Club, p. 135.

11 Rye, H. 1986, 'The Southern Syncopated Orchestra', in R. Lotz and I. Pegg (eds) *Under the Imperial Carpet: Essays in Black History, 1780–1950*, Crawley, Sussex: Rabbit Press, pp. 217–32.

12 Dutordoit, C. 1919, 'Southern Syncopated Orchestra', *Musical Standard*, 2 August, p. 29.

13 'The Southern Syncopated Orchestra', *Cambridge Magazine*, 8, 1919, p. 914; 'Black magic: more about the Syncopated Orchestra', ibid., p. 962.

14 Chilton, J. 1987, *Sidney Bechet: The Wizard of Jazz*, London: Macmillan, p. 87.

15 Demeusy, B. 1978, 'The Bertin Depestre Salnave Musical Story', *Storyville*, 78, pp. 207–19.

16 Swaffer, H. 1923, 'Nigger problem brought to London', *Daily Graphic*, 6 March, p. 7.

17 Public Record Office: LAB 2/1187/EDAR954/1923 (draft reply from Ministry of

Labour to Actors Association), Crown Copyright (quoted by permission).

18 Rye, H. 1988, 'Visiting firemen 13: "The Plantation Revues"', *Storyville*, 133, pp. 4–15.

19 Cochran, C.B. 1932, *I Had Almost Forgotten...*, London: Hutchinson, pp. 219–33; Hughes, S. 1946, *Opening Bars: Beginning an Autobiography*, London: Pilot Press, p. 305.

20 Rye 1984, 'Visiting firemen 9: The blackbirds and their Orchestras', *Storyville*, 112, pp. 133–7; Rye 1984, 'Additional information to previous visiting firemen instalments', *Storyville*, 114, pp. 216–17.

21 Rye 1983, 'Visiting firemen 7: Eubie Blake and Noble Sissle', *Storyville*, 105, pp. 88–95.

22 Rye 1986, 'Visiting firemen 12(a): Ethel Waters', *Storyville*, 126, pp. 219–22; 'For Americans only', *Encore*, 17 October 1929, p. 3; 'London reports: Enormous bill at Palladium', *Encore*, 26 November 1929, p. 4.

23 Gulliver, R. 1977, 'Leon Abbey', *Storyville*, 73, pp. 5–28; 'Cabaret, dancing and bands', *Encore*, 22 December 1927, p. 10; Rye, H. 1983, 'Visiting firemen 8: Leon Abbey and his Orchestra/Eddie South and his Alabamians', *Storyville*, 108, pp. 207–12.

24 'High lights on dark subjects: Negro culture makes its mark on London's dance music', *Melody Maker*, VIII, 1932, pp. 500–1.

25 Rye, H. 1980, 'Visiting firemen 1: Duke Ellington', *Storyville*, 88, pp. 128–30; Rye 1980, '2: Louis Armstrong', *Storyville*, 89, pp. 184–7; Rye 1980, '3: Cab Calloway and his Cotton Club Orchestra', *Storyville*, 91, pp. 30–1.

26 'This week in stageland', *Liverpool Echo*, 13 September 1932, p. 8.

27 Rye, H. 1981, 'Visiting firemen 5: Coleman Hawkins', *Storyville*, 97, pp. 15–25; Stewart-Baxter, D. 1969, 'Coleman Hawkins: a memory', *Pieces Of Jazz*, 6, pp. 43–4.

28 Rye, H. 1979, 'Fats Waller in Britain – some native reactions', *Storyville*, 81, pp. 83–6; Rye 1983, 'Visiting firemen 8(f): Art Tatum', *Storyville*, 108, pp. 216–17; Rye, 1985, '11: Garland Wilson', *Storyville*, 119, pp. 176–93.

29 Rye, H. 1981, 'Visiting firemen 4: Benny Carter', *Storyville*, 93, pp. 15–25.

30 Rye, H. 1982, 'Visiting firemen 6: Teddy Hill and the Cotton Club Revue', *Storyville*, 100, pp. 144–6; Gillespie, D. with Fraser, A. 1980, *Dizzy*, London: W.H. Allen, p. 77.

31 'The profession mourns', *Melody Maker*, 15 March 1941, p. 1; Leon Cassel-Gerard, 'Who is there to take Ken Johnson's place?', *Melody Maker*, 22 March 1941, p. 5.

Chapter 4

1 Some of the relationships between Christmas festivals are discussed by Bettelheim, J. 1979, 'Jamaican Jonkonnu and related Caribbean festivals', in M.E. Crahan and F.W. Knight (eds) *Africa and the Caribbean*, Baltimore, Md: Johns Hopkins University Press, pp. 80–100. For Christmas and Carnival in Trinidad see Pearse, A. 1956, 'Carnival in nineteenth-century Trinidad', *Caribbean Quarterly*, 4, 3 and 4, March–June, pp. 175–93.

2 For some of the forms of folk music see Pearse, A. 1978, 'Music in Caribbean popular culture', *Revista Inter-Americana*, 8, 4, summer, pp. 629–39. A general summary of the development of Jamaican culture (to 1962) is Baxter, I. 1970, *The Arts of an Island*, Metuchen, NJ: Scarecrow Press.

3 Pitts, H. 1962, 'Calypso: from patois to its present form', Independence Supplement, (Trinidad) *Sunday Guardian*, 26 August, pp. 41, 43; *Port of Spain Gazette*, 20 January 1900, p. 5; and the 'White Rose' calypso, *Port of Spain Gazette*, 27 February 1900, p. 5. Spottswood, R. (comp.), 'A discography of West Indian recordings (1912–1945)',

unpublished MS, is the source for recording in this period unless stated otherwise.

4 Jennings, A. 1946, 'Colour bar', *Melody Maker*, 7 December, p. 5; Rye, H. 1986, 'The Southern Syncopated Orchestra', in R. Lotz and I. Pegg (eds) *Under the Imperial Carpet: Essays in Black History, 1780–1950*, Crawley, Sussex: Rabbit Press, pp. 217–32.

5 Chilton, J. 1987, *Sidney Bechet: The Wizard of Jazz*, London: Macmillan, pp. 53–5.

6 Cowley, J. 1985, 'West Indian gramophone records in Britain 1927–1950', *Occasional Papers in Ethnic Relations*, no. 1, Coventry: Centre for Research in Ethnic Relations; Cowley, '*L'Année Passée:* selected repertoire in English-speaking West Indian Music 1900–1960', unpublished MS, discusses the history of *Amba Cay La'* and *Sly Mongoose* in more detail.

7 On Dunbar: the entry in Southern, E. 1982, *Biographical Dictionary of Afro-American Musicians*, Westport, Conn: Greenwood Press, p. 117. Gladys Keep's session is in Rust, B. (comp.) 1970, *Jazz Records A–Z 1897–1942*, Chigwell: Storyville Publications.

8 On Manning: Cowley, J. 1986, 'Cultural "fusions": aspects of British West Indian music in the U.S.A. and Britain 1918–51', *Popular Music*, 5, Cambridge: Cambridge University Press, pp. 81–96.

9 On Johnson's band: Thompson, L. 1985, *Leslie Thompson*, Crawley, Sussex: Rabbit Press, pp. 89–93; *Melody Maker*, 18 April 1936, p. 1; Gray, A. 1937, 'The old Florida', *Melody Maker*, 29 May, p. 2. On his demise, *Melody Maker*, 15 March 1941, p. 1; certified copy of an entry of death. A partial discography is in Rust, op. cit. Details of his 1939 calypso broadcast are from the BBC programme log.

10 On Sowande's band: *Melody Maker*, 17 December 1938, p. 1; on his career, Southern, op. cit., pp. 354–5. On Ros, his (nd), *The Latin-American Way*, London: Rose Morris; and (Trinidad) *Sunday Guardian*, 9 February 1964, pp. 1–2. On Adelaide Hall, Ellis, C. 1970, 'Adelaide Hall – The Singing Blackbird', *Storyville*, 31, October–November, pp. 8–11.

11 Cowley, 1986, op. cit.

12 On Hutchinson's band: *Melody Maker*, 4 March 1944, p. 1; *Melody Maker*, 15 April 1944, p. 5; and his obituary *Melody Maker*, 28 November 1959, p. 4. Discographical information courtesy Brian Rust. On Jennings's band: *Melody Maker*, 18 August 1945, p. 4; (Trinidad) *Sunday Guardian*, 14 October 1945, p. 2; PRO ref: BT26/1215; Jennings, op. cit.

13 Bailey, L. (ed.) 1945, *Travellers' Tales*, London: Allen & Unwin, pp. 128–9, 135–6, 139. *The Edric Connor Collection of West Indian Spirituals and Folk Tunes*, London: Boosey, 1945. Unless stated otherwise, all recordings made in the second period are listed in Cowley, J. and Noblett, R. (comps) 'English-speaking West Indian recordings: an exploratory discography (1945–1965)', unpublished MS.

14 On Campbell and/or Pasuka: *Melody Maker*, 8 June 1946, p. 6; Vaz, N. 1947, 'Berto Pasuka and the Jamaican Ballet', *West Indian Review*, spring, pp. 27–8; *West African Review*, November 1952, p. 1155. Data on 1946 performers/performances courtesy of Stephen Dwoskin and Trish Thomas.

15 PRO ref: BT26/1237 lists the *Windrush* passengers. On Caresser's visit: *Melody Maker*, 2 October 1948, p. 4.

16 On Freddy Grant: *Melody Maker*, 4 December 1937, p. 1; the 'Ragtime' concert, *Melody Maker*, 21 July 1945, p. 2; 28 July 1945, p. 6; the first Parlophone session, (Trinidad) *Guardian*, 31 January 1950, p. 1; *Melody Maker*, 4 February 1950, p. 3; *Jazz Illustrated*, 1, 5, March 1950, p. 6. Average ages of the performers computed from ships' passenger lists and similar sources. On the 'Young Brigade', see Quevedo, R. 1983, *Atilla's Kaiso*, St Augustine, Trinidad: University of the West Indies, pp. 84–8.

17 On Melodisc: *Melody Maker*, 27 August 1949, p. 7; 28 January 1950, p. 2, and the Companies Registration Office file for Melodisc Records Ltd (Company no. 477, 453).

18 On Kalenda (Calinda): Elder, J.D. 1966, '*Kalinda* – Songs of the Battling Troubadours of Trinidad', *Journal of the Folklore Institute*, 3, 2, August, pp. 192–203. On Myler: *Port of Spain Gazette*, 10 March 1905, p. 7; the Myler–Banray confrontation: Jones, C. (Duke of Albany) 1947, *Calypso and Carnival of Long Ago and Today*, Trinidad: *Port of Spain Gazette*, p. 43.

19 Jekyll, W. 1907, *Jamaican Song and Story*, London: David Nutt, p. 219. The name Leslie 'Jiver' Hutchinson is featured on the record label.

20 *Radio Times* (television edn.), 23 June 1950, pp. 36, 39.

21 On King and Maxwell in Jamaica: *Melody Maker*, 3 November 1951, p. 7.

22 On TASPO: *Trinidad Guardian*, 3 July 1951, pp. 1–2; 7 July 1951, pp. 1 and 5; *West India Committee Circular*, 66, 1244, August 1951, p. 193; D.E.R. 'The Steel Band', *Clarion*, February 1954, p. 4.

23 On fund-raising by the calypsonians: *Trinidad Guardian*, 17 May 1951, p. 7; (Trinidad) *Sunday Guardian*, 8 July 1951, p. 9; *Trinidad Guardian*, 11 July 1951, p. 7; 24 July 1951, p. 2. On Lion's trip to Britain: the Roaring Lion, *Calypso: From France to Trinidad*, San Juan, Trinidad: General Printers [*c.*1987], p. 243; PRO ref: BT26/1277 (arrival); *Trinidad Guardian*, 4 September 1951, p. 7 (Festival appearance with TASPO).

24 *Melody Maker*, 3 November 1951, p. 7. On mento: White, G. 1982, 'Traditional music practice in Jamaica and its influence on the birth of modern Jamaican popular music', *African-Caribbean Institute of Jamaica Newsletter*, no. 7, pp. 41–68.

25 Lyttelton, H. 1958, *Second Chorus*, London: MacGibbon & Kee, pp. 106–14; Jones, M. 1952, 'Has the jazz concert come of age at last?', *Melody Maker*, 13 September, p. 2.

26 On Grant's departure: PRO ref: BT27/1723. On King's: PRO ref: BT27/1710. On Shalit's lawsuit: Melodisc Records Limited: 1952 S No. 1178 (Lord Chancellor's Department): affidavit (12 January 1953), Chancellor's Order (23 June 1953); *Melody Maker*, 13 June 1953, p. 1; 20 June 1953, p. 6; 27 June 1953, p. 6.

27 On Hayden: *Melody Maker*, 21 August 1954, p. 1; Invader, *Melody Maker*, 5 May 1956, p. 8; Sparrow, *Time*, 27 February 1956, pp. 47–8; Kitchener, *Music Mirror*, 4, 3, March–April 1957, p. 9.

28 Lawrence's recordings are Starlite 45-022, 45-041.

29 Parlophone MP 112; Lyragon J704; Melodisc 1430.

30 On Terror's victory in 1966: 'Parade of champions 1963–1982', *Trinidad Carnival*, Key Caribbean Publications, 1982, pp. 72–3; and Bryans, R. 1967, *Trinidad and Tobago*, London: Faber, p. 205. On the early history of Notting Hill's street carnival: Cohen, A. 1982, 'A polyethnic London carnival as a contested cultural performance', *Ethnic and Racial Studies*, 5, 1, January, pp. 23–41.

Introduction to Part Two

1 Duke Ellington and Ray Nance appeared at the London Palladium with Skyrockets and supporting artists, including the black singer Pearl Bailey. Others who came to Britain during the period of the MU ban included Ella Fitzgerald and Maxine Sullivan (1948), trumpet player Rex Stewart (1948 and 1949), blues singers Big Bill Broonzy and Josh White (1951), Lonnie Johnson (1952), pianists Mary Lou Williams and Teddy Wilson (1953), singer Nat 'King' Cole (1954). My thanks to

Howard Rye for confirmation of the dates.

2 A full account of the visit of Sidney Bechet and subsequent court case is given in Godbolt, J. 1984, *A History of Jazz in Britain 1919–1950*, London: Quartet Books, pp. 239–65.

3 The partisan positions taken by advocates of different forms of jazz are to be found in the pages of *Melody Maker* and *Jazz Journal* through the late 1940s and 1950s.

4 Mezzrow, Milton 'Mezz' and Wolfe, B. 1949, *Really the Blues*, London: Secker & Warburg, pp. 216–19 and 354–60.

5 *Jazz Music* (edited by Albert McCarthy and Max Jones) was published by the Jazz Sociological Society 1942–53; *Jazz Notes* (edited by James Asman and Bill Kinnell) was published by the Jazz Appreciation Society 1942–3 after which the Society published separate booklets. Many other collectors' magazines were published in the 1940s and 1950s. Other articles were published in the Young Communist newssheet *Challenge* and the anarchist Freedom Press published jazz articles in *Now*. *Jazz Journal* was predictably conservative.

6 Little, K.L. 1947, *Negroes in Britain*, London: Kegan Paul.

7 Hill, C. 1970, *Immigration and Integration*, Oxford: Pergamon Press, Table 2, p. 27.

8 Ibid., pp. 25–8.

9 Khan, N. 1976, *The Arts Britain Ignores: The Arts of Ethnic Minorities in Britain*, London: Commission for Racial Equality, pp. 13–15; Hiro, D. 1973, *Black British, White British*, Harmondsworth: Pelican, pp. 206–13.

10 Deakin, N. 1970, *Colour, Citizenship and British Society*, London: Institute of Race Relations and Panther Books, pp. 282–97.

11 A notable exception is Pryce, K. 1979, *Endless Pressure: A Study of West Indian Life-Styles in Bristol*, Harmondsworth: Penguin Education, ch. 14 'The quest for solutions: black identity and the role of reggae', pp. 143–62.

12 Ibid., p. 151.

Chapter 5

1 Fryer, P. 1984, *Staying Power: The History of Black People in Britain*, London: Pluto Press.

2 Stanley, H.M. 1899, *South Africa*, London, 3 June, p. 558.

3 *South Africa*, London, 13 May 1899, pp. 391.

4 Rye, H. 1986, 'The Southern Syncopated Orchestra', in R. Lotz and I. Pegg (eds) *Under the Imperial Carpet: Essays in Black History 1780–1950*, Crawley, Sussex: Rabbit Press.

5 Willan, B. 1984, *Sol Plaatje, South African Nationalist 1876–1932*, London: Heinemann.

6 Cuney-Hare, M. 1936, *Negro Musicians and their Music*, Washington, DC: Associated Publishers.

7 *West African Review*, London, 5 January 1935, p. 1,498.

8 *West African Review*, London, 31 August 1935.

9 *West African Review*, London, 7 November 1936, p. 1,563.

10 *West African Review*, London, June 1946, p. 681.

11 *West African Review*, London, February 1954, p. 119.

12 Interview with author, London, December 1980.

13 MacInnes, C. 1957, 'City after dark', *The Twentieth Century*, London, pp. 571–3.

14 *West Africa*, 11 March 1961, London, p. 259.

15 Owusu, K. 1986, *The Struggle for Black Arts in Britain*, London: Comedia, p. 107.

16 Conversation with author, November 1988, London.
17 Conversation with author, December 1988, London.
18 Conversation with author, November 1988, London.
19 Conversation with author, October 1988, London.
20 Conversation with author, December 1988, London.

Chapter 6

1 Melly, G. 1970, *Revolt into Style: The Pop Arts in Britain,* Harmondsworth: Allen Lane the Penguin Press, pp. 33f.
2 Chambers, I. 1985, *Urban Rhythms: Popular Music and Popular Culture,* Basingstoke: Macmillan, pp. 24ff.
3 Platt, J. 1985, *London's Rock Routes.* London: Fourth Estate, esp. ch. 3.
4 Burton, P. 1985, *Parallel Lives,* London: GMP Publishers, pp. 26ff; see also Melly, op. cit., p. 150.
5 Popular mod records were 'Can I Get a Witness' by Marvin Gaye, 'Nowhere to Run' by Martha and the Vandellas, and 'The Girl's Alright with Me' by the Temptations (all on Motown, released in Britain on the Stateside label); hard, bluesy records like 'Think' 'Night Train' and other early songs by James Brown; and the terse, choppy rhythms of Booker T. and the MGs on the Stax label.
6 All chart information is taken from Rice, J. *et al.* 1985, *The Guinness Book of British Hit Singles,* 5th edn, Enfield: Guinness Superlatives.
7 The Temptations, Martha Reeves and the Vandellas, and Marvin Gaye all had good chart hits in 1964, and on 19 November 'Baby Love' by Diana Ross and the Supremes reached no. 1 on the chart. James Brown's 'Papa's Got a Brand New Bag' was in the chart for seven weeks in 1965, confirming the fact that it was not only the bright, breezy Motown sound that suited British tastes.
8 See Melly, op. cit., pp. 191f.
9 Hebdige, D. 1987, *Cut 'n' Mix: Culture, Identity and Caribbean Music,* London: Comedia/Methuen, pp. 90ff.
10 See Chambers, op. cit., pp. 161ff.
11 Cummings, T. 1975, 'The northern discos', in C. Gillett and S. Frith (eds) *Rock File 3,* St Albans: Panther, pp. 23ff.
12 See Hebdige, op. cit., p. 93; also Chambers, op. cit., pp. 162f.
13 Bigger and better known hits were 'Back Stabbers' (1972) and 'Love Train' (1973) by the O'Jays, and 'When Will I See You Again' by the Three Degrees (no. 1, 1974). Similar in pace and intent were the many hits of Barry White, the fourth of which, 'You're the First, the Last, My Everything', reached no. 1 in 1974. Most of these recordings were first made popular in discotheques by experienced disc jockeys who had a direct line to the latest American releases. While many disco successes did not reach the charts, plenty (like George McRae's 'Rock Me Baby', 1974) did in fact become impressive hits.
14 Particularly notable in this respect were Ace ('How Long?', no. 20, 1974) and the Average White Band ('Pick Up the Pieces', no. 6, 1975). At the same time a number of British rock stars began flirting with the soul idiom. Rod Stewart covered several Sam Cooke numbers in the early 1970s, including 'Twisting the Night Away' and 'Wonderful World'; Bryan Ferry of Roxy Music recorded Dobie Grey's 'The In Crowd' in 1974.
15 See Chambers, op. cit., pp. 188–90.

16 Heatwave, made up of English and American musicians, had six hits between 1977 and 1979. The first (and arguably the finest) of these, 'Boogie Nights', was in the chart for fourteen weeks, and has since acquired classic status.

17 Though some of the results, like Rod Stewart's 'D'ya Think I'm Sexy' (no. 1, 1978), were exploitative and unconvincing, others were surprisingly successful. 'Miss You' by the Rolling Stones (no. 3, 1978) achieved a feverish, blues-drenched intensity; 'Dance Away' by Roxy Music (no. 2, 1979) distilled the dance idea rhythm into something ethereal and resonant.

18 See Hebdidge, op. cit., p. 95.

19 Bradley, L. 1987, 'Stir it up', *Q*, ii, 3, December, p. 74.

20 Shortly after this recording, Paul Weller, guitarist, singer and songwriter, disbanded the Jam to form the Style Council, a group that has thrived into the late 1980s, writing and playing songs inspired by black music.

21 In 1987 Jackie Wilson's 'Reet Petite', Ben E. King's 'Stand by Me', Percy Sledge's 'When a Man Loves a Woman' and Nina Simone's 'My Baby Just Cares for Me' all reached the top 10 on the British chart.

22 The early hits of such groups as ABC ('Tears Are Not Enough', 1981), Spandau Ballet ('Chant No. 1'), and Wham! ('Young Guns', 1982) employed variations of the funk style as a vehicle for very modern pop songs. Other groups played dance rhythms on drum machines and synthesizers: Heaven 17's 'We Don't Need that Fascist Groove Thang' and Soft Cell's 'Tainted Love' (both 1981) are more solidly in the funk tradition than in any other genre, and were perceived by the record-buying public as such. A case in point was the phenomenal success of the Human League, whose album *Dare* (1982) yielded substantial hits on both sides of the Atlantic.

23 For a detailed history of hip-hop see Toop, D. 1984, *The Rap Attack*, London: Pluto Press.

24 Bradley, L. 1987, 'Morgan Khan: a chastened man', *Q*, i, 10, July, p. 11.

25 Other rap hits at this time included 'Give it a Rest' by the She Rockers, the Coldcut Crew's 'Say Kids What Time is it' (1987), and 'London Posse' by London Posse (produced by Tim Westwood, 1987). The rise to the top of the charts of 'Pump Up the Volume' by M/A/R/R/S/ (1987) signified the commercial cross-over of hip-hop.

26 There have been only a few successful go-go records; Trouble Funk's album *Trouble Over Here, Trouble Over There* is among the best. Some British records have adapted its lumbering beat, most notably an excellent remix of Hot Chocolate's 'I Believe in Miracles' (1987), and Scritti Politti's 'Philosophy Now' from the album *Provision* (1988).

27 Garratt, S. 1986, 'Chicago House', *The Face*, 77, September, p. 19.

28 In the late 1980s a surprising number of small record labels (including Wham! in Liverpool and Kool Kat in the Midlands) and new clubs sprang up in response to the demand for house and related styles. The independent label Rhythm King had considerable commercial success in both the USA and Britain with records by Bomb the Bass and S'Express.

29 See Bradley, December 1987, op. cit.

30 Others include Simply Red, whose first LP sold well in both Europe and the USA, and was awarded a platinum disc; it was produced by Stewart Levine, a black American who had previously worked with, among others, Cecil and Linda Womack. The group's lead singer, Mick Hucknall (from Manchester), wrote several songs with Lamont Dozier, formerly one of Motown's chief songwriters. Floy Joy's single 'Weak in the Presence of Beauty' (1986) was scored by Harry Bowens, once vocal arranger

for the O'Jays. Wet Wet Wet recorded in Memphis with Willie Mitchell (Al Green's producer).

Chapter 7

1 Musicians listed in Prospect, G.A. 1968, *The Steel Band*, Trinidad and Tobago, p. 11.
2 Noel, T. and Scarfe, J. 1988, *Play Pan: Learn Music the Steel Pan Way*, Stoke-on-Trent: Trentham Books.

Chapter 8

1 I should like to acknowledge with gratitude the help and support of Ranajit Banerji and Arild Bergh in researching this contribution.
2 Grateful acknowledgement is due to the Leverhulme Trust, London, for the award in 1988–9 of a grant in aid of research which began in 1986. For this contribution in particular, my sincere thanks are due to Bhangra musicians, among them especially Mr Manjit Kondal of Holle Holle, Mr Jagjit Singh Gill of Mela, and two others who prefer to remain unnamed; and to Bhangra listeners, among them especially Ms Sarbjit Lal, Ms Harprit Bagha, and Mr Balbir Nandra. My local research has been greatly helped by the nation-wide coverage of Bhangra in *Ghazal and Beat*, the first Asian music paper in Britain and itself a milestone in the professionalization of South Asian music journalism in Britain. It is edited by Arik Farhan and published by Derbar Ltd, 61a King Street, Southall, west London.
3 Quoted in Ace, V. 1988, 'The Valentine's Day Gig Massacre', *Ghazal and Beat*, 2, p. 4.
4 Quoted under rubric 'Boliyaan', *Ghazal and Beat*, 7, 1988, p. 4.
5 Dubashi, J. 1986, 'Cassette piracy: high stakes', *India Today*, 31 March, p. 112.
6 Laing, D. 1988, '[Review of] Phonogram and Cultural Communication in India, by J.M. Ojha', *Popular Music*, 7, 2, p. 227.
7 Manuel P. 1988, 'Popular music in India 1901–86', *Popular Music*, 7, 2, p. 174.
8 Dewan, V. 1988, 'Pirates! Chori Lok', *Ghazal and Beat*, 6 p. 4.
9 These figures represent averages as estimated by four commercially competent musicians.
10 Quoted in Dewan, V. 1988, 'Culture shock', *Ghazal and Beat*, 1, p. 10.
11 Interview with Mr Manjit Kondal, 7 September 1987.
12 The long-established group Azaad, for instance, is reputed to play 'daytimers' only during school holidays.
13 Shiv Kumar Batalvi (d. 1973) emancipated Punjabi poetry in both traditional and modern genres and reformed the literary idiom of the language in the face of Soviet influences during the 1950s and the hegemony of Bombay writers in the 1960s.
14 Thus the song *'Is daj noo band karro'* on their highly successful album *'I Love Golden Star'* (1987) is an explicit protest against abuses of the dowry system, and yet a favourite request at many weddings.
15 Nirmal quoted in Mistry, T. 1988, 'Shava Shava', *Ghazal and Beat*, 6, p. 8. Annil quoted in Dewan, V. 1988, 'Culture shock', *Ghazal and Beat*, 1, p. 10.
16 Dr Richard Middleton, Open University, in a personal communication.

Chapter 9

1 There are useful summaries in Farmer, H.G. 1929, *A History of Arabian Music*, repr. 1973, London: Luzac & Co., pp. 20–38; Robson, J. 1938, *Tracts on Listening to Music*, London: Royal Asiatic Society; Roy Choudhury, M.L. 1957, 'Music in Islam', *Journal of the Asiatic Society, Letters*, XXIII, 2, pp. 43–102.

2 Baily, J. 1988, *Music of Afghanistan: professional musicians in the city of Herat*, in (Cambridge Studies in Ethnomusicology), Cambridge: Cambridge University Press (with accompanying cassette), p. 152.

3 See, for example, Farmer, H.G. 1930, *Historical Facts for the Arabian Musical Influence*, London: Panther.

4 Sakata, H.L. 1983, *Music in the Mind: The Concepts of Music and Musician in Afghanistan*, Kent, NC: Kent State University Press (with two accompanying cassettes), pp.79–81.

5 Neuman, D.M. 1980, *The Life of Music in North India: The Organization of an Artistic Tradition*, Detroit, Mich: Wayne State University Press.

6 Baily, op. cit., p. 118.

7 Qureshi, R.B. 1986, *Sufi music of India and Pakistan: sound, context and meaning in qawwāli*, (Cambridge Studies in Ethnomusicology), Cambridge: Cambridge University Press; Currie, M. 1978, 'The shrine and cult of Mu'in al'Din Chishti of Ajmer', D.Phil. thesis, University of Oxford.

8 Manuel, P. 1988, 'Popular music in India 1901–86', *Popular Music*, 7, 2, pp. 167–8.

9 About 60–70 per cent, according to Khan, V.S. 1977, 'The Pakistanis: Mirpuri villagers at home and in Bradford', in J.L. Watson (ed.) *Between Two Cultures*, Oxford: Basil Blackwell, p. 57.

10 Khan, op. cit. Ballard, R. 1988, 'The political economy of migration: Pakistan, Britain and the Middle East', in J.S. Eades (ed.) *Migrants, Workers and the Labour Market*, London: Tavistock; Ballard, 1989, 'Migration and kinship: the differential effect of marriage rules on the processes of Punjabi migration to Britain', in press.

11 Ballard 1988, op. cit.

12 Ballard, personal communication.

13 Jones, P.D. 1984, 'An investigation into curriculum music in middle schools and the role of music in the lives of Muslim children, as a basis for development of a music education more relevant to a multi-cultural society', B.Ed. dissertation, Bradford College, UK.

14 Ibid., p. 70.

15 Ibid., p. 37.

16 Ibid., p. 55.

17 Sakata, op. cit., pp. 78–84; Baily, op. cit., pp. 102–3.

18 See also Banerji, S. 1988, 'Ghazals to Bhangra in Great Britain', *Popular Music*, 7, 2, pp. 207–13.

19 Neuman, op. cit.

20 Baily, J. 1986, *Lessons from Gulam: Asian Music in Bradford*, 16 mm film (or as VHS video), 52 mins, in colour with study guide, London: Royal Anthropological Institute.

21 Khan, S., Huma, F. and Shaikh, S. 1978, Libretto, translations of six poems sung by the Sabri Brothers on their 'Qawwāli Music of Pakistan' tour of the USA, New York: Performing Arts Program of the Asia Society.

22 Gulum Musa, edited conversation.

Recommended Recordings

Early recordings of black music in Great Britain are rare. Some were originally on 78rpm discs, but only a few of these have been reissued on long-playing records. More recent recordings are uneven in their representation. Recordings listed below have been recommended by contributors, and many are 'anthologies'. Their inclusion is no guarantee of availability, nor is the list in any way comprehensive.

Chapter 1

Introduction to Gospel Song (RBF 5)
Includes single examples by the Fisk University Jubilee Singers, the Tuskegee Institute Singers and Pace Jubilee Singers.
They All Played Banjo (Retrieval FG 403)
Early banjo styles recorded by white musicians in London, 1907–16.
Too Much Mustard (Saydisc SDL 221)
Includes 6 titles by Jim Europe, including the 'Hell-Fighters' Orchestra, 1913–19. Others by Arthur Pryor's Band.

Chapter 2

Quintet for Clarinet and Strings (CHAN CH T003)
Quintet in F Sharp Minor by Samuel Coleridge-Taylor, 1895.
Petite Suite de Concert (EMI CDM769689-2)
Orchestral Suite, Opus 77 1910 and *Hiawatha's Wedding Feast*-Cantata, Opus 31/1 1898. Important early works by Samuel Coleridge Taylor
Thou Art Risen My Beloved (EMI Ex 2909-11-3)
Song, 1925 by Samuel Coleridge-Taylor. None of his 'African' compositions are currently available.
Green Pastures (ASV AJA 5047)
Miscellany of Paul Robeson's best performances, including 'St Louis Blues'.

Lonesome Road (Academy Sound & Vision ASV AJA5 027)
Paul Robeson singing Afro-American spirituals and songs.
The Record of Singing (EMI Ex 2909-69-3)
Roland Hayes included in boxed set of 'Anglo-American and East Europe'.

Chapter 3

Harlem Comes to London (Swing SW8444)
Includes The Plantation Orchestra, 1926 and Noble Sissle, 1929.
Americans in Paris, Vol. 1 (Jazz Time 251276-2 [CD])
Stretton's Orchestra, Sam Wooding and Mitchell's Jazz Kings.
Noble Sissle's Sizzling Syncopators (Classic Jazz Masters)
Americans in Europe 1931–38, Vol. 2 (Tax m8035)
Garland Wilson, Louis Armstrong's British band, 1933 (Armstrong absent).
Swingin' at Maida Vale (Jasmine JASM2010)
Benny Carter and his Orchestra in London.
Swing is the Thing (Swing SW8555/56)
Two LP collection of all Valaida Snow's British recordings.
Fats Waller in London 1938–39 (Swing SW8442/43)
Ridin' in Rhythm (Swing SW8453/54)
Includes British recordings by Coleman Hawkins, two with Jack Hylton.
Dancing the Night Away (London RECDL16)
British dance bands, includes '*Snakehips Swing*' by Ken Johnson's Orchestra.

Chapter 4

Barbados Blues (Collectors Items 015)
Sam Manning and Wilmouth Houdini, vaudevillian and calypsonian.
Where Was Butler? (Folklyric 9048)
Tiger, Atilla, Radio and Executor; calypsos on an oil strike in 1937.
Jazz and Hot Dance in Trinidad (Harlequin HQ 2016)
Mainly instrumental recordings made between 1912 and 1939.
Calypso Pioneers (Rounder 1039)
Calypsonians, vaudevillians and instrumentalists, 1912–37.
Port of Spain Shuffle (New Cross 005)
Black music in Britain in the early 1950s compiled by John Cowley.
Caribbean Connections (New Cross 006)
Another compilation by John Cowley of musicians in Britain in the 1950s, includes
Kitchener, Beginner, Lion and Trinidad All Stars Steel Band.

Chapter 5

Woyaya (MCA MCG 3506)
By Osibisa, Britain's biggest-selling Afro-Rock band of the 1970s.
Abio'sun Ni (Hot/Cap 1)
Modern African sound from a veteran London-based Nigerian percussionist Gasper
Lawal.
Oh Africa (African Records International ANM 1228L)
Do-it-yourself hi-tech album from Kofi Busia, Oxford-based Ghanaian.

Ashewo Ara (INK 1228)
Roots-Funk 12 inch by Kabbala, led by Michael and Isaac Osapanin.
C'est la Danse (Ovalt 28/12)
African Connexion's Zairean sound with Abdul Tee-Jay and Mwana Musa.
Chimurenga (African Dawn AD300)
Poetry and music by African Dawn, synthesized from the African diaspora.
Life in Bracknell and Willisau (Jika LP ZL2)
Azanian funk-jazz synthesis by South African and British musicians.

Chapter 6

The Front Line Vols 1 and 2 (Virgin FLB 3000/1)
Collections of reggae by Jamaican and British artists including Prince Far-I ('*Foggy Road*'), I-Roy, Rocking Trevor and Culture, 1976–9.
20 Mod Classics Vol 1 (Tamla Motown STML12125)
20 Mod Classics Vol 2 (Tamla Motown STML12133)
Favourites of the Mods, compiled from original hit singles, 1962–5.
Love Train: the Best of Philadelphia (PIR 25316)
Classic soul discs that were UK hits: O'Jay, Billy Paul and Harold Melvin.
Casino Classics Chapter One (Casino Classics CCLP1)
Northern Soul by the All Night Band, the Ron Grainer Orchestra *et al.*
Anthems (Street Sounds Music 5)
Some of the most popular suburban 'weekender' recordings.

Chapter 7

Steelband: Antigua (Playa Sound PF 804)
An accessible introduction to neck-slung steel pan music of the 1980s.
Original Trinidad Steel Band (Polydor SPE LP 38)
8-piece steel band from Trinidad on tour in the USA in the 1960s.
Steel Band Panorama 1974 (Tropico TSI 2016)
Recordings by participating bands in the Trinidad Panorama Festival.
Panorama 1984-Live (Carotte [no number])
Steel bands who played in the same event, ten years later.
Steel Band des Caraibes (Arion ARN 33612)
Variety of bands recorded for a French label, 1981.
Phase One (P and C 1983)
Recordings by British bands are rare. This collection of Classical and Caribbean music is by the Phase One Steel Orchestra of Coventry. On 12 inch 45rpm.

Chapter 8

Abhimaan (HMV D/MOCE 4183)
Hindi film soundtrack by Lata Mangeshkar, Kishore Kumar, Mohd. Rafi.
Shakti: A Handful of Beauty (CBS 81664)
Indo-Jazz fusions by John McLaughlin and L. Shankar.
Indipop Music and Dance Compilasian (Indipop INDU 5)

Examples of characteristic Indipop by various artists of the 1980s.
Najma (Cassette SNMC1274)
Light Classical *ghazal* by a popular singer.
Nehin Sikheya Nundey Ne (HMV TPHVS 19089)
Sital Singh and Seema perform semi-traditional *ghazals*.
Nach Mundeya (Multitone MUT 0359)
Bhangra Beat by the very popular band, Alaap from 1987.
Ark of the Arqans, Heaven and Hell etc. (Scarface M FACE 11)
East-west Indipop synthesis from the multi-instrumental Suns of Arqa.
Bhangra Fever (Arishma ARI 1005)
Remixes of chart-making Bhangra hits by Heera, Kalapreet and Holle Holle.

Chapter 9

Ghulam Farid Sabri (Angel LKDA 20050)
Magbool Ahmed Sabri with Ghulam Farid Sabri and Party perform *qawwālis*.
Qawwāli: Sufi Music from Pakistan (Nonesuch H-72080)
The Sabri Brothers and their ensemble playing traditional *qawwālis*.
Bahauddin Qawwāl (Angel LKDA 20021)
More *qawwālis*, with Bahauddin and Party.
Sufyana Qawwāli (Angel 3AEX 13001)

Lessons from Gulam: Asian Music in Bradford.
This film, made and directed by John Baily is available for hire or purchase in video or 16mm print. An extensive study guide is also available. Distributed in the UK by the Royal Anthropological Institute, 50 Fitzroy Street, London W1P 5HS and in the USA by Documentary Educational Resources, 101 Morse Street, Watertown, MA 02172.

Index